TRYING TO BE
... AND NOT QUITE SUCCEEDING

TRYING TO BE ORTHODOX ... AND NOT QUITE SUCCEEDING

MICHAEL LOMAX

DARTON·LONGMAN + TODD

First published in 2020 by
Darton, Longman and Todd Ltd
1 Spencer Court
140 – 142 Wandsworth High Street
London SW18 4JJ

ISBN 978-0-232-53452-8

A catalogue record for this book is available from the British Library

Typeset by Kerrypress, St Albans
Printed and bound in Great Britain by Bell & Bain, Glasgow

To Irina Gorbunova-Lomax, my wife, without whom neither my blogs nor this book would have happened.

CONTENTS

INTRODUCTION

Almost any newcomer to Orthodoxy initially tries hard to be 'properly' Orthodox: closely following the fasting rules, going to regular confession, learning when and how to bow and cross oneself, ask a blessing from the bishop and, more prosaically, to stand for two hours at a stretch without violent pain in the knees. One has, one is told, entered a particularly privileged, and (according to many Orthodox) the only grace-filled part of the Christian church and needs to behave accordingly. Perhaps this is why I have never totally succeeded in becoming a pattern Orthodox. Ever since entering Orthodoxy officially in 1995 I have been unable to contain my religious identity within its tight bounds. I remain simply and stubbornly Christian.

While I cannot fault God on the road that led me into the Orthodox Church after already 40 years of Christian practice, it has been and remains a difficult journey. I have seen the good sides and the bad sides of Orthodoxy, its glories and its disgraces. I have been in the Russian Orthodox Church since 1995, and a deacon since 2010. I have watched the Russian Orthodox Church develop from the new awakening and rather chaotic enthusiasm of the Yeltsin years, through to the well-organised, vertically integrated monolith it is today, with a vision of 'traditional morality' and 'unchangingness' which its clergy are expected to uphold. During the same period I have also watched 'Western Orthodoxy' spring up fast, too fast, and wither and die for lack of root.

As a deacon my job in the Church is to read the gospel and say the services out of the book, no more. 'Ours not to question why, our just to do and die' I quoted to my fellow deacon the other week. 'Not to question': this with a good education and an English dissenter background, I find impossibly restrictive. It is the need to speak and discuss as an – I hope – intelligent Christian that led me to start blogging on LiveJournal in 2010 and shortly after on Facebook. The resulting dialogue – mainly with Orthodox from Russia, but also with a couple of hard-hitting US correspondents, has been valuable, and has carried me further on my Christian path.

The bulk of this book consists of a selection of these blog postings. Unless otherwise indicated, they are on LiveJournal. It is introduced by a spiritual autobiography of sorts I wrote in 2014 and is followed by three longer key texts I have written over the past ten years.

In publishing this book I recognise that I am highly privileged in two areas. The first is living in a part of the world which has a relatively free religious press, with a tradition of honest dissent and the right to question, and a publisher ready to take a risk on an unknown author. It is a privilege that is probably not available to my opposite number in Russia.

The second is having first-hand experience of Christianity outside Orthodoxy. Just as I speak English, French, German, Dutch and (after a fashion) Church Greek and Russian, I 'speak' Methodist, Anglican, Roman Catholic, Orthodox, Quaker and Protestant charismatic from personal involvement. This includes also a more than nodding knowledge of European church history, including the different spiritual trends of the past thousand years. This gives me a vantage point which very few – too few – people in the Russian Orthodox Church have. It has obviously coloured my outlook on many aspects of current Orthodox praxis.

I am acutely aware that on occasions I can sound harsh. I have no wish to condemn – that is for God – but when in any church I find approaches and practices which to me seem to impede people's progress to fullness in Christ, I find it difficult to keep silent.

By the same token, I hope I do not sound too despairing. Yes, by many traditional measures the situation of the Christian church, and more particular its Russian Orthodox version, raises serious questions of praxis and governance. At the same time I firmly believe in God's love for His people and His creation. He continues looking for His own, I suspect more concerned with deep integrity and sense of justice, and with the ability of His people to reciprocate His love in their life and worship, than for liturgical accuracy, perfect hierarchical systems and 'traditional morality'. He may indeed be leading us into new places, and we must not be afraid to follow Him.

I have to state, as I do at the front of my LiveJournal blog, that these are my personal opinions and bind no one but myself. I am not writing as a deacon of the Russian Orthodox Church, but as Michael Lomax, that rather strange religious mongrel who somehow strayed into the Russian church in Belgium and stayed there.

And finally, two debts: the first, of thanks, to my wife Irina Nikolayevna, a top-class iconographer and indefatigable blogger, who nearly twenty years ago left St Petersburg to marry me, and who, as well as guiding my feet around the complexities of the Russian religious psyche, pushed strongly for this book. She also provided the line drawings in this book, which, like good icons, express the spirit of this book better than the words themselves. The second debt, this time of memory, is to Jeff Blake ('Bardcat' on LiveJournal), who died in 2019 of cancer. We commented regularly on each other's blogs. We did not always see eye-to-eye, he being more 'liberal' in certain fields than I, but there was an integrity in him and an honesty in our exchange which remain a treasured memory. 'Eternal memory', as we say on my side of the confessional divide.

SOME PERSONAL BACKGROUND

This autobiographical piece was written in February 2014 under the title 'Christianity Beyond the Structures', for possible inclusion in a book to be entitled 'World Book of Faith', for which at the time I translated/corrected a number of articles. As far as I know, the book was never published.

I have been Christian throughout my life. Yes there have been some cold patches, but I don't think I have been away from church for more than one month since I started Sunday school in a Methodist Church in the London suburbs at age three. At age 64, this adds up to over 60 years.

That was then a very different world. These were the swansong days of 'Christian England'; it was, it seemed, a world in which everyone was Christian, with prayers every morning at school, Scripture lessons twice a week (with extra for those of us who could not sing and were excused from choir) and weekly Sunday school.

I 'got God' seriously at age 13 in an inter-denominational Protestant boys' Bible class, run by one of the most holy of men I have known: a jobbing printer who simply loved God, his Bible, and the boys who came into his care. It was pretty primitive stuff: pure Bible-based, penal substitution Protestantism. For all its limitations, it gave me a rock with which to weather a world which was falling apart both outside and inside: outside the Beatles and This Was the Week that Was smashing the moral and social certainties of the 1950s post-war consensus, the British Empire reducing in size by the month, and the threat of nuclear Armageddon vividly brought home by the Cuba crisis. Inside, my family background was not happy: my parents were an odd couple: my father a pacifist who had spent the war in China with a Quaker ambulance unit; my mother had been part of the Alpha codebreaking set-up at Bletchley Park, of which she never breathed a word until the secret was out. He was Methodist from the industrial Midlands, she Church of England from the better London suburbs, an insignificant difference today, but in the class-conscious England of the 1950s, a social mismatch. I think he married her on the rebound and she never forgave herself, falling prey at regular intervals to the depression that finally killed her.

By good fortune, at age 11, I got a state scholarship to an elite school in London, which in those days was a straight path to Oxford and Cambridge if you were academically good enough. Which I was. I arrived in Cambridge just turned 18, planning to study German and French for one year, change to theology, then two years of theological college and ordination into the Church of England. Priest by age 24.

Priest I never became. Deacon at age 61 ... What happened?

I could not really find my feet in establishment Christianity. Deep down I was uncomfortable with Cambridge Anglicanism, which seemed to be the rich merchant class at prayer, more moral than really spiritual, trying to hold onto the best of both God and mammon. They were probably equally uncomfortable with me. The more so when, my academic development having outrun my emotional development, I nosedived into depression in my third term, and no longer looked likely to bring the college in a first in the honours list. My second year in Cambridge was probably the most miserable in my life. I kept my faith, using evening chapel as my religious backbone, but was stuck. Later I drew from this the lesson that most of the plum places in religious structures go to those to whom the system (or an important person in it) takes a liking at an early age, and decides it is worth their time and effort to co-opt into it. If this matching process does not work, if you do not 'join the club' at this stage, there is almost no second chance: the best places are already taken. It's not nice, doesn't sound very 'Christian', but is I fear an accurate description of how things happen.

I moved sideways; not too badly in fact; I got off tranquillisers fairly quickly, spent a year out in Germany teaching – my first year ever in really mixed society – returned to Cambridge, got a decent degree and then went into banking in London and Germany, picking up en route an MBA from a top European business school, which I got into probably thanks to a high intelligence test score and as the only English candidate who was really trilingual.

The salary from the ensuing job with an American bank in Germany was good, too good. But something was nagging stronger and stronger. I am not a businessman at heart. At age 32, I quit in quick succession a job I did not believe in and a relationship that had no mileage. I will leave the precise details to any biographer, but by what seems at once a miracle, but where I had that inner certainty of knowing I was doing the right thing, I found myself, within two months, as a postulant in a French Roman Catholic monastery.

It lasted two years. I loved it at first, an almost idyllic setting in western France, a good library and the novice master away sick half of the time, leaving me to get on with things myself. I read, prayed, wrote and thought, putting together the basis of a personal Christian philosophy which still underpins my faith. The real reasons why they asked me to leave were never explained to me convincingly, though yes, a year and a half in I could see it coming. The zealot in me was unhappy. I had expected monks to be men of courage and deep prayer. Yes, there were one or two, and the abbot, whom I loved, was outsized physically and spiritually. But there was an awful lot of second rate and of minor neurosis, including, I suspected, psychosomatic reasons for the novice master's sickness. At the same time, it had become clear that I myself was carrying wounds from an unbalanced home background that would need time, space and good guidance to heal. The monastery was unwilling (and probably unable) to provide these. I could not square the inability of a monastery – supposedly a treasure-house of Christian wisdom and spiritual practice – to untie the inner knots of myself and other psychologically underperforming brethren with the deep inner healing which I believed (and still believe) to be a key promise of the Christian gospel. I clashed with the novice master badly on this. It became him or me, and he was stronger, organizationally, and I had to go. This episode taught me hard lessons: that any ecclesiastical structure is, for many of its members, a provider of security and identity. Threaten these and the structure will throw you out, and fast. Nor are monasteries very good places for deep spiritual healing.

Back on the periphery again, and the second most miserable year of my life. The good Lord was merciful, and within a year I had found my way onto my feet in translation in Brussels, self-employed, which I hated at first, but for which for the past ten years I have thanked Him daily. I married, bought a house, we had two kids, but then the marriage broke down. A Protestant pastor from the charismatic movement held my hand through some very difficult months, and forced me to look God hard in the face again. I did so, though not in the way my pastor friend expected. I could not root in Protestantism and was not happy with the Roman Catholicism which had thrown me out. One day I looked up *'Église orthodoxe'* in the Brussels phone book, visited three churches, and stayed in the third one for two years. I started postal studies at the Orthodox seminary in Paris, and felt once again very comfortable. A couple of years later my wife left for England with the boys. I stayed in Brussels, got on with my translation work, and moved into the Russian part of the Orthodox Church.

I had learnt my lesson in the monastery: don't rock boats; so I came very gently into the Russian community, with a priest who spoke reasonable French and, I think, was glad to have someone who was socially well-placed in his rather ragamuffin and largely refugee community. By this time I had got myself, via the seminary, a proper spiritual director who, to my surprise, insisted on my getting remarried.

Almost simultaneously three things happened. I remarried, to my present wife, a Russian artist I met when she was here for an exhibition, and loved me enough to go through all the hassle to uproot to Belgium with me. Second, I went to Mount Athos. I loved the place, and have returned every year since. There I was among people with whom I could be openly zealot, in the good sense, people for whom God and their commitment to Him was the only thing that mattered, and who were prepared to engage with Him seriously. Third, to use Orthodox parlance, I came into the altar, first as second acolyte, then later as subdeacon, and unexpectedly, three years ago, as a deacon.

Ten years later, I can say that the marriage has worked. I still marvel at how my wife puts up with me day by day. What has certainly helped is that she has in the meantime found her niche, setting up an icon-painting school which is proving very successful, and an excellent source of quality Christian contacts.

Eighteen months ago I signed up for a carpentry course. It is in the family. Two years away from retirement age, it was my way of handling the fact that my earlier dream of retiring into non-stipendiary priesthood was not to be, and that I needed another occupation if I was not to remain translating full-time till the grave.

I am often asked: why are you Orthodox, in a church far away from your own cultural roots? The answer is that I have found in its spirituality a way, over time, to face and work through my own inner hurt and to start to advance, I hope, towards full Christian maturity, in the words of St Paul, towards the 'perfect Man, into the measure of the stature of the fullness of Christ' (Ephesians 4:13, KJV). This said, I do not side with Orthodox zealots who insist that Orthodoxy is the only Christian way to salvation. Much of the best of Orthodoxy spirituality can be found elsewhere, if you look hard enough. Orthodoxy is a curious jumble of the very best and the very worst in Christianity, of marvellous saints and some really tawdry churchmanship. I have had to learn to take courage from the first and put up inner defences against the latter. Orthodoxy is not an easy option and I would not recommend it to everyone, especially in its often degraded Western diaspora form. But despite all this, it remains the best way for me and I thank God for introducing me to it.

Mine is the rare experience of having spent time in each major part of the Christian church: Nonconformist, Anglican, Roman Catholic and Orthodox, with minor forays into Quakerism and charismatic Protestantism. In each of them I have found deeply saintly people, in nearly every one incompetents and charlatans. To each of them I owe something: to Protestantism a love of the Scriptures, to Anglicanism a sense of decency and good order and of liturgy properly done. My experience of monasticism in the Roman Church has given me a sense of disciplined spiritual life, while parts of its spirituality, especially the fourteenth-century German mystics and the sixteenth-century Spanish ones continue to challenge me. My really close spiritual friends are as much outside Orthodoxy as in it. With them, my primary identity is 'Christian'.

What my Christian experience has taught me is that, regardless of one's particular confession, there is for many of us a critical point where we have to be able to leave the comfort and safety of structures and move towards Christ Himself. I am reminded here of the biblical image of St Peter, who with Christ's blessing, gets out of the boat he is in with the other disciples, and walks across the lake to Him. It is the experience of having got out of the boat at a couple of critical moments and, like Peter, to have been caught by Him as I started to sink, that gives me a certain inner freedom which enables me to exist within often sorely inadequate structures.

Like anyone the wrong side of 60, I realise I am not eternal, and it is time to separate out the essential from the non-essential. Outward rank and position are not essential. A bishop leaves his fancy vestments, his expensive ornaments, and his social pre-eminence at the judgement throne. Nor is there any fast lane for Orthodox there. What remains essential for me is to maintain the freedom, inward and outward, to act and speak my faith in a world which is much less sympathetic to Christianity than 50 years ago. But above everything else, what matters between now and the grave is to gain real spiritual depth, the 'fullness of Christ' I mentioned earlier, achievable only through a disciplined prayer life. Maybe a bishop still decides to make me a priest sometime between now and the grave, 40 or 50 years after the originally planned date. Maybe he does not. But that's not that important. What counts is 'to know God' and to 'be known by God' (Galatians 4:9). The rest is secondary.

2010

My wife started blogging first, and I followed. For me it seemed an opportunity for dialogue on shared ideas and concerns, which I lacked in my immediate Christian community – the Russian Orthodox cathedral parish in Brussels.

By now I had been 15 years in Orthodoxy, and in the same parish for 13 years. I was long past the neophyte convert stage, and clear in my mind as to Orthodoxy's strengths and weaknesses. I was already expressing doubts as to convert Orthodoxy, doubts confirmed since then with the closure of all local language churches within our Russian diocese in Belgium.

More importantly I was already beginning to sense the need for a more mature Christianity, especially for lay people. My 23 November posting was my first serious posing of the question, which has been a recurrent theme since.

And right at the end of the year I was ordained a deacon. This was unexpected: I had thought my previous divorce had excluded this. It began a long process of mastering the services and of learning Church Slavonic sufficiently well to read in church.

Sending God wafting out with the incense...

27 May 2010

I watched with interest the YouTube video of a traditional Latin mass by the dissident SSPX group in Antwerp that a friend of that persuasion sent me. I have a certain sympathy with the old-fashioned East-facing celebration of the mass as recognising the might and glory of God. Yet I am uneasy: it can push God out into the 'yonder' – conveniently distant.

West-facing celebration forces the 'God with us' – we have to come to terms with the fact that this God of glory wants to be with us, to become very tangible to us in our midst and in our very depths, individually and perhaps also corporately. Rather than have Him waft out of the east window or to the apex of the reredos in clouds of incense, we meet this *Deus tremens et timendus* (God of fear and trembling) when we really start to search for God in the depths of our hearts and experience the mixture of fear and hope as we come closer to the place, the *morada*, where the Trinity dwells in us.

Intelligentsia and Church – an uneasy co-existence

26 July 2010

Throughout its existence, the Russian intelligentsia has found itself in loosely networked dissent against an authority seen to be (and which was) sophisticated only in its brutality. From the mid-1980s onwards, led by figures like Fr Alexander Men and the group in Moscow which became St Tikhon's Orthodox University, part of the intelligentsia found its way into the Orthodox Church. But 20 years on the Christian intelligentsia remains edgy, often deeply believing and extraordinarily well-read in theology and church art and history, but unwilling to commit fully into mainstream church life. It is viscerally anti-power, and the Orthodox Church has quickly been perceived as a power structure which, notwithstanding the faith element, is little different to any other in Russian history.

My English sense of fair play tells me that it is unjust to place the entire blame on the central church hierarchy, which includes men of considerable spiritual and intellectual vigour and pastoral concern. Indeed I at times ask myself – as have others in the Western press – just how much they are masters in their own house, given the blurred frontiers between secular and spiritual power, including a deep-rooted nationalist and anti-Western populism, in which church and state are hopelessly fused.

Coming back to the intelligentsia, the Roman Catholic Church has perhaps been wiser: it has parked its intelligentsia in organizations like the Jesuits, Dominicans and Opus Dei, which are answerable directly to Rome and not the local bishop, as are the monastic orders. A possible new development in the Russian church is that many competent clergy are staying away from the church power centres of Moscow and St Petersburg, a position that the Internet, Skype and the blogosphere are making increasingly tolerable.

Why don't we Orthodox convert Belgium?

28 July 2010

He was an intense and rather abrupt young man, from somewhere in the former USSR, completing a doctorate somewhere in England. I am by now used to intense young Russians, so I kept my cool. Why, he asked me, was the Russian Orthodox Church not doing missionary work in the Belgian community, challenging the Catholics and Protestants? He had a point. Why indeed not?

The straight answer – and at the risk of spitting in my own soup – is that the results are not convincing. Even if there are certainly individual cases of holiness, they are not reproducible.

It has to do, I think, with the inevitable mix of religion and culture: simply, the Russian Orthodox or the Greek Orthodox or the Romanian Orthodox Church are the way the Russians, Greeks and Romanians have dealt with God within their existing cultural frameworks. I am not sure that Orthodoxy really matches with the cultural framework of either Belgium (my host country) or England (my home country).

Almost the only way to become an Orthodox and survive in the long run, is either to adopt another culture (I know a couple of priests who have adopted the Russian culture pretty successfully) or to adapt it to your own culture. And when you do, I do not really know whether it is distinguishable from Roman

Catholicism (in Belgium) or the best in (Anglo-) Catholicism. I remember here a conversation with a fellow English exile, also a convert to Orthodoxy, a few years back, where, well into the second bottle of wine, we decided that Orthodoxy was the best way to be Anglo-Catholic outside England.

There is a third version, which is carrying around a sort of tailor-made culture all of one's own, a bit like a snail carries its own house everywhere with it. This culture is good for one's own personal spiritual life, for a small circle of like-minded friends, and eventually to the odd visit to Mount Athos, but totally unrelated to the cultural environment in which such Orthodox converts live and work. Very often you recognise them by their full shelves of Orthodox books, or their presence at yet another conference on the repetitive theme of how to be Orthodox in Belgium. But ultimately, they are hermaphrodites, and spiritually unable to reproduce. But that's the subject of another post...

Ecumenism as an excuse

20 November 2010

I drove out today to the annual conference of the National Catholic Commission for Ecumenism being held in Ciney, Belgium, south of Namur, as the Russian Orthodox Church representative. (...)

As I remarked to my Anglican compatriot, this is not really about ecumenism at all. What this really is – and why we are here – is one of the few occasions in the year in which the Christian intellectual élite can get together and be intellectual in top gear. Indeed our confessional differences are not so much a problem to be thrashed out as an excuse to get together, and to breathe a bit of fresh air outside our own parish and confessional boundaries. Among ourselves we reached unity a generation ago...

Freedom and structure in the church

23 November 2010

Increasingly I see a problem of church structures blocking the road to spiritual maturity. Let me test out a hypothesis on spiritual development. The consequences are different in Russia and in Western Europe, but the underlying pattern is the same. I tried it on our mixed-confession group of English-speaking clergy in Brussels, and they reacted positively.

Let me start with a basic three-stage model of Christian development, for both lay people and clergy outside monasteries...

Stage one: An initial stage, in which the structure is largely provided by the church, its services, its feasts and fasts, its standard patterns for home and private prayer.

Stage two: After a period, there is a shift from external to internal structure. We begin to develop a structure based more directly in Christ, rooted in Him, in which we are less dependent on the outer structure. We thirst for Christ in a different way, and slowly come to know Him independently of the external structures. The process can be a messy one: we feel dissatisfied with the outer structure, may go into reaction against the church, become less regular in our churchgoing. Western Christianity knows this as the 'Dark Night of the Soul'.

Stage three: At the end of this period we have gained sufficient spiritual freedom to return to the structures, but now as mature people, moving towards the 'stature of the fullness of Christ' (Ephesians 4:13, KJV), psychologically free and able to maintain a critical distance from the formal structure where necessary. This includes being able to differ with one's priest or bishop without walking out of the church.

My contention is that, in both Russia and the West, until the 1950s, the overwhelming majority of lay people traditionally spent all their lives at stage one. Today, however, in particular as a result of large-scale higher education, many lay people feel the urge to move further into stages two and three. I would argue that this is a normal psycho-spiritual development for intelligent and educated people. Stage one is a natural place, for both lay people and non-monastic clergy to be in until, perhaps, their mid-thirties. After about that age, it is time to move beyond. If one is still in stage one by age 50, one is heading for serious trouble.

In Russia, a major problem seems to be that most parish priests are ordained while still in stage one, and have great difficulty themselves in moving beyond it. What a Russian seminary teaches you, first and foremost, is to be a guardian of the structure. If a priest cannot move beyond stage one, individual members cannot do so properly, and either remain immature and unhappy, or simply quit. Tragically, some people are made bishops in this stage (no one should really be a bishop unless and until they have safely landed in stage three). The result is spiritual stagnation for themselves and their flocks.

In Western Europe the problem is different: intelligent lay people want to move directly to stage two, without the thorough grounding in liturgy and word that stage one provides. But without stage one engrained, one will not get through stage two.

In both Russia and Western Europe, there is often insufficient flexibility for a priest who is ordained while still in stage one, but is naturally moving beyond it, to make the necessary adjustments. He has to remain the guardian of the structures, even if he is losing his own belief in and dependence on them. It may be that many priests need to move out of parish ministry for a few years into teaching or social work.

Stage three is the goal for all, bishops, priests and intelligent lay people. But for priests and bishops it means accepting to deal with intelligent lay people who have their own maturity, who do not go running to *batushka*[1] for everything, who can largely structure their own spiritual lives, who are co-workers with them, rather than their servants. For most Western priests this is generally not a problem; in Russia I suspect it can be a very serious one.

2011

They say that the devils arrive soon after ordination, and I was no exception. For me they came with my translating Patriarch Kirill of Moscow's book 'Freedom and Responsibility' into English, also negotiating its publication, and helping with its launch at that year's London Book Fair. I was correctly paid, but the insights I got into the way 'Moscow' works were disturbing and left a bad taste which remains till today.

This starts a long period of increasing unhappiness with Russian Orthodoxy, and of questioning its practices, its approach to society, and, locally, its witness and relevance in Belgium. This will be a repeated theme.

Orthodoxy has also given positive impulses to my thinking. It has heavily shaped my ideas on the relationship between Christianity and democracy, and led me to question the tacit assumptions of many Western Christians that democracy is the only valid form of government in God's eyes (17 October; 20 December 2014).

It has also exposed me to popular religion, Volksreligion, in which, like in pre-Vatican II Catholicism, people visit church services in languages they do not understand and rarely take communion. The priest is the absolute authority, the preaching is heavily moralistic. The church is politically conservative and allied with the powers that be. On the one hand this type of religion risks acting as a brake on a more committed Christianity, on the other hand if the majority church of a country does not provide this social glue, nastier forces will fill the gap. This too becomes a constant theme (23 November; 1 February 2015), extending more recently to the role of ritual, something I sense to be vital to the homo religiosus, and which Orthodoxy retains, however impurely, better than most (29 April 2019).

Christians in exile – openness or ghetto?

31 January 2011

(...) Christians find themselves in exile situations, living outside their home countries for a variety of reasons: political, economic, psychological and so on. Where this exile looks to be permanent, it is in my eyes incumbent on the exile to integrate into Christian life in the host country, and to become part of the witness of the host country's Christian community to the wider world. This means learning the host country (religious) language and understanding its Christian structures. Unless theologically or morally impossible, it also presupposes a positive attitude towards the host country's majority church.

This also imposes a duty on the churches representing the (old) home confession in the host country. Once that church in a particular location has a majority of members who are permanent residents of the new country, it is incumbent on it to orient its member's life and witness to the host country. Trying to pen exiles into the old country's religious patterns and language not only does not work (my best guess is that 80% of the next generation will marry locally and quit), it is in fundamental dereliction of the duty of every individual Christian and worshipping community to witness to Christ in the society in which it finds itself.

Yes, there may be doctrinal reasons which prevent full cooperation with the host country's majority church, in which case it is fair and honest to maintain a separate identity. But these must not be used, or worse, exaggerated (as they too often are) as an excuse to maintain a cosy – but spiritually sterile – apartness and a refusal to integrate.

An Orthodox Church in the diaspora which can witness to the essential Christian message to the world around it, and enrich the local Christian church with its particular liturgical or ascetic contribution, is acceptable, and can indeed be a blessing. An Orthodox Church which shuts itself off behind high walls of language or liturgical practice (or simply not providing seating for outsiders unable to stand for two hours at a stretch) in order to retain a redundant identity, is simply failing in its basic duty, to its own flock, to the host country's Christian community, to the wider world and to God.

Kirillus absconditus (or wrestling with the Patriarch's thought)

19 May 2011

I continue to wrestle with the Patriarch's book ('Freedom and Responsibility', published by DLT in 2011, and which I translated into English). The devil is in the detail – in sentences which sound good but prove hard to piece together into a coherent system, at least for my Western mind. In particular I am having a hard time trying to get the 'morality' and 'tradition' to which he is constantly referring to lock together. If I understand the Patriarch right, he says that we all have a moral sense planted deeply in us, from the very fact of our being created in the image of God. *Capax sensus moralis quod capax Dei.* So far, so good. But then he talks of the church as 'securing morality', and acting a guardian of morality, in particular through its tradition.

Here I feel uncomfortable. Rather, it seems to me that the church's role is to direct and help individuals to the purity of heart and mind which will give them the mind of Christ, which will give them a correct moral sense and enable them to make the right moral judgements, especially in those difficult cases (divorce; what is and is not corruption in a business or administration setting; in situ reactions to alcoholism, family violence or homosexuality) which do not fit into neat categories. And since moral sense belongs to that inner, private sphere in which we meet God, any morality, or indeed any religion, imposed from the outside, by church (*batushka*), state or neighbours, without genuine consent, becomes very quickly violation and violence. We can warn, we can exhort, we can hopefully give a good example, but it stops there. As does Christ.

And where do tradition and 'traditional morality' (even if the latter term is not, I think, the Patriarch's) come into the picture here? Traditional morality very quickly evokes a bygone system of social control, very largely predicated on making sure that women were not left with unwanted children and without financial support and men did not catch VD (outdated by contraception, the welfare state and penicillin), in which 'what the neighbours say' was of paramount importance and where the local priest ruled in terror from the confessional.

On the other hand, if by 'tradition' we mean more a general approach to life, with God included in any view of the world, and with the 'mind in heart' (νους ἐν καρδία) rather than the rational mind as supreme arbiter, the practice of which the church is instrumental in passing from one generation to another, then we may be closer to getting these two pieces of the jigsaw – morality and tradition – to fit. But then can we please use a term like 'tradition-supported moral sense' rather than 'traditional morality'.

Orthodox in the diaspora – essentials and trappings

21 August 2011
As I try to think my way forward, within a local Orthodox diaspora situation (the Russian Orthodox Church in Belgium) which is going nowhere in particular, I find myself increasingly making a clear distinction between two aspects of Orthodoxy. The first aspect is the core essentials or kerygma of Orthodoxy. For me these lie in the emphasis on deification and the associated ascetic path, with a constant reference to monasticism somewhere in the background, and a sense of a deep prayer that is highly salvific, not only for the one praying, but for his or her wider entourage.

The second aspect is the external trappings (music, vestments, architecture, priest-people relationships, patterns of interaction between the different levels of the hierarchy) which reflect the particular social cultures in which Orthodoxy has grown and has influenced and been influenced by.

Increasingly I conclude that the Orthodox kerygma can travel fairly easily and cross-culturally, but that the cultural trappings travel badly. So badly in fact that I am having to seriously ask myself whether Orthodoxy is currently 'saleable' in Western Europe, at least in its Russian form. It is one thing to convert to the Orthodox kerygma, quite another to convert to Russian culture, especially in its post-1990 form, with patterns of authority, expectations of deference and a display of 'power' which are at odds with general Western Christian standards. With respect I would point out that what successes there have been (Metropolitan Anthony of Sourozh, Archbishop Vassili Krivoshein or Elder Sophrony Sakharov) were mainly pre-1917

Russian in style with a heavy dose of Mount Athos, and also had a holiness that could lift above cultural differences. Post-1990 Russian Orthodoxy, often appearing more brash than holy, has on the contrary made relatively little headway in my part of the world.

This ultimately raises the question: does one have to convert to Orthodoxy – and quit one's whole social-cultural background – in order to buy into this Orthodox kerygma? I am increasingly believing one does not. I know people in the Roman Catholic Church whose prayer feels close enough to Orthodoxy as to make no difference, and for whom I would see no point of moving out into an Orthodox ghetto. I can sense how the Orthodox kerygma could be introduced into the Church of England, or the Church of Sweden, even if female clergy are one step too far for Orthodox sensitivities. In the case of the Church of England, it would feel very close to the best of Anglo-Catholicism, of the non-exaggerated kind where, I will admit, part of my own heart still lies. Certainly 'Orthodoxised' Roman Catholics or Anglicans, well introduced into local structures, can pull a lot more weight than they can by moving out into the little Orthodox ghettos, which with one or two rare exceptions (Ennismore Gardens in London, Bussy monastery in France, possibly the Orthodox seminaries in Paris) count for zero in the wider Christian life of their host countries.

What I am noticing is that, without saying so explicitly, many of the spiritually more mature Orthodox I know in and around the Russian church, both Russian and local convert, are taking their lead less and less from the main Russian centres and more and more from Athos, or from Athos 'proxies' like the Monastery of St John the Baptist (Maldon) in England.

Is this giving us a message we need to be heeding more closely?

An unhappy parish

3 September 2011

Right now, I would describe our cathedral parish where I serve as a deacon as a Christmas tree on which each member has come and hung his or her own decorations. Originally the decorations were all pretty similar and matched: that of a refugee congregation seeking human warmth and identity in the economically difficult 1930s. How really 'Christian' they were is another question. Most of those who placed decorations are long dead and buried. The present set of decorations now hanging on the tree are a badly matching set put there by the children of the 1917-1923 wave of *émigrés*, a large group of Polish masons/cleaning ladies who came in the 1980s, and a few mixed marriages. Probably, though we don't say so, what unites us most is a dislike of the style of the former parish priest (*batushka, batushka*-type autocracy) who went off with 70% of the parishioners ten years ago to found a bigger church elsewhere in town and get as far away as possible from the bishop. We preferred to stay.

The problem right now is that there is no pattern among the present decorations. To be fair, we are on average more Christian and less 'ethnic-identical' than a generation ago. We more or less know and accept our individual and diverse histories, but we have no picture of where we are going as a group.

For 40 years we have dodged the issue of what we are here to do once the Russian memories fade, once we are integrated into Belgian society, once, as will inevitably happen, Russian is no longer a lingua franca. Until we grasp this nettle by the root; until in our minds and souls we are living in Brussels in 2011, and not in a church summer camp of the 1950s where they still spoke Russian, or in a remaining Russian aristo enclave still playing the worn-out 'if only there had been no 1917' record, or in our eastern Polish village where we return every summer, or in the Athonite monastery where we hole up once a year to get 'real' Orthodoxy; and, probably most importantly, until we confess to God our corporate failure to grasp this nettle and agree with Him that our primary duty is for an Orthodox Christian witness in the Belgian here and now, we are going to go nowhere. Nor probably do we deserve to.

A lesson from a strange conference

28 September 2011

It was a strange conference. The name of the organization 'Philosophy and Management' told me that it would be free-thinking rather than Christian. But the subject interested me, the organization is part-sponsored by my largest customer, and with a dearth of Christian intellectual life in Brussels, why not, I thought.

At one stage I was asked 'What do you think of this as a Christian theologian?'. I refused to comment. I can see many well-meaning Christians saying 'You should have taken your chance to witness – in season and out of season'. The more I think back, the more I feel I was right. The other people at the table had been more open about themselves than usual. Importantly they were using their own and not borrowed language. OK, it was still a bit shallow, but no matter. If I had spoken as a theologian at that stage, in standard Christian religious language, they would have closed up, gone into argument mode, and we would have got nowhere. I am convinced that if we say that the image of God is already in people, then our role as theologians and pastors is to enable them to find their way back to this, in their own time and using their own language. The language of their truth.

Justice, not democracy

17 October 2011
It was a disappointing debate at the big Catholic bookshop, where an up-and-coming Catholic priest, Erik de Beukelaer, former spokesman of the Archbishop, presented his book 'Credo politique'. He is a competent speaker and clearly has a good head on his shoulders. I left dissatisfied, not able to put my finger on why. It was only in the metro on the way home that it became clear why.

He had strongly defended democracy, to the point of nearly making it an article of faith. This for me is wrong: the article of faith should be justice, and democracy as a possible way of making it happen. There is indeed a strong democratic culture in Belgium, but it is undermined by two things: by ethnic cleavages, and by a lack of social mobility.

Basically there is, as nearly everywhere in the world, a 'ruling establishment' which pretty much runs the country into its own pocket. This phenomenon is not as crass as in many other places in the world: first because the circle is much larger, including a large upper middle class; and second because it is not obviously corrupt. But social mobility is seriously limited, including by poor public education (outside a few elite schools largely squatted by the establishment) and by a tax system which makes it very difficult to accumulate new wealth and very easy to retain it if you already have it. In my bad moments I wonder whether, for all their talk, this class really wants first-class education to be available to all: bright and well educated kids from outside their social circles threatening the position of their own children, especially if these kids came from the Muslim or other ethnic communities, which represent today some one in three of the Brussels school age population.

No, I don't teach my kids democracy: I try to encourage values of justice, stress the importance of hard effort and delayed satisfaction, and insist that they work out exactly how the system works (largely self-interest) and not how it is theoretically supposed to (democracy).

καλος *and Christianity*

25 October 2011
Since being in Athens for the first time last week, I am thinking a lot of the relationship of the Greek notion of καλος (beauty and goodness – physical and especially moral) and Christianity. I suspect καλος is key to understanding the educational tradition, with its heavy Greek and Latin emphasis, that produced the Anglican and Lutheran elite from 1850 to 1950. The ethical discourse of this elite was so imbued with the classical pre-Christian tradition, that one is not always sure whether this is Christianity in a toga or chiton, or Socrates or Cicero in a preacher's gown. The embodiment of this is probably the brilliant classics-educated Dean Inge, whose writings, with those of Bishop Charles Gore, dominated the Anglicanism of the pre-C. S. Lewis and pre-William Temple era. On its own, this tradition quickly becomes cold and arid (an impression borne out by photos of Inge himself), and yet its absence in modern Catholicism and Orthodoxy is probably a loss.

Volkskirche and the elect

23 November 2011

Last Monday evening the Roman Catholic cardinal Walter
Kasper gave a well-reported speech in Munich in which he
said that the period of 'social Christianity' or *Volkskirche* was
coming to an end in Germany and Europe, and that the Roman
Catholic Church in this part of the world is in the birth pangs
of something new.

I blow hot and cold on this one.

The biblicist in me says: 'Of course, the message of Christianity
goes beyond the national, tribal aspect of religion and into new
waters', quoting either St Peter: 'you are a chosen race, a royal
priesthood, a dedicated nation, and a people claimed by God for
his own, to proclaim the triumphs of him who called you out of
darkness into his marvellous light' (1 Peter 2:9 NEB) or St Paul:
'there is no question here of Greek and Jew, circumcised and
uncircumcised, barbarian, Scythian, freeman, slave' (Colossians
3:11, NEB) or again 'so as to create out of the two [Gentiles and
Jews] a single new humanity in himself … to reconcile the two
to God in a single body' (Ephesians 2:15–16, NEB).

But the socio-political observer says: 'Careful, any search
for a common purpose and identity at a national or supra-
national level inevitably takes on a religious component, and
if Christianity vacates the space which has traditionally been
assigned to it here, something else very much less pleasant may
take its place. For the last 40 years, in our rather comfortable
identity-less existence halfway between national state and
Europe, this need for religion as a factor of identity and common
purpose has shrunk. But with a major shift in identity patterns
and/or a period of economic and social difficulty possibly
ahead of us in Europe, the need for religion could return with
a vengeance.'

The historian in me is reminded of the way Hitler harnessed
this underlying and unsatisfied need for the religious, and the
cynic in me adds that he was German and that it looks like
Germany and other 'Germanic' peoples will be setting the
agenda for the new Europe. Which is why I instinctively give
more time of the day than most to Russian Patriarch Kirill and

his desire to keep the patriotic *Volkskirche* idea alive, even if I have a hard time justifying it by Scripture or the Fathers.

The tricky thing here then becomes maintaining the 'church of the chosen' (the ἐκλεκτοι) and the *Volkskirche* together so they do not go off into separate orbit, as they did in Russia with the Old Believers *raskol* (schism), or as happened in late-eighteenth-century England where the Methodists and the Church of England parted company.

Bound by a girdle

27 November 2011

I am having a hard time with my religious instincts in reacting to the phenomenon of the huge crowds in Moscow queuing for up to 24 hours to venerate the Girdle of the Virgin relic (the girdle or belt that is supposed to have fallen from the Virgin's waist as she was taken up to heaven, and is one of the most treasured relics of Vatopedi Monastery on Mount Athos).

I ask what is going on in the mind and soul of the Ivan or Olga or Natasha, who probably rarely goes to Sunday liturgy, but who will queue for hours in the freezing weather to venerate a relic brought in from outside Russia (and will not know that there has been another relic of the same girdle in Moscow for several hundred years). I suspect that the answer will be something like 'we felt bound to do it'. That something deep down in their subconscious told them that this was right.

This is an area that the Orthodox Church, and in particular the Russian church, plays heavily to. We are in the area of the primitive 'religious' – a word that by its very etymology has the idea of being 'bound', 'linked' into something very deep and beyond us, in that area of the subconscious that probably includes patriotism, which certain members of the Russian hierarchy emphasise strongly.

The question is whether this 'boundness' is always right in the Christian understanding. Or as a friend put it to me: 'Will people who have venerated the girdle come back "sanctified in soul and body ... enlightened ... saved"' in a way we hope that they would on taking communion in a proper state of mind. I sense that a lot of Christians, particularly Protestants and many

Catholics, will say that it is not; that this is a 'boundness' that Christ has come to set us free from.

I myself feel mixed on this one. I believe very much in the existence of this deep religious subconscious, possibly on a 'group-subconscious basis' as defined by Carl Jung, and I strongly suspect that a lot of the prayer of the church, and in particular of the *startsi*,[1] operates at this level. I suspect that Protestantism has largely lost it and is the poorer for that. Yet I am far from convinced that all this area is 'clean', that one can evoke and use it all the time. At the very least there has to be a relationship between venerating a relic and partaking of communion. When this link is lost – as it seems to be to a large extent in the present situation – I think one has the right to ask questions. Exactly of whom, I am not sure. Of Ivan, Olga and Natasha, of why they do not go to the liturgy? Or of our hierarchy, for putting the Christian label on something that is in fact part of a general religious subconsciousness, and the 'boundness' of which does not always include the sense of 'freedom' and 'life' which we associate with a fully lived Christian existence.

Two questions to Patriarch Kirill

18 December 2011
Following a speech by the Patriarch Kirill of Moscow, two questions arose...

The first question: Who defines truth in the Russian church, both in theory and in practice? The magic word *sobornost* which we learnt at seminary flutters into my mind. But what does it mean in practice? Should it not somehow be the 'mind of the church interpreted and expressed by the synod', which seems to me to mean some sort of process of consultation, and, ex post, some sort of validation through its wide acceptance by the faithful. This consultation process does not have to be 'democratic': few in the church would disagree that a wise old confessor of 60 should weigh more than an 18-year-old student. But one can be excused in the present situation of asking whether the 'mind of the church' is not becoming the mind of a very small inner circle, to the point of being not far off a 'papal infallibility' in disguise.

The second question: How does the Patriarch really want Russia to be ruled? My impression is: by a nomenklatura of people who have decided among themselves that they have a right to hold power, who self-police themselves morally under the guidance of the church, opt capable people into their group, and possibly get themselves mandated by the common people in some sort of more or less managed elections ever so often. I'm not saying this is right or wrong. But to work over the long haul it does demand a high moral level and quite a measure of self-sacrifice. And indeed people of such high moral calibre and self-sacrifice do exist at the high levels of the Russian nomenklatura. I have met a couple of them personally – deeply Christian men – and have been impressed. But the fact remains that 'absolute power corrupts absolutely' and two terms of office is enough for anyone short of a saint. And that two or three levels down – the level of the praise-singers and 'snouts in the trough' – it gets pretty unpleasant.

2012

From now until about 2014 our parish passes through a slough of despond, which we seem unable to get out of. I am told, in an inappropriate way, that I will never be ordained priest. I had assumed that, once made deacon, priesthood would be only a matter of time. At the same time several men with considerably less religious and general education are priested. This hurts. Slowly I come to accept the fact and seek an alternative role (26 March 2013; 8 March 2014; 7 July 2018).

In 2012 we celebrated 150 years of Russian Orthodox presence in Belgium. This included a conference together with the Jesuits on Orthodoxy past and future, which I orchestrated. The conference, which drew heavily on talents from other Orthodox churches (we lacked the local talent for the level of audience), was a success, and earned me a church medal.

The anniversary drew the usual crowd of praise-singers, with articles and a TV reporter from Russia flattering the Russian church in Belgium to the sky. Finally, sickened by the whole affair and without telling anyone, I wrote a 'corrective', entitled 'Orthodoxy in Belgium – Towards what Future' (see pp. 221), which, pretty miraculously, ended up being published in a serious Russian Orthodox journal in Moscow. It cast me as the rebel thinker, and some say put pay to any hopes of priesthood.

At the end of the year, acknowledging that I would not be ordained priest and not be spending large amounts of time on this after retirement, I started an evening course in joinery (2 September), which I continued through to gaining my state joiner's certificate in 2018.

The real art of comparative theology[1]

3 January 2012

Ultimately, unless you take the line that God walked out of the Roman Catholic Church in 1054, you have to expect a similarity of spiritual experience in East and West, that of people seeking the same God based on a largely shared body of texts. In that case the art of comparative theology becomes not one of finding the difference between Eastern and Western theology (which any first year seminary student with a good head can do) but of having the spiritual, linguistic and historical sensitivity to find the bridges and commonalities between the spiritual experience of the Eastern and Western church (including Northern European Pietism), despite very different forms of linguistic expression.

Another fascinating task, which requires much the same sensitivity, is to find out why certain spiritualities 'break down' and run into the sand. Why did Nil Sorsky's movement die out? Why did the Ecole Française lose its wind? Where did Anglo-Catholicism go wrong? What (in my opinion thankfully) has calmed the charismatic movement in the Roman Catholic Church?

Orthodoxy's burden

18 February 2012

I asked the Catholic bishop at our symposium: 'If we put the Pope, the Patriarch of Moscow, Metropolitan Hilarion Alfayev, yourself, and a few members of the Roman Curia together on the famous desert island, with a decent supply of water, vodka and good Italian wine, and with no press around, how long would it take you to agree on intercommunion?'.

He sidestepped the question elegantly. My own guess is maximum one week (unless that is that you put two Orthodox patriarchs on the island...). But the question for me gets to the heart of the problem: that the division between Orthodox and Catholic has really very little to do with doctrine, and everything to do with identity.

Identity is, I am beginning to think, Orthodoxy's burden – that is, a situation in which the gospel and of the organization which ensues from it, the church, have become instrumentalized for purposes that have very little to do with the Christian message, and which may in fact block it.

Orthodoxy has turned into a badge of national identity, especially in Slav countries, a component of a myth of uniqueness which would be seriously threatened if Rome and Moscow were to sign up to intercommunion.

Orthodoxy in the diaspora acts as a rallying point for refugees, in an initial period giving an identity and sense of dignity to those who have lost their home bearings, and a generation later providing a mooring for those still unable to identify with their host culture.

Orthodoxy in convert churches offers the psychological benefits of belonging to a special society, an apart group with its own rites, rituals and vocabulary (with similar dynamics to convert circles in English Catholicism, or to Pius X communities, or possibly the Freemasons).

Once religious confession (Orthodox, Roman Catholic, Methodist or whatever, rather than straight 'Christian') becomes identity, it becomes part of people's internal structure and defence mechanism, and you attack it at your peril. And indeed, in a lot of cases, it would be un-Christian to do so: many people need the protection this structure and identity offer.

Yet the Christian call is ultimately a call away from this first level of identity into a new one, rooted not so much in shared origins or chosen group, but in a real Christian experience. Once this experience has weakened the need for this first level of identity, then with people from other confessions one finds one shares a largely common spirituality, even if with different externals and with different labelling.

Indeed our 'ecumenical gatherings', where we pray '*ut unum sint*' (that all may be one – John 17:21) are in fact a contradiction in terms. *Iam unum sunt* (They are already one). Their real use for many of us is rather to provide an opportunity for those who already essentially 'unum sunt' (are one) to get together. That is me with my friends Fr Dominique from the Catholics, pastor Bernard from the Protestants and Captains Jacques and Yvonne from the Salvation Army, who know that we have all answered the same call to holiness and want to recognise and support each other on the path.

In other words, the barriers to Christian unity have precious little to do with doctrine, and an awful lot to do with confessional structures as a provider of identity.

Rethinking the Orthodox witness in Belgium

18 March 2012

For the last four years I have been co-responsible in Belgium for relations between the Russian Orthodox Church (Moscow Patriarchate) and other Christian communities. I am now convinced we need to radically rethink our approach. I'll try to explain…

The specific spirituality of Orthodoxy, largely centred on divinization (God became man so that man might become God), is consistent and coherent. When lived properly, it is deeply attractive. In and around Belgium we have had Orthodox bishops, priests and monastics men whose holiness, borne of an Orthodox approach, have exercised this attraction: Archbishop Vassili Krivoshein in Belgium, Metropolitan Anthony of Sourozh and Archimandrite Sophrony Sakharov in London, Fathers Serguei Schevitch, Serguei Bulgakov and Boris Bobrinskoy in Paris. They brought men and women from their host countries into the Orthodox Church. They were not without their faults, which history is beginning to show, but they put Orthodoxy on the map as a spiritual force to be reckoned with.

Those 'heroic' days are past. Spirit has given way to structure, which can be either organised or disorganised. The need in Belgium to look after a mass of seekers of a better life – first Greeks, then Poles, then 'refugees' from the 'stans', then Romanians and, more recently, Russian-speaking Moldavians entering en masse with Romanian passports – most of them in the skilled worker/cleaning lady class, has made Orthodox communities less attractive for the university-educated class among whom Orthodoxy traditionally draws converts. The mixing of religion and politics, with diaspora bishops in and out of embassies, is not attractive to the West. The quality of the Orthodox clergy in Belgium is very uneven, from very good to downright shabby. Priests of deep spiritual level, which is what Westerners look to Orthodoxy for, are rare. In short, Orthodoxy is attractive in books but not on the church floor.

In other words, a good product has been rendered unsalable by its packaging. How do we continue to sell the product? It seems to me that there are fundamentally two ways…

The first approach is to say: forget trying to convert local people into Orthodox structures. Rather give them the Orthodox kerygma and let them live it in their existing (Roman Catholic) church structures. Increasingly I believe that Orthodox spirituality can be lived in a Roman Catholic surrounding. It is perhaps not an ideal solution, but neither is their joining the existing Orthodox churches in Belgium, where they will always be second-class citizens, struggling with the liturgical languages, or, in the few local language convert churches, with the temptations of New Age, crankiness, 'religious feminism' (this needs a discussion of its own) and simply being too far from the 'flow' of the church. In this respect, our recent conference entitled 'Orthodoxy between yesterday and today' in conjunction with the Jesuit seminary in Brussels, may point to a way forward. The audience, in the majority good quality Roman Catholic seminarians plus a large contingent from the 'new communities', were genuinely enthusiastic. But I just cannot imagine them 'converting' to Orthodox structures. But I can imagine them picking up the message of theosis and trying to live it out and bring it into their own structures. The other thing that the conference did was to identify a small group of clergy and lay people – Russian, Romanian and Greek – who have the necessary mix of theological competence and spiritual level to be able to present the Orthodox way to educated Christians of other confessions. We need to work on this further.

The second approach is to have an Orthodox monastery somewhere in Brussels, working either in French (the majority local language) or English (increasingly the lingua franca in Belgium) on the style of an Athonite metochion. It would have to fiercely guard its independence from those who would want to take advantage of it for national pride reasons (no financing out of state budgets). It would need priests who can be politely but brutally firm with the gnostic and feminist set, and who can confess properly. English would also have the advantage of maintaining a certain social-intellectual level. I for one, as the one native English-speaking clergyman in Brussels, would be sorely tempted to make it my spiritual base.

Nobility and a simple life

22 March 2012

I have just finished reading Ernst Wiechert's 'Das einfache Leben' (*The Simple Life*). It is part of a small library I inherited from my German 'second mother' when she died in a car crash 20 years ago. I read right through nearly 400 pages in under two weeks.

I rarely read books through to the end. Gustav Freytag, the 'German Dickens' was a recent such casualty after 150 pages. At least three Thomas Mann novels lie unfinished – behind the linguistic brilliance is an emptiness he lacks the courage to face.

Wiechert has that courage: through the novel's main protagonist, pensioned sea captain Thomas von Orla, who quits the emptiness of early 1920s city life for a semi-hermit existence on the Polish border, he faces the German 'death of God', that is the collapse of a whole interlocking social and belief structure held together by twin loyalties to the Emperor and to the Protestant Church (the German equivalent of the Byzantine symphony), following the military collapse of November 1918. It is a harsh book, part novel, part philosophical excursus. You sense that terrible void that comes with loss of a meaning-giving system. Wiechert was widely read in the 1930s, but as *non grata* with the Nazis, to be careful with what he wrote. 'Das einfache Leben' was published in 1939 and one senses the 'inner emigration' typical of non-Nazis of this period. It is, delightfully, written in a German which still has not yet lost its consistency and creativity to multilingualism.

Throughout the book is a strong sense of underlying nobility, in the sense of duty to calling and calling to duty, backed by tradition, a nobility that maintains continuity when both religion and political systems fail. A nobility that is in many ways religion. A nobility that is probably essential to religion, and without which religion becomes quickly cheap and tatty.

Into fifth gear – finally

18 April 2012
We met, six of us, last night, to discuss the book 'Remember Thy First Love', by Archimandrite Zacharias of the Monastery of St John the Baptist (Maldon, Essex).

We were three Roman Catholics, including one religious sister, two Anglicans and myself, Orthodox, all native English speakers. I led it.

It was a moving exercise in the ability of Orthodox spiritual language to carry people closer to God on paths that are either less well mapped out or less travelled in other confessions. The sense of unitedness in our common search was enormous. For me it highlights three things.

First, it is in this area that there is a real thirst, and the real possibility of Orthodox witness, in Western Europe. We have tools which can be of real use at a more advanced stage of spiritual development. Second, to talk ascetic theology, there has to be a certain existing stock of Christian experience and a certain ability to express oneself. We were average age of a little over 50, with, I guess, an average of 30 years serious Christian commitment, and we were all graduate level. We could not have done this with 25-year-olds. Third, to work in this area, you have to have at least a basic knowledge of and respect for the ascetic language of other confessions. You need to know the basics of Meister Eckhart, St John of the Cross, the Ignatian method, have a feeling for the 'École Française', German pietism and so on, and be able to use these 'languages' when appropriate. I can do so – very badly and crudely – but I am one of the only people in Orthodoxy in Belgium who can.

But the joy of being able, for once, to speak at this level. It was like getting out onto the freeway and finally being able to put the car into fourth and then fifth gear, out of the second gear in which I crawl along most of the time in institutional Orthodoxy in Belgium.

Glorious, but...

26 May 2012
Last Tuesday we had the festive liturgy to mark the one-hundred-and-fiftieth anniversary of Orthodoxy in Belgium.

It was glorious, but somehow it seemed so unrelated to what is happening around us in Belgium. We could have been on Mars.

This is my personal struggle with Orthodoxy right now: I want it, and my own Christian life, to be relevant to the country I live in. However glorious the occasional big event, and however much I can vibrate to it personally, there is nowhere in the Russian church in Brussels where I can happily say to a Belgian friend: 'come and see for yourself'.

I managed to make my way in, yes. But I already had 30 years Christian experience, was Bible and liturgically literate, and have a Russian wife who helps with the language and psychology. I am not sure how someone with minimum Christian experience, no Bible literacy, no Russian and a Belgian wife or companion would fare. I don't think they would get very far. And that's wrong somehow.

Russian blues

17 July 2012
From 1995 to 2010 I went to Russia (or Belarus or Ukraine) at least once a year. Last year for the first time I did not. My wife's Russian passport had expired and renewing it proved a miserably slow process. This year she has a passport, and is going, but I'm not.

(...) It is as if I sense also, from somewhere very deep down, that something has to change in Russian Christianity. There was

. of ferment in the Russian church for about 20 years from 85 onwards.. But the dynamism seems to have juddered to a halt. Perhaps this ferment was more wide than deep – too much outer rebuilding and restoration of structures. Too much prominence taken by a rather crude type of preaching which lacks the finesse needed for a deep spiritual life. Too great a temptation to institutionalization and autocracy, which sit uneasily with full, adult, Christian freedom.

It is as if now a new inspiration, new shoots, are needed, taken from the very core of Christian experience and from a very deep prayer. A prayer far from unknown in Russia, that of, among others, St Serguei, St Nil Sorsky, St Seraphim of Sarov. This new ferment will be deeper, perhaps also discreet and hidden, and away from the main monastic centres. I am pretty sure it will come – it is the way God works in history – indeed it may already be coming (and I note in passing the interest of many educated Russian Christians for Mount Athos, possibly standing for something Russian Christianity senses it needs but it does not find coming from Russia itself).

It is this change which interests me. I have little interest in tackily rebuilt churches with their expensive gilding, in bland spiritual writing that lacks real depth and the fresh language of individual experience, and, as an Englishman, I loathe autocracy. They are not worth the trouble and discomfort of travelling to Russia. But when I really sense something fresh happening, the Spirit of God on the waters, then I will be back. It might be worth learning Russian for.

Where angels fear to tread – on Orthodoxy and English spirituality

14 August 2012

We drove yesterday to Ely. This must be one of the most magnificent cathedrals in England, in a quiet city an hour's drive north of Cambridge.

English cathedrals are a complex experience for those with the spiritual and historical background to read and interpret them. The different building styles – Ely, like most English cathedrals, offers the full gamut of medieval architecture, from Norman (Romanesque) to Perpendicular (the particularly

English form of late Gothic) – and the later monuments and stained glass narrate a rich and often difficult spiritual history, into which the native observer like myself also has to fit his or her own. Ely Cathedral was, like many other medieval cathedrals, saved by the Victorians, who had the necessary combination of piety, money and engineering skills to renovate buildings eroded by three centuries of minimum maintenance since the Reformation.

The Victorians restored the buildings but were unable to restore English Christianity into a semblance of unity and uniformity. English Christianity was already badly fractured – in the previous century Methodism had made the running, owing largely to the slowness of the Anglican 'establishment' to take the measure of the nascent industrial and social revolution. At its simplest and crudest, traditional wealth remained Anglican, 'trade' and the working class went non-Conformist. The Oxford Movement of the 1830s and 1840s was a noble attempt to revive a more 'Catholic' spirit which had never quite died out (maintained largely in cathedral worship – its choral tradition takes over the medieval tradition without a break), and return to a more ascetic theology. It failed, in my opinion, first and foremost because the reinstatement of the Roman Catholic hierarchy in 1851 deprived it of vital oxygen. To which we can add the 'drag' factor of being an established church, and the ambiguities of the Gothic revival movement, often more decorative than in depth, and soon using medievalism as a cloak for some rather nasty spiritual undercurrents (Dante Gabriel Rossetti, Edward Burne-Jones...). Anglican attempts at monasticism, from the 1850s onwards have, despite examples of individual sanctity, been a failure, with the possible exception of the Franciscans, some small women's communities, and a very discreet but substantial anchoretic movement. And yes, I had better mention it, there is women's ordination, seen by many on my side of the confessional divide as the 'abomination of desolation' and a breaking point for many outsiders.

In many ways you feel that the cathedrals are waiting for something, for a spirituality with a beauty and spiritual strength to match that of the stonework.

I can already sense the hot breath of some young, keen Orthodox down my neck, saying: we can do this. Some, I am pretty certain, would love nothing better than to be given a large, empty, historical church building (and ample funding from a wealthy sponsor) and to be told: Go ahead.

Beware. As we say in English: 'fools rush in where angels fear to tread'. Like transplant surgery, or tree grafting, putting two religious traditions together is a complex and delicate process, and the reject rate is high. It could be an interesting challenge, but demands enormous wisdom and sensitivity.

Into a new church year

2 September 2012
(Note for non-Orthodox friends: the Orthodox church year runs from September to August).
I go into the new church year in muted mood.
There is a sense of a gathering of energy deep inside, which if I am unable to gather it and direct it usefully within my own Christian terms of reference, could turn into anger or, worse, depression.

I no longer believe that the Russian church in Brussels, in its outward form, has anything useful to offer to the Christian world. Diaspora Orthodoxy (maintaining the outward forms of a left-behind culture in a new cultural space) as practiced here is a contradiction in terms and carries the seeds of its own failure. I believe even less in convert Orthodoxy of the type that flourished here in the 1970s and 1980s, which is dying fast.

(...) Something else is working to the surface, which I would describe as liturgy in a broader sense of the term. It is the sense that the essential role of redeemed humanity is as an intermediary in bringing the creation to God: if you like, so that it can sing to its creator. Without this 'God-pointing' of ourselves and creation, we are mired in futility.

For this we have to be 'grounded', and I am beginning to think some sort of handicraft may be an essential part of this: creatively taking the very elements of God's creation and working with them: whether earth in gardening, wood in carpentry and carving, thread in weaving, food in cooking. This is why I have registered for a course in cabinet-making at the

Institut des Arts et Métiers in Brussels. I am not sure that a computer keyboard is grounding enough.

It is a wrench: for me somewhere it is saying goodbye to the secret hope of being ordained priest. But if I were to be a priest, it has to be for something better than consoling exiles unable to adapt to their host country. There are others who can do this better than I, and if it gives them the identity and status they want – including taking them off the building site into the security of a state-paid job (priests are paid by the state in Belgium) – let them have it.

The homosexuality debate – a proxy (cultural) war?

12 October 2012
You know the idea of a proxy war: America and Russia don't fight directly, but support opposing sides in a local conflict, say Vietnam or Afghanistan.

I can't help feeling that the 'battle' around homosexuality is basically a similar phenomenon. It is rather a convenient field for a proxy battle between two opposing cultural forces. And just as proxy warriors show scant concern for those whose territory they borrow as a battlefield, so the fighters show pretty scant pastoral concern for those who are gay. Indeed if there were no gay people in the world, they would have to go and look for another area into which to confront themselves. Certainly the amount of firepower – as it was at a conference I have just returned from – seems out of all proportion. It is overkill several times over.

Finesse

12 October 2012
I am reading 'Counsels from the Holy Mountain', by Elder Ephraim, former abbot of the Monastery of Philotheou on Mount Athos – they gave it to me as a gift when I visited Philotheou seven years ago with my son Ben.

Solid stuff. But there is one thing which irks me here, and in other Orthodox spiritual writing also: no sense of beauty comes across, no finesse.

I compare this with the medieval Welsh poem, 'The Loves of Taliesin', which an English Anglican friend sent me this week:

The beauty of virtue in doing penance for excess
Beautiful too that God shall save me…
The beauty of a faithful priest in his church…
The beauty of a strong parish led by God…[2]

This sense of beauty, of finesse, of καλος, which is part in particular of the Celtic tradition, remains important to me, and, yes, I fear losing it in certain parts of the Orthodox world.

I remember the words of the late Dom Paul Grammont, my abbot when I was a Roman Catholic novice 30 years ago, who once said to me of very strict women's monasteries that where the life is too harsh and regimented, people can lose something, a certain finesse, a certain humanity. I think he was right…

Exhausted (theological) mindsets

13 October 2012
I spent time at the World Public Forum 'summit' at Rhodes last week with Hans-Peter Dürr, a leading German nuclear and quantum physicist who worked closely with Werner Heisenberg. In a paper he gave me he describes the process of exhausting a particular way of thinking and having to change radically: in the case of physics moving from conceiving the world in terms of 'matter' to seeing it as 'energy'. I quote: 'Quantum physics marks the farewell from an Aristotelian world view, in which everything still appeared explainable and takes us into a Heraclitean world view, where everything is in flow.'

Speaking with him and reading his paper brought back acutely a sense that I often have, even if I perhaps try to repress it, as a theologian. That certain ways of thinking, certain mindsets – not least in moral theology – are rapidly exhausting themselves, requiring us to change, 'de-structure', re-rhythm … perhaps at some stage even to take a quantum leap. That we need to be talking in theology, certainly in ascetic theology, much more in terms of divine energy and of its patterns and logic.

It is all a bit like in the history of art. There are periods where you sense that a particular style has exhausted itself, is starting to turn around in circles and has to make way for something new.

You have it in Netherlandish painting around 1520 (just before the jump into Renaissance) and again in 'Byzantine' church art in Russia in the seventeenth century (before the jump to 'Academic' painting). There is something in the discourse of the Russian church right now which feels strangely similar, a certain turning around in circles which needs to make way for another mindset, another style.

Sex, economy, freedom and community

18 October 2012

I've just spent a couple of hours reading an essay by the U.S. essayist and poet Wendell Berry entitled 'Sex, Economy, Freedom and Community' in a collection of essays with the same title.

Berry has a sharp and independent mind and chronicles and comments, it seems to me pretty astutely, on the breakdown of community and its effects on morality, especially sexual. He gives his reader the pleasure of reading nicely turned, fresh-baked moral aphorisms, spiced with a yearning back to a small-town yesteryear where everything was that much more structured and safe. The opposition, the baddies, are the big government-business machine, which allows Berry – and you reader, if you follow him – to find his identity in his opposition to it, rather like sixteenth-century Protestants used the Roman Church to create individual and group identity through opposition to it. Or indeed the Pilgrim Fathers the established Church of England.

But, I wonder whether identity by opposition, or indeed in Berry's case, making a living off criticism of others, is not ultimately a mug's game. The question I want to ask Berry, if he is a real moralist, is not whether the surrounding system is moral – we know that it is not – but rather how, very practically, do I define and preserve the highest degree of morality and freedom, for myself, my family and possibly some group which I might want to call community, within the space appointed to me?

Perhaps we need to accept, rather than bemoan, the fact that our outward space for freedom and morality is limited, and start looking for this space inwardly. Perhaps one feature of the U.S. spiritual mind is the idea that there is always outward space to escape to somewhere. But I am not sure this makes for spiritual depth. Some of the greatest European and Russian spiritual writing has come from precisely the lack of space to move, whether voluntary in a cloister (St Teresa of Avila), or imposed (Dietrich Bonhoeffer), or both (St John of the Cross).

Liturgical celebration – privilege for the few or right for all?

17 December 2012

A priest friend of mine tells me how important celebrating the Eucharist is for his own spiritual life.

Whoops! Wait! Yes, like a lot of priests, he has built his spiritual life around being able to celebrate. Nothing wrong in that. Being a co-celebrant as a deacon has also become to me very important, much more than I expected when I took on the job. Something in a sense very primitive, but no less licit for that. Indeed, it seems to me that celebration is hardwired deep into the religious psyche.

But what about all those others standing in church Sunday after Sunday who presumably have it hardwired into their psyches too, but for whom, in the context of Orthodox church services, outside of the choir, there is almost no opportunity to celebrate actively?

I had a similar conversation with our choir-leader, who complains that the church is nearly empty for the Saturday evening vigil service, other than the altar party, the choir and the reader. Would you be ready, I answered, to stand for two hours doing no more than listening (in a language you badly understand) and occasionally crossing yourself?

For me there is a very fundamental question at stake. Simply, whether it is right to have a situation – as it exists currently in the Orthodox Church – where active involvement in Christian religious celebration is the 'privilege' of the choir and the altar-party? Does not this somehow go contrary to how God made us to be? Will we not, in the kingdom of God, all be celebrants in one way or another? And if the Church is supposed to mirror the kingdom, to be its first fruits on earth, shouldn't we already be reflecting this in the way we structure our worship?

2013

The years 2013 (and 2014) were for me the 'pits' in my relations with Russian Orthodoxy. I sense that those in power in Moscow have laid down a party line, and that dissent is increasingly unwelcome. There is nothing fresh, nothing new. I continue as a deacon in the Russian church, but increasingly my loyalties are to the Christian church in general. Any sense of specialness or greater worthiness of Orthodoxy has long gone out of the window. Mount Athos, which I visit regularly every year, provides comfort. A key article here is my 'Idaho potatoes' (7 February 2013). Another, 'When church fails' (23 September) is me preaching to myself in this situation.

Perhaps precisely because of my 'polite despair' with Orthodoxy, and having given up trying to defend it, I sense I am venturing into new areas, beyond traditional patterns. My 'Priesthood – type A and type B' is an example (26 March) as is 'Religion with a Swedish flavour' (14 September).

O dear, it's Christmas ...

4 January 2013

I find Christmas rather weak beer. Would the Christian story be so much the poorer without the shepherds, the manger, the wise men, the slaughter of the innocents, the flight into Egypt? Neither St Mark nor St John seemed to think so. The action that counted was both before: Mary's vital 'yes' (*fiat mihi secundum voluntantem tuam*– Luke 1:38) and after: Christ's acceptance of His role, baptism and anointing with the Spirit.

The liturgical texts are middling at best. As starters (Vespers of the Nativity): 'The peoples were enrolled by the decree of Caesar; and we the faithful, were enrolled in the name of the Godhead'. This play of ideas may have sent Cassia the Nun, who penned it sometime around the sixth century, into ecstasy, but not me. Much of it is a bit over the top: 'Thou hast come to plunder the strength of Damascus and the spoils of Samaria, turning their error into faith beautiful to God ... As dew upon the fleece hast Thou descended into the womb of the Virgin' (Canticle Four of Mattins). Or beyond, as in: 'Behold, the Virgin comes like a young heifer, bearing in her womb the fatted calf that takes away the sins of the world' (Mattins of the Forefeast). Mercifully almost no one will be in church, and the reader will gallop through it so fast in Slavonic that only he (perhaps) and God will understand...

Making sense of Christmas

5 January 2013

State the problem and you may start to get the answer. What should Christmas mean to me? I had been asking myself all last week (see yesterday's posting). The dawning of an answer comes perhaps in two lines from the nineteenth century Anglican hymn 'O little town of Bethlehem': 'The hopes and fears of all the years / Are met in thee tonight'.

In other words, a hope, maintained throughout Old Testament Judaism and indeed inherent in humankind, that there is something more for which we are made, another level of meaning than the daily humdrum. A hope that God says, in Christ's birth, is genuine, valid and worth building on. A hope that, after the Christmas narrative, goes silent, emerging temporarily in the incident of Jesus with the doctors in the Temple, and then entering another period of silence – 18 or so years until Christ's baptism. This tells us that Christmas is only a beginning, a glimpse, a foretaste. Hope needs to root and develop over a long time before it becomes adult and can usefully 'go public'. The real beginning is Epiphany.

There are twelve days to Epiphany. The progress from babe to adult, hopefully from spiritual infancy to spiritual adulthood. The time to 'put away childish things', including the mawkishness and cheap joy of much of the Christmas experience, and prepare for the adult world of Epiphany, with its harsh demands of repentance and rebirth. Only then can the story really begin, in us.

Unity in disunity

20 January 2013
We spent the afternoon with some of the Sisters of St Mary in Namur. (…) We stayed for Vespers in their simple chapel (four icons, the reserved sacrament…). Afterwards we shared tea and cakes with the whole house around a large table. We were eight or so sisters, my wife Irina and myself. And, because it was the Week of Prayer for Christian Unity, yes, we spoke of how we saw the situation between the Roman Catholic and Orthodox Churches. These were women, all Belgian, each with between forty and sixty years' religious life, much of it spent teaching in Africa, often in difficult circumstances.

In such a situation you don't talk theology: *filioque* or the Immaculate Conception. There is no question of Orthodox superiority. You simply share some of your experience of being Orthodox in a Catholic country, the bits you like, the bits you find difficult. You complain, rather apologetically, about the way most of the Russian church in Belgium acts as if no other Christianity exists, and the way convert Orthodox are so wrapped up with their Orthodox identity as to be little use in spreading God's kingdom. The overwhelming concern, from both sides (all of us, apart from my wife, being the far side of 60), is to 'complete the race' and to do what we still can for the coming of God's kingdom. Committed Christians together. That's all. Unity in disunity.

The Russian diaspora church and Idaho potatoes *

7 February 2013

Yes, I can get exasperated at the management of our diocese, bitter at the way that some of my colleagues sacrificially work their butts off for very little – or no – money, while others, on salaries (the Belgian state pays the salaries of Roman Catholic priests and some Orthodox ones), come and go as they please or build up power positions, and Moscow does not seem to give a tinker's cuss. But something tells me that this may be symptomatic of something much deeper: of a fundamental incoherence in the position of the Orthodox Church outside its 'home' territories.

Remember the story of McDonald's and the Idaho potatoes?

When McDonald's first came to Europe, they imported their potatoes from the U.S. This proved a pretty expensive exercise, so they decided to grow them locally in Europe. They signed up a couple of Dutch farmers and sent over a ton of seed potatoes. The result was a disaster: the seed potatoes which produced lovely large potatoes in Idaho, produced miserable, gnarled stubs in Holland.

I am beginning to suspect that Orthodoxy, like the Idaho potato, does not travel well. I would describe it as a particular form of Christianity moulded to a particular cultural setting. When that cultural setting for which it was shaped is lost, it quickly goes to pieces and becomes an inferior and not very tasty product.

One solution is to try to maintain the cultural setting in the diaspora setting. This worked pretty well for a generation or so after the 1917 revolution in big cities like Paris. But then this émigré group was large and culturally and socially homologous; it entered the host society at a high social level, already speaking the local language; and was already churched in Russia and expected to go back. The modern Russian diaspora came here largely unchurched, low down the social scale, and in most cases with no intention of returning home. Its 'church-Russianness' is largely what it has picked up here from a very, very small number of people. But other than a common language (which already many of the second generation cannot read), there is precious little culture – nothing inherently valuable to pass on to the following generation.

For converts, other than those who have absorbed large doses of Russian – or Athonite – culture, the soil is equally very thin. Many converts have a curious cultural rootlessness about them. Yes, there was an attempt to revive a pre-1054 culture, most notably with the 'Liturgy of the Gauls' which appeared about 30 years ago, a reconstruction of a tenth-century Western liturgy. And, yes, they make pilgrimages to the tombs of local ninth-century saints. But the whole effort quickly lapses into silliness: you cannot construct a Christian culture out of a poorly documented era – and a pretty uncivilised one to boot – of a millennium ago. (…)

Basically, Orthodoxy as it is currently lived here in the Russian diaspora, without a viable cultural base, is going nowhere. It is incoherent, logically flawed. Locked in on itself and largely unable to do the job of being Christ to the world which is what the church is for. Unless that is, in my opinion, it links into the broader Christian culture of this part of the world. This it is scared to do – for fear of losing its identity.

And in such a dead-end situation everything eventually sours. Actually, I rather suspect the smartest heads in Moscow recognise this. Which is why they seem really quite happy to let things quietly rot. And while of course they will not say so, they confirm it by their inaction.

Richness and barrenness

3 March 2013
I watched with considerable interest the funeral of Fr Pierre-Marie Delfieux, which took place last Wednesday in the Cathedral of Notre-Dame in Paris. He was the founder in Paris, along with the then Cardinal Marty, of the Fraternités Monastiques de Jérusalem, a series of Roman Catholic contemplative monasteries, now to be found in various cities of Europe.

After my usual struggles with not-always-well-read Slavonic, it was delightful to be able to hear and understand every word.

And the Cardinal-Archbishop of Paris spoke very well: not a word out of place, in a French that was at once cultivated and understandable to the simplest. And the movement itself has a clear logic within the history and culture of the Roman Catholic Church in France.

Yet one thing leaves me uneasy, both about the ceremony, and perhaps about the Fraternités themselves: a bareness, bordering on barrenness, which I find too harsh. It is very much the 'ecclesiastical minimalist' style of the 1980s, very much what I knew as a monk in France 30 years ago. Extremely simple dress, very simple vestments, very heavy emphasis on 'word'. It is the same barrenness which turned me off the box office success film 'Des Hommes de des Dieux' (Of Gods and Men) based on the Trappist monastery of Tibhirine in Algeria.

I am not sure how much headway the Fraternités are making in Belgium: last time we visited the Sisters, a couple of years back, they were all French, Italian, Polish … Would it be unkind to suggest that it is because this somewhat 'Cistercian' style does not work here in Belgium? Our tradition here is richer. Belgium must have more (quality) religious art, architecture and artefacts per square kilometre than any country outside Italy, including a string of late medieval churches and another less well-known string of large Baroque churches (often with excellent woodwork). Plus of course the Flemish Primitives and a lot of good still-figurative art in the late nineteenth and early twentieth centuries. And not forgetting that up until 50 years ago Belgium supplied stained glass, quality vestments and excellent liturgical printing across much of Northern Europe.

It may be a 'richness' that is inherent to the Belgian Christian tradition, which we have lost, and which we need to find again. I say 'we' intentionally, putting myself, as an Orthodox cleric, in the same boat as my non-Orthodox Christian brethren. Simply because, as a Christian, I have to be concerned with the progress of the Christian gospel and witness in my adoptive country. A progress that in my judgement, the Orthodox Church in its present constellation is currently contributing very little to, and perhaps never will. Whose fault this is – after all 'it takes two to make a ghetto', those inside and those outside – I will leave for another time.

Me struggling with English

14 March 2013

At today's BESPA meeting I struggled with differing
varieties of English. (BESPA is the Belgian English-Speaking
Pastors' Association – a meeting of Christian pastors of all
denominations). Start with two varieties of black African
English: that of our guest speaker from Malawi, and that of
Peter, our very excitable Pentecostalist pastor from Nigeria.
Add to this the thickest Irish accent I know from Fr Patrick,
a native Gaelic-speaking priest from the Franciscans (our
hosts), a lovely man, but I'd understand him more easily if he
spoke French(!); the delightful Afrikaans accent from Wim,
a missionary to Muslims (including Tadjiks in Moscow); and
the educated American accent of the new Episcopalian female
priest.

But it was a good meeting, on prayer and mission. And we
shared hard, with a rare level of honesty and openness among
mature Christians. I remember Wim came in heavy with his
'Don't pray for anything if you're not ready to be part of the
answer.' John, another pastor said, 'Don't go out on mission
work till you cry to God both for your own sins and for your
target group.'

But what struck me equally as much was the joy to be
swimming way out beyond denominational differences. It
mattered very little that we are Protestant, Catholic, Orthodox
or whatever. We were most of us mature Christians, men and
women who have had to fight hard and take risks for our faith.
We all face the double duty of pastoring expatriate flocks
outside their national and cultural contexts and asking ourselves
what is our relationship and responsibility to the wider Belgian
population, large parts of which seem as obdurate as steel
against the Christian gospel (or at least to the version we
want to give to them). In this context I am no longer 'Mr
Orthodox', supposed to put across a 'party line', as I too often
am, but simply a committed Christian with others, able to
contribute with a certain level of Christian experience and, I
hope, maturity, to a critical debate.

Priesthood – type A and type B

26 March 2013

There is a priesthood function we all know – embodied in Vladika X or Father Y, whom we may love, hate, admire or whatever. On him we rely for leading our church services, being able to take communion, and where this is a prerequisite for communion, hear our confessions. I will call it 'type A' priesthood.

There is, I am increasingly convinced, another form of priesthood, which I will call 'type B', which is equally, if not more, important in the overall spiritual economy. This priesthood joins with Christ's priesthood, not by presiding or co-celebrating the Eucharistic liturgy ('offering the sacrifice of the mass'), but of oneself passing through the Christian process of death and resurrection at a depth in which one carries through, not only oneself, but a part of broader humanity as well. In so doing one takes part in, and completes, the priestly function of Christ's own crucifixion and resurrection (see Colossians 1:24).

Yes, of course, every Christian is supposed to go through the process of death and resurrection. It is the very sense of baptism, as expressed in the epistle of the baptism service: 'that like as Christ was raised up from the dead by the glory of the Father, even so we also should walk in newness of life.' (Romans 6:4, KJV). In both Orthodox and Roman Catholic ascetic theology, this dying and rising again is seen as an iterative process, as the inner cleaning and healing moves deeper into the heart. And at some point in this process – and I suspect this is a critical point and the opening into the second form of priesthood – we become acutely aware of and cry out to God, not just for our own sin, but that of our fellow humans. We realise that we cannot separate ourselves from the sin and the consequent pain and sufferings of the human race of which we are part. And the accepting to bear this 'more than ourselves' in our own iterative deaths and resurrections has a salvific value well beyond our own individual souls.

It is probably the acceptance or not of this type B priesthood which largely determines whether a type A priest is a good priest or not. The priests I really respect combine A and B. Type A on its own is, in my opinion, little more than a necessary evil, to keep the church-machine running.

But it is equally important to recognise that Christians can play a vital type B priestly role without being type A priests – in particular women, religious and not. It would not harm if this were said more clearly so that the concept of priesthood is seen as something much wider than ordination. It might serve to brake people – both women and men – who want to become type A priests at all costs. It is this second priesthood, I believe, not the first, that will save the world.

Homo religiosus belgicus

5 April 2013

These few lines, on religious feeling in Belgium, started as a reply to another dialogue. But I think they sum up the situation pretty well. I am coming to a variety of conclusions, coming from different angles, but pointing in the same direction…

First, it is possible, providing you are reasonably integrated socially and not psychologically damaged, to live a pretty satisfying life in this country without reference to organised religion. Especially if you have an interesting and/or demanding job. I note that many business corporations, government offices and educational institutions seem to be taking on an increasingly 'religious' and meaning-providing function.

Second, the religious element remains strong in an 'underground' way – it expresses itself at times in a very strong sense of morality and justice, especially when the police or courts act badly. Despite what our Russian Patriarch Kirill wants us to think, the debate on euthanasia, abortion and homosexuality in Europe has been often of a high moral level – even if starting from different premises and leading to different conclusions, and even if the results of high moral discussion have been widely abused by less moral people.

Third, much of the remnant of 'traditional Christianity' remains either among the top and bottom social classes, i.e. those who clearly 'govern' and those who are clearly governed and dependent (very often non-ethnic Belgians and including much of the Russian Orthodox population here). It is the in-between who want to keep their private lives out of other people's governance, who stay away.

Fourth, I suspect that the 'cry' of the world towards the church in this country is 'treat us as adult individuals'. Unless and until we as a church do so, I believe we are sunk. Even if in the longer process, as one progresses along the religious path, one realises that one is perhaps not as deeply free and adult as one would like to think one is. I come back again and again to Bonhoeffer's concept of '*Mündigkeit*', a world that has come of age.

Me – extremist?

29 April 2013
Let me share my reply to a LiveJournal friend who in response to a comment of mine called me extremist Orthodox. It came out sharp and hard, which normally means it's for real...

Me, extreme Orthodox? My fear is being thrown out of the church for liberalism: for saying that Orthodoxy is perhaps not the only one true Christianity, and perhaps not even the true Christianity at all in certain parts of the world. For saying that you need proper pastoral care for homosexuals, rather than hounding them, or using anti-gay as a definition base of Orthodoxy. For saying that episcopal autocracy as practised in my church has more to do with feudalism than Christianity. For expressing doubts as to whether our practice enables people to grow into mature, discerning adult Christians (Ephesians 4:13), or represses them as servants of a power-holding oligarchy.

Disconnected

13 May 2013
I have a pretty clear and very real idea of what Easter means to me personally, the experience of being buried with Christ so as to rise with Him. But there were times (during the Holy Week celebrations) when I was hard put to link this personal experience with what was actually happening liturgically. (...)
I rather envy the early monks: at the start of Lent they disappeared into the wilderness with just enough food to keep themselves alive, lived through, each in their own way

and at their own rhythm, what Lent and especially the 'Entry to Jerusalem – Gethsemane – crucifixion' sequence meant to them personally, and then reconvened for the Easter Vigil itself. Instead of them I am faced with an almost indigestible flood of language I cannot always identify with, not to mention physical near-exhaustion, due to nervousness, attendant bad sleeping and poor ventilation. Nor is there leeway for any creative expression: absolutely rigid texts, rigid movements, rigid dress, the same music since the 1920s ... Is this the only way of doing things, is it un-Orthodox, if not heretical, to suggest that there may be other approaches?

I shot my mouth

15 May 2013
I shot my mouth last night (colloquial English for: said exactly what I thought) on the situation in the Russian church. I am still slightly stunned by it, that feeling of having gone further than I expected, but I still stand by what I said.

It was in a situation of a small group of mature, English-speaking Christian friends, where I am not linguistically disadvantaged nor have to fear ecclesiastical censure. The essential thing I said is that I feel the Russian church to be in a situation similar to that of the Roman Church in around 1505, just before the Protestant Reformation (Martin Luther's 95 theses appeared in 1517): that the traditional structures are outdated and at breaking point. As then, the hierarchy is too closely linked with an outdated and exploitative social-economic system (then the feudal system, today the petro-rouble rent system) and is fast losing favour with a rising independent and freer-thinking middle class. Spiritually, the temperature is low: there are few people of really deep spirituality around, there are plenty of loudmouths of rather poor spirituality who have largely monopolised the media, while much of the episcopal college is a) too young and b) totally beholden to the Patriarch. Among the people, especially the urban middle classes, there is a lot of 'we want God, but we don't want it in the way it is being offered to us'.

For the past 25 years the Russian church has lived on the prayers and 'merits' of the previous two generations who went through the persecution. My own sense is that this capital of 'merits' is drying up fast: that we in the Russian church have to live on the strength of our own prayers (with the help of the saints if we invoke them), and that these prayers are simply not strong enough, because, in large parts of the church, we have not reached the honesty with God and the readiness to self-sacrifice for them to be really strong.

A church which functions well is a giving church: my feeling is that right now the structured church, very much like the Soviet system, is a sucking-in system, in that too many people are using it to be served, rather than to serve. The difficult balance that the church has always had to preserve between organisation on the one hand and the deeply spiritual/prophetic on the other is once again tilting dangerously towards organisation.

The question for me is increasingly not whether this system will break, but when and how. I am neither a Kremlinologist nor a 'Danielov-ologist', and the really useful and accurate information coming from Russia (other than the damning figures on parental choice of type of religious education in schools) is scarce, piecemeal and often anecdotal.

If the Protestant Reformation is anything to go by, the challenge will be mounted away from Moscow, possibly in St Petersburg, possibly in one of the big eastern cities like Krasnoyarsk, possibly in the diaspora. The small group of Christian oligarchs, with a sense of how power works in both church and state, could, like the German princes of the 1520s, play a decisive role here. Popular support, once the dam breaks, could be massive.

14 June 1963

13 June 2013

This was the day, 50 years ago, and a week after my fourteenth birthday, when I was confirmed, in the Church of England, by the late Mervyn Stockwood, Bishop of Southwark, at 'Christ's Chapel of God's Gift', which is the school chapel of Dulwich College, then and still one of the top London secondary schools, which I then attended.

It was not a big event. There was not the same fuss as there is around a Catholic first communion or solemn communion.

Nor was it a family event. Religion was a difficult subject in our family, my mother being Anglican and my father Methodist, and neither comfortable in the social structure of the other's church (Methodism was one to two steps lower down the social scale in those days). Also, there are no photos. Photography was expensive then, the equivalent of two dollars for each photo shot. We were four kids and cash was tight. But confirmation gave me access to Holy Communion and put the seal on a personal commitment which has remained intact to this day, 50 years later. God has remained faithful; me, more or less.

At that time the plan was to study for the ministry and be ordained priest by age 24. This did not happen, for reasons which lie in part with me, and others totally out of my control. I do not regret this (though I will admit to occasional twinges) and I think God and my guardian angel were wise in keeping me out of the priesthood (where at least three friends of mine came to grief for various reasons).

From those days I have my love of Scripture, and of English hymnody (something I miss badly in Orthodoxy). Prayer and liturgy came later (and are still coming). My horizons were totally Protestant then; Catholicism came in my late teens with trips to continental Europe, Anglo-Catholicism at university, then my two-year stint at a French monastery. I'm not sure that I even knew what Orthodoxy was, and to imagine then, in the early Brezhnev years, that I would end up in the Russian church and married to a Russian would just be inconceivable. But I did and God is still there and so am I.

> My song is love unknown,
> My Saviour's love to me;
> Love to the loveless shown,
> That they might lovely be.[1]

Tillich et al

11 August 2013

I got a broadside the other day from a correspondent whose hackles I had raised. He asked whether I actually read the Bible (I do actually) and whether I read the important modern theologians, like Paul Tillich.

To which the honest answer is that I read Tillich 35 years ago, in my late twenties, when living in Germany. Last night I took down his 'Shaking of the Foundations', blew off the dust, and spent an hour skimming through passages I had underlined back then.

The man is powerful, and faces squarely the powerless of the Protestantism of his younger days to handle the demons of post-WWI Germany (Tillich himself quit Germany for the USA in 1933 at age 47, persona non grata). He fights against a Christianity that has become superficial, tepid, and has lost the experience of God of the depths. Only by going through to the 'depth of being', and taking the pain that this involves, does one meet God, and thus oneself, or equally, oneself and thus God.

However powerful and prophetic Tillich is, what scares me is my impression that for him (and the German/American Protestantism of which he is part), this 'depth of being' is largely terra nova. In fact, as I see it, it is land that the other two main confessional blocks, Roman Catholicism and Orthodoxy, had mapped out centuries before and maintained a tradition of operating in, largely through monasticism, which the Protestant Reformation abolished. Operating at this 'depth of being' has included fighting with the demons which have produced phenomena like Nazism, rather than hiding them under veneers of 'civilization'. Rather than knock on the door of these confessions and ask to borrow the maps, Tillich sets out to produce his own.

Frankl, God and me

25 August 2013
I have just reread Dr Viktor Frankl's 'Man's Search for Meaning'.

Frankl (1905–1997), for friends who don't know him, was a Jewish psychiatrist and neurologist from Vienna who survived Auschwitz. He was also the founder of 'Logotherapy', a form of psychotherapy based on helping people to find meaning (*Logos*) in their lives. The book, originally published in 1946, is his account of the psychology of the concentration camps, with particular emphasis on what enabled people to survive by continuing to find 'something to live for'. My edition

(Touchstone 1984) includes a valuable 'Introduction to Logotherapy' by Frankl himself.

To quote a couple of lines: 'Any analysis […] tries to make the patient aware of what he actually longs for in the depth of his being. Logotherapy deviates from psychoanalysis insofar as it considers man a being whose main concern consists of fulfilling a meaning, rather than in the mere gratification of drives and instincts, or in merely reconciling the conflicting claims of id, ego and superego, or in the mere adaptation and adjustment to society and environment' (p. 108).

Reading this, I was asking myself how this 'longing for in the depth of my being' and 'fulfilling a meaning' pans out for myself. For me it has been interrelated with God, as far back as I can remember in childhood (I started Sunday school at age three). Put a bit more accurately, interrelated with this something/someone that pushes me, needles me, often hurts me, and with which I fight in the depths of my being, which I know that I have to 'get right', come what may, which seems more or less coterminous with the God (Father, Son and Holy Spirit) of the Christian Scriptures, which I am able to relate to within the theological language and structures of the Christian church, and my experience with which seems to have quite a lot in common with the experience of certain people the Christian church calls saints

That being said, I have never been a good churchman and never will. An awful lot of what I find in a church service seems fairly irrelevant to this search, like the wine counter in a supermarket for a teetotaller, and often what I do need I have to go looking hard for in specialist stores. I hesitate, à la Billy Graham, to serve God as the answer to all man's existential woes: certainly not in the form (Orthodox, Catholic or Protestant) in which He is often packaged. A lot of the 'comfort' which people went to church for when I was a boy you can get elsewhere. Whether God is the ultimate answer for everyone, I don't know, all I know is that, for some reason, I cannot track through the depths of my own being without engaging with Him.

With my cornflakes…

29 August 2013

I have been reading Dorothy of Gaza's *Spiritual Works*[2] with my breakfast cornflakes for the past few weeks. This is a practical book of spiritual instruction, written in the sixth century, aimed at novice monks. It is down to earth and in very easy Greek, and to this day prescribed reading for novices on Mount Athos.

Two small things struck me this morning. The passage is from Instructions X § 106: 'This is why we say the virtues are a middle way. For example, courage is the middle way between cowardliness and reckless audacity, humility between pride and servility; respect between shame and insolence; and in the same way all the other virtues.' First was the Greek word used for 'courage' (ἀνδρεια), which uses the root for man (ἀνδρος), if you like 'manliness', important in any man on a serious spiritual journey. Second was the positioning of humility midway between pride and servility. All too quickly the distinction between humility and servility is lost in Orthodoxy, with the latter often both expected and offered.

Religion with a Swedish flavour

14 September 2013

I am right now reading in Swedish a small book entitled 'Frälsarkransen',[3] which translates into English as lifebuoy. It is by an older bishop of the Church of Sweden, Martin Lönnebo, who has devised a set of prayer/meditation beads (a bit like a rosary/prayer rope, though in the hand more like Muslim worry beads), and he explains how to use them.

What am I doing anywhere near the Church of Sweden some will ask. The COS, with gay marriage and (currently) a coupled lesbian bishop (of Stockholm), is not exactly flavour of the month in the Russian Orthodox Church. Yet there is something in the book, written extremely simply, which attracts me. I can best describe the approach as giving people space and time to find their own way to God, with a strong emphasis on silence, and with reference to the European mystic tradition. It is an approach in which, if I have understood it right, morality and ethics come out of this silence and the relationship with the

Trinity which it leads into. This silence is something I miss in the Orthodox tradition, which quickly becomes a barrage of words, with no space for silence (if there is a gap of more than three seconds in a two-hour Orthodox liturgy, someone has made a mistake) and where morality is imposed and policed heavy-handedly. The Swedish approach restores a balance...

When church fails

23 September 2013

If my own experience is anything to go by, there can come a time in a committed Christian life where church does not work. One has ten, fifteen years or more of committed Christian life, attends church services regularly, has a pretty steady personal prayer life, knows the Scriptures and several of the Christian classical authors. Then there creeps up a feeling of unease with regard to one's churchgoing. Something difficult to express. What was once a joy has become an unwilling drudge. One continues to go, it would be wrong not to, but the outward results seem negative. One returns home unhappy, tired, wondering what went wrong.

No, one has not lost one's faith. Not least because the words of Scripture, or of the services, read in one's private corner at home (one's 'cell') still make deep sense, as does one's own prayer. But church itself does not work. Everything seems wrong. Coming back from the service you complain about the bishop's poor preaching, or about your fellow-deacon who is brown-nosing in order to get priested, or the fact that you found yourself at lunch after church next to a set of Polish bricklayers you cannot connect with. But somehow you know that this is not the real reason. That the real reason lies elsewhere.

At this stage it is important not to panic; not to listen to the evil one's *logismos* that you are losing your faith or becoming a bad Christian; not leave the church. What this rather confused unease may in fact be telling you is that it is time to take a further and major step towards Christian maturity – to hit a deeper level of relationship with the Trinity, which is of vital importance for yourself, for the church and for the world.

The hard fact of the matter is that the spiritual level of most parishes in not particularly high, especially those where an important part of their role is to provide social support or identity, as in first generation diaspora ones. To (over-)simplify, under the old system, in both Orthodox and Roman Catholics, the senior clergy (bishops and rectors) held the social, organizational power, monks had the spiritual competence, and everyone else paid, obeyed and crossed themselves from time to time. While this system flew out of the window in the Roman Catholic Church in the 1960s and 1970s, it remains the default situation in much of the Russian church.[4] If one moves to a deeper spiritual life, one is inevitably going to move ahead of most of the pack, including, as laypersons, into areas traditionally reserved for monastics and clergy. The art is to do this without damaging, but rather benefiting, the pack and yourself.

Let's be clear: at this stage there is no quick fix. This transition process takes time. We may easily be talking two to five years. To get through it and out on the other side is going to take patience, and a certain degree of discipline. Obviously the evil one is around, and if he sees you trying to respond to a call to 'go deeper', he will try to block the process and lead you off down a blind alley. Here it is important to make sure that your personal spiritual life is balanced. It is this, rather than church, which is going to provide the permanence. Yes, you will need to take communion ever so often, and go to confession from time to time (but be careful with choice of confessor – see later), but the continuum will come from the 'cell'.

If it is the cell which provides the balance, don't be afraid to dictate its language. My own continuum language, in which I read the Bible, pray, and to which I translate back the Slavonic liturgy, has since the age of 14 been contemporary English, i.e. the language of which I correctly understand every word. For church purposes I have variously used seventeenth-century English, French, German, Dutch, Italian, Latin, Greek and Slavonic, but it is modern English that provides the continuum.

A certain amount of ascesis will be necessary, especially if you are older. Keep food consumption limited and balanced, be careful with alcohol, limit computer use, exercise properly. One key feature of the process you are going through is almost invariably going to be to face up to the nastier sides of your character which are hidden inside you: irateness, sexual desires, greed in terms of food or money. Alcohol and overeating are traditional ways of avoiding facing them, as are overwork or wasting time on the computer. That is why we restrain them in Lent (even if I remain far from convinced of the present Orthodox way of living this).

You may need to lighten your involvement in the local parish. Especially if you are the sort of person who tends to sweep up after others, do the jobs which the others are too busy, or lazy or proud to do: checking the vestments, removing the cobwebs, helping with liturgies at awkward times like Saturday mornings, etc. It might do no harm to pull back a bit and say clearly what you are and are not ready to do. You will need to have a certain discipline so that you continue to take communion fairly regularly. Less than once a month is, in my opinion, dangerous.

You will need somehow to express your disaffection with church. But you have to be careful not to damage those for whom the outer structure is very important. And more important, not to get entangled in that sort of permanent cynicism which is so undermining, especially for Westerners (in my experience, Russians can handle it better, but I'm not sure it does them any good). I have found writing to be important, shared with a few carefully selected friends on LiveJournal. I am not sure how far the Russian church monitors what I write, but I am instinctively careful, especially not to attack any identifiable person.

Another two dangers you have to be aware of: if (like me) you were a child in a malfunctioning family, you may be either transferring one's childhood reactions to a weak father onto a bad bishop or rector, or subconsciously preferring a malfunctioning to a well-functioning community, because, paradoxically, you feel more at ease, and are better able to find your way around, a malfunctioning one.

Your prayer life is going to change. You will have to start to meet God face to face. Much of this will be in reaction to more difficult situations, and you grow increasingly aware of the continuing existence of evil in yourself and the world around, and their inter-reaction. One learns in this sort of situation not to pussyfoot with God. My language with Him has not always been kind, but in these cases it has been clearly me, and there was clearly Him at the other end.

A particularly delicate part of the process is to get sacramental confession right. The standard wait in a queue for 20 minutes for a two-minute 'to allow me to take communion' confession is, in my humble opinion, at this stage pretty useless. My advice is to get the most experienced confessor one can find within easy physical reach, and come to an arrangement with him, how often to take communion, how often to go to confession (this does not have to be every time one goes to communion). Fifteen minutes a month at a prearranged time can be much more fruitful. There seems also to be a natural cycle in it: the really deep things which need to be 'exorcised' come up slowly, and my own experience is that I need to 'clean the filters' every four or five weeks. Truth to tell, I use confession as much as anything to place in front of Christ what I am uneasy with. By doing it in a confession format, it keeps it – and me – in the church. I would add here that there will inevitably be situations as one advances in one's Christian life, and also simply gets older, where one is going to be spiritually more mature than the confessor, especially if he is young and has not passed through certain life cycle changes (especially the one which hits most men around 40 to 45). I insist that if you do not feel comfortable confessing something to the priest in front of you but are honest to God about it in private, your confession is good. One also has the right to deflect any question from a confessor one deems too clumsy or indiscreet. I am a firm supporter of the Roman Catholic rule that one has the right to choose one's confessor, and wish it would be formalised in the Russian church.

It is also important to tell oneself that one is part of the church even if one does not particularly feel it. Including praying for the hierarchy, even, and perhaps especially, when you do not agree with them.

It may be that, at the end of this period of disaffection, when you have moved to a new depth, that you reintegrate organised church life more fully. But it is equally possible that God may want you to remain a bit on the sidelines. This can be painful, if for example one has secretly hoped for priesthood, but has to let this slip away to younger and less experienced men. I suspect that a very large part of the real work of the church, the bringing of the world to God and reducing, or at least keeping in check, the evil one's rule over it, takes place on the altar of the Christian's own heart, ex-centrically, and away from the limelight.

Englishmen and Russians

24 November 2013

An educated Russian friend of mine and my wife visited us recently from Moscow. We are both deeply involved in the Russian church, I in the diaspora, she in Russia, and discussion inevitably turned to church news. We spoke of situations where church bodies are clumsily managed by authoritarian and incompetent people.

What struck me was the difference in our reactions: mine was to be horrified, 'one more nail in the coffin', one more reason to withdraw from the Russian church sooner or later. Hers was a sense of inevitability and a willingness to continue to give of herself sacrificially in the situation, regardless. For me our different reaction points to a fundamentally different approach...

Russians expect any organization of any size, including the church, to be corrupt and/or incompetent, to be led by second-class people, co-opted into an inner circle of power by those already enjoying it, in return for loyalty to this circle. This is unacceptable to us English. Competence and a clean style are essential for public life (even if not always achieved), along with at least a degree of real choice in who leads us and speaks on our behalf. And this includes the church. Indeed to English ears, very use of the word 'power' in a church setting sounds wrong and anti-gospel, whereas in the Russian church, the episcopacy – an unelected, self-perpetuating body, drawn from a very small pool (celibate monastics) and very difficult indeed to call to order when it misbehaves or underperforms – is still viewed largely in terms of power, both inside the church and outside. Russians survive this situation with a sort of inner barrier, by creating an inner area, sometimes shared with a few close friends, but many times going no further than the boundaries of their inner souls, where they are honest and clear-sighted. For many, outside these boundaries, it is legitimate to lie and cheat and do dirty deals. For them, honesty and integrity, as we English understand it, is reserved for a much smaller and more intimate group.

Englishmen, thrown into the Russian situation, are lost: we have been taught that integrity and honesty are essential social virtues in every situation, and lack this second inner line of defence. A Russian churchman will pick up on and accept a situation when a senior cleric is overtly lying – in particular painting a situation as much better than it really is – because the situation seems to demand it, while to an Englishman such lying is abhorrent. My classic example of this is the Archbishop of Canterbury's angry remark to Metropolitan Nikodim Rotov during an official visit of Patriarch Alexis I to England during the Brezhnev era: 'I can understand, Metropolitan, that you may have to be sparing with the truth, but I refuse to accept downright lying', following which the Metropolitan was severely downgraded in the seating arrangements at the official banquet. All my deepest English instincts side with the Archbishop.

My midnight mass

25 December 2013
It is Christmas Day today everywhere except Russia, Mount Athos and perhaps one or two smaller Orthodox countries. Even if you are supposed to wait another 13 days, Christmas is in the air today and you sense it (including, right now, the delicious silence of Christmas morning).

Last night, rather on instinct I decided to go to a Latin midnight mass. Something to do with acknowledging that, even if Russian Orthodox, I belong to Christianity in this part of the world and to its traditions. Something to do also with a need for quiet decency and anonymity, a service I could quietly relax into, rather than my usual nerve-tautening and tiring participant role as a deacon, and perhaps a reaction to the inner coldness of the musically exquisite Christmas Carol service from Kings College, Cambridge that I had heard a few hours before on the radio. Whatever. I ended up at the Society of Pius X (SSPX – Catholic schismatic) church in the centre of Brussels (the only 'legal' midnight mass in Latin was at the other end of town, and an expensive taxi ride back home).

I am not a great friend of the old Roman mass: the way the priest does the consecration in a huddle with the deacon and servers at the far end of the church, with only a couple of '*in saecula saeculorum*' and hand-bells to tell you where he is at (though to be fair in many Orthodox churches it is no better). I sense also with the SSPX the need to do everything 'by the book', with no space for real creativity.

What I like though is the space and the pace. A large church, built in what in the 1860s was the chic quarter of Brussels, the stately houses of which were demolished in the 1950s and 1960s and replaced by concrete and glass office buildings, it has those old-fashioned chairs-cum-kneelers which are a bit low to sit on and a bit high to kneel on. The service is taken slowly and with discipline. The servers are male only, in cassocks, cotta, and proper black shoes. They are well-behaved at the altar and have a sense of dignity with what they were doing. A good choir, not too large, were singing from the organ loft, mostly Gregorian. The priest's vestments were of the old variety, of good quality. The service progressed slowly – what a relief from our 'if there's a three-second gap, something has gone wrong'. There was a properly prepared and delivered sermon.

I was surprised by the large male presence, over 60%, including many in their twenties. Maybe schismatic churches tend to attract a certain type of male which needs a 'harder' and sharper-edged religion than what the 'regular' Roman Catholics offer.

The SSPX is a thorn in the side of the official Roman Catholic Church. I am rather glad they are there. While their anti-modernism can be a bit extreme, they preserve certain values, decency, decorum, and simply good behaviour, as well as a certain sharp edge, which need to be preserved somewhere. And yes, a place where an exhausted Orthodox deacon can just flunk out anonymously and let someone else do the work...

Cowards

27 December 2013
Who, in the book of Revelation, gets thrown into the 'second death, the lake that burns with sulphurous flames'? 'Murderers, fornicators, sorcerers', of course. That we knew. But they are only four to six in the list (of eight). Surprise, the number one place is not for them.

No, the number one place (Revelation 21:8, NEB) is for the 'cowardly' (the word can also be translated as 'fearful' or even 'timid'). I suspect this includes us when we toe the line rather than risk the discomfort of saying what we believe to be right. Each of us can imagine situations this includes, in church and outside. No need to give examples.

It is clear from this passage and from many others, as well as Christ's own example, that God hates it. We need to be careful about what we don't say.

2014

In 2014 I reach 65, retirement age. It takes a long time for this to sink in. The notice from the pensions office remains on my desk unanswered for several months. I am still in good physical and mental shape and continue working nearly full-time as a translator, while saying goodbye to a couple of customers who had become burdensome.

In the same year I have had enough with the despondent situation in my own parish and diocese and, with the approval of my spiritual director, request formally to leave the Russian Orthodox Church and move to the Ecumenical Patriarchate, which is prepared to receive me. My archbishop refuses dimissorial papers, for canonically flimsy reasons, and my sponsor from the Ecumenical Patriarchate is unwilling to fight a fellow-bishop. I am stuck, organizationally at least. Yes, I could have stormed out into the Roman Catholic Church or even the Church of England, but that just did not feel right.

Rereading my posts from this period, I am struck by the move away from organizational concerns to more spiritual ones, with an emphasis on man's fundamental spirituality and a question of whether Christianity is doing it justice (2 November).

.

People who live in glass houses

11 January 2014

I am pretty glad that the news of gross sexual misconduct at a Russian seminary (in Kazan) with the local bishop clearly implicated, is out into the open, and, I gather, also outside Russia. It will, I hope, put an end to a certain type of moral grandstanding directed at Western Europe and America from certain quarters of the Russian church. People who live in glass houses should not throw stones.

In a Western-style country (and assuming the information I have received is accurate), at least two Russian/Ukrainian bishops would by now have been in court for misconduct with minors/forcing people into unwanted sexual relations from a position of authority, and probably behind bars. In Russia, where unfortunately those in power are above the law, it is unlikely ever to happen, even though this is punishable criminal behaviour according to the Russian statute book. The Russian church also has its own church courts system, but as the ultimate judge in such cases is the bishop himself, these are toothless against episcopal sexual malfeasance.

We had a case like this in the Roman Catholic Church in Belgium a couple of years back. Once the facts were clear, the man, a senior bishop, was out of his position and into a monastery within 48 hours, with a press conference by the presiding bishop putting the facts plainly on the table. An example to follow.

In my opinion, any 'alliance for traditional morality' between the Russian Orthodox and Roman Catholic Church must be preceded by serious housekeeping. The Roman Catholic Church seems to be doing a pretty good, though painful, job at this. The Russian Orthodox Church must follow suit.

On the refusal of God

28 February 2014

(*My contribution in an email exchange with a friend on the question of damnation for those who refuse God:*)

'The anguishing part for me is when people refuse God, not because they inherently refuse God, but they refuse the way He is presented to them in the church. If right now I were outside the church, like my two brothers, for example, and looked at the church, went to a few services perhaps, I am not sure that I would "bite" on God. In many ways I am Christian despite of the church. I exist more happily on its boundaries than at its centre. God has got me, yes, and continues to "get" me, but as much outside as inside the church structures. Many times, when I go into the cathedral, I ask myself, are we really bringing salvation in the full Christian sense of the term? Do we have the courage to really want people to grow into their full Christian divine-human maturity?'

Forgiveness Sunday

2 March 2014

It is Forgiveness Sunday in the Orthodox Church, which marks the start of Lent. Today's gospel centres on Christ's order to forgive each other's sins: 'For if you forgive other people when they sin against you, your heavenly Father will also forgive you' (Matthew 6:14, NIV). And today our parish priest gave the standard sermon on how unforgiven sin creates bitterness and distances us from God. It was a decent sermon as far as it went. But listening to him I was wondering whether this command of Christ's to forgive does not need to be crossed with another: 'If your brother or sister sins against you, rebuke them; and if they repent, forgive them' (Luke 17:3, NIV).

This adds to me a vital dimension: any real process of forgiveness starts with the naming of the sin or unhappiness, between the hurter and the hurt. God willing, if the two are serious in their Christian faith, there will be a way of reconciliation, of removal of bitterness. The problem comes when this process is short-circuited because the aggrieved or hurt person is not allowed to rebuke. Bitterness grows, and can explode, either outwards or inwards. We know this too often from politics. Unfortunately, it extends into many churches, where laymen are not allowed to rebuke clergy, junior clergy not senior clergy, or do so at their peril.

Wiechert's men of God

4 March 2014
German writer, Hans Wiechert combines a fine sense of nature, of the slow, deep movements of peasant life, with a profound religiosity, within a totally Protestant reference framework. It is largely this peasant sense that allows him to move beyond the cold and formal Lutheranism of the pre-1918 establishment, and face the disarray in Protestant society at the collapse of the old order after World War I.

He delivers three magnificent men of God – two in 'Die Jeromin-Kinder' from the 1910–1914 period, and a third in 'Das einfache Leben' set in the early 1920s – each of whom is able to shatter a narrow mould and so give meaning to others.

The first man is Agricola, a Protestant pastor who cannot handle the upholder of public morality position expected of him. He leaves his wife whose small-town social pretentions he does not share, and retires to a country ministry. There he faces a diphtheria epidemic which kills 70 small children in the village communities he serves. This is too much for him, he hits the bottle and retires to a small island, but remains deeply loved by his former parishioners, who turn out en masse to his funeral after he is killed protecting a child from a drunken knife-grinder. He loses his faith outwardly, but cannot quite get away from God, with whom he quarrels continuously.

The second is the senior church official, named only by his functional title of '*Oberkonsistorialrat*', who grasps what is happening with Agricola. His speech at Agricola's funeral is a masterpiece: 'He had deposed him as a God who has strangled his children, but the deposed one stood in front of his door. And he sensed that he stood there. He smashed his image and cursed him, because he had suffered a lifetime for his name's sake. His book was a lie and a great deception, but he never ceased reading it. [...] He trod the dead one into the earth, deep into the earth, and rolled stones over his grave, but sometimes, in the dusk, in front of his hearth, he turned round abruptly, sensing that the dead man was in front of the door.'

The third is the pastor (again unnamed), a huge, tired bear of a man, whom Thomas von Orla visits somewhere in a Hamburg suburb at midnight, trying to get meaning into his life after forced retirement from the navy after World War I. 'You were not looking for "God's word", as they call it. You were only seeking confirmation, that things are not right with your world. And you thought that a pastor, if he is still up at midnight, might know [...] Become pious? Believe? How do you get such ideas. One must work, work! Only work [...] Four years long we have misused his name, now we need to be silent for four years. We have killed, and now we need to work, heavily, panting and sweat-covered, nothing but work. And only then let's see whether we are again worthy of speaking his beloved name.' Thomas takes the advice, leaves wife and child and lives as a semi-hermit, working hard physically as a fisherman in the forests of Eastern Prussia.

Each of these men of God has in his own way moved beyond structure, touched God, and from this experience been able to communicate something of Him, and change a situation, create resurrection, the *Konsistorialrat* getting Agricola's life and death into focus, the Hamburg pastor setting Thomas out on a life of meaning and relevance. The dialogues/sermon in question total no more than 20 pages, but carry a primitive and real religious depth, absolutely true to the environment in question, that I have rarely encountered.

Priests and prophets

8 March 2014

During Lent the Orthodox daily lectionary quits the New Testament for the Old, with a mixture of historical narrative (Genesis), prophecy (Isaiah) and wisdom (Proverbs). Of these it is the prophecy readings which engage me most.

For me, prophecy and priesthood go side by side, complementary functions if the people of God is to fulfil its role on this side of eternity. Christ was both.

The prophets' role is essentially, through their direct experience of and communication with God, to keep the general body of the church constantly confronted with the full truth when, as is perhaps inevitable with any establishment, it functions on reduced levels of it.

Right now, in my part of the church, priesthood is the fashion. Our pocket-sized diocese has nearly doubled its priestly quota in the past two years. The main qualifications, as far as I can see: piety, ability to do liturgy well, and loyalty to the system in the person of either the bishop or the senior priest in the diocese.

The bishop has not ordained any prophets. Nor can he. There is no 'Ordination of Prophets' rite in any service book I know. God ordains them. At best the bishop blesses their choice of a particular form of life; often (semi-)eremitic. And yet in today's church theirs is a vital role: they are the men and women able to receive and carry that deep word of God that cuts through any nonsense; who have the pluck to tell a senior priest or bishop he is off-beam; who ask the awkward questions, like whether the church's role is to create comfort zones for the happy few or face the great discomfort of a world whose rejection of Christ often expresses a desperate search for Him; and who are dissatisfied with the half-truths that the descent into establishment inevitably brings.

No, being a prophet is not much fun. The fatality rate is pretty high, in particular in the high places of establishment religion – 'Jerusalem, Jerusalem, you who kill the prophets' (Matthew 23:37, NIV). But it remains a vital function in the Christian world.

On the desert...

8 March 2014

The desert is a necessary part of a committed Christian existence. It is a *lieu de passage*, which one is called to pass through in order to find something much richer, a deeper well from which to draw. The goal is an experience which, like blossom after a hard winter, is overawing in its beauty. However, a desert that does not bloom sooner or later is a place of death. No one, I suspect, should enter into the desert without knowing roughly where that secret well is. And probably not without the tools to express the beauty when they find it: whether in painting, song, poetry or another art form.

But desert should not be a permanent style. A church should not look like a desert. Its walls and its liturgy should rather reflect the beauty of the desert encounter – hopefully the faces and bodies and voices of its clergy and laity as well.

As Easter approaches

16 April 2014

Was it Jakob Boehme who said that 'Christ is not risen, if He is not risen in you'? This expresses perhaps in part a certain trepidation and unease with which I go into this Easter period.

If done well, as liturgy it can be magnificent, anywhere where you have a set service, a good choir and space. But what has beaten me in past years is the sense of distance between what is going on 'out there' and what is happening inside me.

For me the Christian message stands or falls on what it does to me, and others. That is to produce, providing I stick more or less to the rules, a real life-turning change, a living out of another depth, a loving which I do not have naturally in myself, a joy and a peace that spring up from elsewhere. This process includes a death and resurrection, a taking up my cross to somehow, mysteriously, resurrect precisely through doing so. This is basically what Easter is all about, at least to me. A (start of the) resurrection of the soul already before that of the body.

I will admit that when I try to square this 'what it is all about for me' with what is going on inside me as a co-celebrant during the period from Maundy Thursday through to Easter night and on to Easter evening Vespers , I do not always succeed . Some years, Easter has been a decidedly 'de-resurrecting' experience. Quite a bit of this may be because I have almost no idea how those around me – fellow clergy, choir, congregation – are really experiencing Easter, deep down. Our words are common, but the rest? Resurrection must somehow be a shared experience of going into something deeper, being grasped and changed by something more than ourselves. This sharing is impossible without communication, either in our own words, or the tonality we give to the set words we speak.

Only with this sense of sharedness, with the set words matching what we really do feel and experience, does the whole long liturgical sweep, from Thursday through to Sunday night, make sense. Otherwise it becomes an exhausting crawl, relieved by copious alcohol and cheesecake when it is all over.

And indeed, who ordains that the particular liturgical format, unchanged for 1,500 years – originally intended for a mixture of largely illiterate peasants and a literate clergy, all able to put the world on hold for four or five days – is the one that enables me and my Christian brothers and sisters to pass through the cross-resurrection process together? That the sole permissible format is the excruciatingly long 12 lessons service on Thursday night, the long 'Praises' on Friday evening in front of the Epitaphion (a 176-line meditation on the crucifixion alternating with the 176 verses of Psalm 118, with the author running a bit short on inspiration at times) or indeed the gaudiness of the Midnight Service, with clergy and choir basically on autopilot.

Good Friday

18 April 2014

On that Thursday evening, the system failed. The Jewish religious structure, more intent on preserving the 'system' – in particular the privileged position of a few key families – crucified the man Israel was waiting for. But Christ continues on His way, beyond the structure, true to something else, a deeper truth (in St John's Gospel the word 'truth' is central both in Christ's last discourse and His dialogue with Pilate). To borrow the words of St John of the Cross, He continues: '*Sin otra luz y guía/ Sino la que en el carazón ardía*' (With no other light / Except for that which in my heart was burning). It is in the framework of this deeper truth, outside and beyond the religious structure, that the key act of salvation took place.

Ascension

29 May 2014

Ascension is perhaps the Christian feast that speaks to me most. It is for me Christ saying to His apostles: 'Over to you now. I put myself in your hands, and with the help of my Spirit, you will get it right. Yes, there will be bumps and upsets along the way, you will get it wrong at times and hurt yourselves, and worse, may hurt others, but it is essential that I retreat if you are to grow into spiritual maturity. Which is what I want most for you.'

Russian cold shower

10 August 2014

Two weeks ago I was helping with emergency repairs on the summer church in a village 1,000 km north of Moscow, shoring up the main roof and removing several hundredweight of bird droppings weighing down on it. Our time slot was far too short and we left with the roof still leaking badly onto the floor.

The building was curiously attractive – with good light and proportions – even though far too big, probably already when it was built around 1890, and certainly now with the village at probably under half its pre-Revolution size in summer, and no more than 20% in winter.

For me, in terms of Christianity, the whole exercise was something of a cold shower. People had visibly got their lives back together after the trauma of the early 1990s, when the local wood factory went bust and much of the younger population decamped to the towns: the houses were often quite smart, the gardens tended. But no visible attempt to get the church back functioning. We did a prayer service in the church itself, importing the local priest from the next village, but with no more than five local persons present. I had served as deacon with the same priest that morning in his home church, ten kilometres away, with perhaps five people present, no choir, and giving communion to one person only, a struggling four-year-old.

This is the reality of the Russian countryside – not the mythical 'Holy Russia' in which everyone has Orthodoxy in their soul – but a place where God seems to be a fairly distant memory, where people get on with their lives pretty much without Him.

It will be an uphill struggle to get Him back. Yes, the church can quickly be brought into use by converting the narthex, which has a proper roof, into a church and leaving the leaking barn of a main building to later. But for this to make any sense the village needs a permanent priest, and not just a summer visitor or a missionary team from one of the seminaries, but a man – and perhaps more importantly his wife – ready to stay the course, including bitter winters and substandard health facilities. A man who does not just do the services and expect people to come – as I rather expect the next village's priest does – but one able to go out and engage with his potential flock, especially the younger ones.

'Normality' and salvation

14 September 2014

As we think about the church's role of bringing salvation, we are confronted with a dramatically changed situation from two generations ago. Put simply it seems to me that, traditionally, the preaching and teaching on conversion/salvation has worked on the presupposition that the target audience consists of persons who are basically functioning 'normally' as human beings. Yes, they can cuss, swear, fight, lie, steal or cheat on their wives, but basically they are 'normal' and can move beyond this behaviour towards Christian holiness through conversion and a period of repentance. This presupposition, it seems to me, no longer holds water. A significant percentage of persons who present themselves in our churches seeking for something in the Christian message, are not functioning 'normally': either they have not passed through the usual stages of development, including in particular for males the 'initiatory' process into adulthood, or they carry severe internal wounds, often connected with broken family backgrounds.

This must, if we are to be any use to anyone, force us to radically rethink our pastoral-missionary approach, not least in the Orthodox world. At first sight, the English-speaking, and especially the American world, seems to be at least two generations ahead of us here in tackling these areas. On the question of handling the failure to initiate, I think of Richard Rohr; on that of wounded memories, I think of Lynn Payne. While we may want to be cautious with their therapeutic practices and perhaps question some of their underlying assumptions, these persons and their like present the virtue of describing and making a first attempt to address these issues. We could do well to listen to them

Love, community, Carthusians

25 September 2014

The biblical images of heaven show men and women directed totally towards God. Each is fully caught up in the same thrust towards God. Nothing is said of their relationship one with another (other than Christ's comment to the Sadducees that 'in the rising again they do not marry nor are they given in marriage'). The uniting factor, which allows them to sing – we suppose – in harmony, is their common impetus Godward.

It may seem strange therefore that current preaching on Christianity places such a heavy emphasis on this horizontal, interpersonal level. The most widely used here is 'Love', which has become one of the key sales propositions of Christianity: in the Christian community you will find the love you long both to receive and to give in order to be fully human.

Somehow I am not quite convinced. Quite apart from the fact that my experience of Christian community has often been pretty mediocre, I sense that we are missing something. That is that, just as it will be later in heaven, what binds us and makes real 'love' possible is this common striving for God. Our relations with others are really meaningful in so far as we are helping each other on the way to God, enabling each other to get face to face with God, including confronting that emptiness and destructiveness which are critical parts of the pathway. It is this face-to-face that is the ultimate source of our humanity (even if those who attain it may have a surrogate role to play for those who cannot). Too much emphasis on horizontal, inter-human love can thwart this thrust, both by giving a promise of love that cannot be fulfilled, and by filling a gap which needs to be left open. The image which still speaks most to me is that of the Carthusians, with their mini-apartments dotted along a huge cloister: their primary raison d'être is their being alone with God: the community is there to support this, not to replace it.

Identity – in Christ or church?

27 September 2014

As previously mentioned, my request to change from the Moscow Patriarchate to the Ecumenical Patriarchate was refused by my local bishop. The only way out, I have been told, is by laicization.

I am biding my time, reducing my appearance in church as far as I can just to the Sunday liturgy, avoiding in particular the 'nonsense' services – those which do little or nothing to spread the Christian gospel and improve the Christian life of the faithful. It is a pretty painful process. But what it is forcing me to do is to find my Christian identity solely in Christ, and not in any clergy function. I insist that the only real identity one should have in the church is as a Christian. All the rest – bishop, priest, deacon, acolyte, churchwarden – is service to one another, helping each other along the Christian way.

The bitter lesson I have learnt over the past four years since being ordained is just how dangerous it is when church becomes part of a man's identity kit. Once this happens, if position in the church increases his sense of identity (and worse – the loss or questioning of it threatens his very being) he will start to use others to maintain this identity. Or will seek position to gain status. The free communication of people jointly serving a single master is jeopardised. The freedom of the gospel life is blocked. Church in the full sense of the term cannot happen. Put at its crudest: nobody's role in the church is to be players in other people's psychodramas, or to fulfil needs for identity, sense of importance or belonging which ought to be fulfilled elsewhere, or the need for which should be surpassed by being rooted in Christ. I have had too much of this in the past and am happy to retreat.

Praise

29 September 2014

Praise in the Christian context has never come easy to me. The ' worship services' of the more charismatic end of the Christian church have always struck me as a bit artificial, but even at the Orthodox end of the confessional rainbow, I struggle, as we start Vespers with Psalm 103: 'Bless the Lord, O my soul. Blessed are thou, O Lord. O Lord my God, thou are become exceeding glorious'.[1] For me this is too close to the language of sybaritic praise-singers in a despot's court; especially if I have had a bad day.

Again, to take the words of the General Thanksgiving from the Anglican prayer book: 'We bless you for our creation, preservation, and all the blessings of this life; but above all for your immeasurable love in the redemption of the world by our Lord Jesus Christ'. Do I thank my earthly father and mother for creating me? Indeed can we really think of God as father in any other way than redemption? If, as an earthly father, you forgive your children almost everything and pick up the bits, is God's redemption anything really special or not rather in the very nature of fatherhood?

Something tells me I need to look deeper. My guess is that somehow the praising, or blessing of God, has to be a pretty natural movement, something innate, inscribed into our very being. In the next life, according the chapters four and five of the Book of Revelation, this praise, this singing 'blessing and honour, glory and power' is inherent in 'every creature which is in heaven, and on the earth, and under the earth and such as are in the sea' (Rev. 5:13, KJV). Maybe what we have is a natural inbuilt momentum, one that extends beyond humans to the very creation, directed towards God, that we have lost in our fallen world, and especially in one which strives to be sufficient to itself without the divine. A momentum which is independent of our moods of the moment, and which can be rediscovered, even if blocked temporarily by nurture and circumstances. A momentum which may be intimately related with the sex and other human drives (or a more fundamental drive, an *élan vital*, into which the sex and other drives are subsumed) and which, like them, when blocked, breeds depression, bitterness and cynicism, and makes song impossible. A momentum that can come alive again somewhere along the healing-divinization path towards Christian maturity.

If I am right, praise, it seems to me, cannot be forced, at best nudged. It is a song you can join in when the time is right, when you have 'picked up the tune' again. But only then.

Leading people to Christ

2 November 2014

We were speaking last week with a Catholic priest on our travels. He used the phrase 'leading people to Christ' as a major part of the Christian vocation. This was the language that I would have used as a fresh teenage Bible class Christian. And missionary activity is part of what the church is all about. But it is language which I have since lost and have a hard time recognising myself in, although as a Christian, and an ordained one (deacon) at that, I suppose I should. Why? I started to think hard.

While moments of doubt have been rare, much of my 50-or-so-year career as a practising Christian has been difficult, and often uncomfortable. Sailing against the wind, if you like, under a lot of grey sky. A certain amount of my early Christianity was in a sense 'forced' on me and not terribly free: it was more a sense that the Christian gospel is 'right', something I could not honestly escape, than a sense of a call to fullness and freedom. I remember once rather unhappily referring to Christian practice as 'an additional tax'. I did not have an easy childhood, and facing up to the resulting anger and hurt inside (which I finally learnt to do as part of my own Christian discipleship sometime between age 40 and 50) has been uncomfortable.

And yes, I have to admit, I have met relatively few people in my Christian life who have really impressed me: my Bible class leader, my abbot as a novice monk, my spiritual director, and a scattered handful over the succeeding 30 years, many of them monastics, some on Mount Athos. Otherwise various shades of grey, who failed (and still fail) to enthuse, especially those with a strong personal interest in 'established' Christianity.

I think that I am now finally catching the scent of what 'deep' Christianity is about, with a love and a joy and a peace that come from elsewhere, that bespeak more than just a naturally happy disposition and a natural ability to preach and theologise. A love and joy and peace that are marks of the '*dilatato corde*', which St Benedict mentions in the prologue of his rule, even if I do not feel myself to be a terribly good representative of it and am far from sure that the church I am in is the place for it. But it is the only Christ I could preach, and the only Christianity I would want to try to lead people to, knowing that the way is often long and hard.

For a church that reflects the gospel

11 November 2014

I have just finished Monique Hébrard's new book 'Pour une Eglise au visage de l'Evangile' (For a Church that reflects the Gospel). Hébrard is France's leading French religious journalist. An early book of hers, 'Les Nouveaux Disciples' on the (then) new religious communities, was one of the books that led to my own monastic experience 35 years ago (1982–1984).

She quotes no less an authority than Cardinal Danneels (the former head of the Roman Catholic Church in Belgium, a mild, thinking man now in his eighties, who comes across better on paper than in the pulpit) as saying that 'In the last few years in particular, Christianity has been reduced to a moral system' and that many are tired of this. Somewhere else she has the telling phrase of a lay person to a bishop: 'Stop talking about sexuality and start talking of spirituality'.

In my language: I suspect there is a very large number of people on the edge of Christianity, who basically feel the need for spirituality but a) are not going to be fobbed off by the miserable low quality of much of what comes from the pulpit and confessional and b) want to leave questions of sexuality in abeyance until other more basic questions are answered (and then some of the sexual ones may answer themselves in the process).

I am increasingly coming around to the opinion that (most) people are deep down spiritual, and this is something the church should encourage fundamentally and make space for. We who have managed to 'stumble towards God' within the structures of the church (often thanks to people who were more open to human failings than others – I owe my very Christian survival to one such man) should perhaps be more tolerant of those who stumble outside the church. We need to accept that perhaps a large proportion of what we think as specifically Christian spirituality is in fact shared by people of other faiths (Islam, Buddhism). At times it may be appropriate to teach the rules of this 'general spirituality', such as the danger of spiritual pride and the real existence of a force of evil, the use of disciplines of fasting, spiritual reading and silence, before moving into the specifics of Christianity.

In particular we need to take people where they are in their intimate and family lives, including having the courage to say that the 'happy family' (mother, father, permanently married, with at least two and preferably more kids) which remains a standard in the Roman Catholic Church and (more or less) in Orthodoxy is probably at this present time in Western Europe unreachable for a majority of the population, in the present socio-economic-moral environment. There will of course be heroes, but most of us are not.

In this context I increasingly rile against the strictures placed by both Roman Catholic and Orthodox on taking communion in 'non-standard' situations. Basically in many areas (including also fasting rules during Lent and before communion) I believe that this should be a matter of individual freedom (and only when you take responsibility for your own actions in front of God can you be mature), though a priest has the duty to warn of taking communion 'unworthily'. To refuse communion to a person whose marriage has fallen apart and who is hurting from this is for me straight wrong. Whether priests should systematically refuse communion to people in gay relationships (which according to the book they should) I am less than certain. As to whether one should follow the church's fasting rules to the letter, my answer is, outside of a monastery, no.

History of our British Orthodox cocoon

6 December 2014
I have watched four times today the DVD 'Orthodox Christianity in the British Islands', introduced by Metropolitan Hilarion of Volokolamsk, originally produced last year in Russian and now to be re-edited with English subtitles (my job to check them).

I have not yet quite worked out who is the real target audience for the film, nor why the Russian Federal Agency for Press and Mass Communication co-funded it. But leaving that aside, the DVD is tastefully done, the historical information given is accurate (bar one howler), and the subtitles sensitively written in British (as distinct from Russian) English. I had to look hard to find bits to correct.

A good half of the film is devoted to the three 'giants' whom, to quote the blurb: 'England gave to Orthodoxy', the late Metropolitan Anthony of Sourozh, the late Archimandrite Sophrony (Sakharov) and Metropolitan Kallistos Ware of Diokleia. And indeed the best bits are precisely little snippets of the Metropolitan's personal experience of all three men when still a humble student, including his tactful handling of the fact that Anthony and Sophrony were very far from friends...

Where I did feel short-sold was where the film jacket promises: 'The film features bishops, parish priests and simple parishioners, native Britons who are taking the challenging path back to their spiritual roots, that is to Orthodoxy.' In total these take up no more than five minutes of the 44-minute film: two bishops, four priests and just one layman. The latter is a very well-introduced member of the London upper set, close to the British court, now a trustee of the Russian cathedral, and is filmed in his London club. A charming man (I know him personally) but hardly a 'simple parishioner'.

If I had to subtitle the film it would be either 'England through Russian spectacles', or less kindly, the 'history of our British Orthodox cocoon'. 'History' because the film looks backwards rather than forwards. Two out of the three 'great' figures are dead, the third just celebrated his eightieth birthday (though I of course wish him many more). One of the big temptations of Orthodoxy outside its home countries is to live too long on its past, re-editing books and talks of spiritual giants of 20, 30, 50 years ago, rather than encouraging a new generation of spiritual men. 'Paris Orthodoxy' made this fatal mistake, so, I suspect did the Russian church outside Russia. Orthodoxy in Britain is in danger of going the same way. Certainly, of the three 'greats' mentioned, only one, to my knowledge (Sophrony) has produced a worthy successor, who is continuing the tradition (Archimandrite Zacharias).

I say 'cocoon' because the film gives the impression of a very closed and separate world, very much outside the mainstream of both English church life and, despite all the very 'British' shots (Queen, Prince Charles, Tower Bridge, horses in Hyde Park), of English life in general. Much of the comment on existing English Christianity, and in particular the Church of England, is the eternal Russian lament against gay marriage and female priests and bishops. Yes, I understand this, but somehow I feel that if someone in England is going to have again the effect that either Metropolitan Anthony or Archimandrite Sophrony had, they have got to come at things from another angle. For me these are symptoms of a malaise, not their root causes. And good spirituality, by its very definition, goes for root causes.

A *different drum-beat*

20 December 2014
Something is telling me louder and louder that we have got it wrong, or that it is going wrong. I mean the system we generally sell as 'European values'.
It is like over recent months I have been constantly catching snatches of another song, with a beat that penetrates deeper than the daily musical diet of the last 60-odd years...

From reading various German authors up to about 1960 (Jünger, Wiechert, Andres), all born before WWI, I get strains of another, older value system, that has been nearly smothered out of existence. Essentially 'aristocratic', at times unashamedly elitist, with a deep sense of honour and loyalty, and its moral code closely linked into the established church.

I pick it up also in the traditional Spanish system, for example from the accounts of the family of the late Belgian Queen Fabiola. Historically it was monarchist and anti-Republican and welcomed Franco's putsch of 1936, even if it and the Franquist regime kept each other at a cautious distance. I pick it up in the traditionalist Catholics of the Society of Pius X (Lefevrists), which seems to have made particular inroads into the French aristocracy, many of whose more Catholic members may be more in favour of Marine Le Pen (the French far right leader) than they would want to say publicly. I am getting it from Russia, whose propaganda machine is making a pretty good job of making European values look spineless and unfocused, a society in which a basic human right is to have no values.

Against this what we seem to have in Western Europe right now is a system that, while it works well in terms of economic goods, general law and order and bureaucratic efficiency, fails to meet a deeper hunger. You can talk about a missing religious element if you want. Yes, the Christian church has been talking for the past 40 years of the need to re-evangelise, as church congregations wither. But it has preached a distinctly individual Christianity, missing out on a basic human need for religion at a group and identity-giving level.

I am beginning to think that this need for a 'religious' foundation to society is something fundamental to the way we are and are meant to function, and we neglect this at our peril. This is something the European political establishment is really scared about: with memories of Hitler, Mussolini and Degrelle, it does not want mass movements which get out of its control (demagogy is a top 'fear word' for this class), and is unhappy at certain moral strictures that such a mass movement could call for (stronger emphasis on family, stricter abortion laws, keeping LGBT activity off the streets), and has the problem of avoiding such a movement turning into immigrant- or gay-bashing.

Modern Christian theology too has a problem with religion at this level, as it means concentrating much of the energy of one's elite on maintaining a broad-based religion, inevitably in some sort of inter-action with the powers that be, that keeps religion on a very 'low' level, with a constant danger of being used for political ends. For these theologians, Christianity becoming the official religion of the Roman Empire in AD 380 was a major wrong turn.

2015 TO DATE

Since 2014 there have been no marker events in either my personal or spiritual life. I have reduced my workload as a translator, with some of the time freed up going to woodworking. I remain a deacon, now in number one slot since the previous proto-deacon was priested a year ago.

During this period I have been fortunate with two dialogue partners. The first is various persons from the Roman Catholic organization 'Notre-Dame de Vie', which I was introduced to by one of my wife's icon-painting pupils. Founded by Blessed Marie-Eugène de l'Enfant-Jésus, it concentrates on helping lay people to advance spiritually in the Carmelite tradition. His signposting of advance into spiritual life into the contemplative/theoria stage I have found very valuable and has given me useful language with which to share with spiritually mature people. The second is Fr G, a Greek Orthodox priest in Brussels. We meet under the cover of my improving his English and he my Church Greek: most of the time we are sharing our concern to live mature religious lives in a contemporary context. His knowledge of Orthodox patristics has been particularly valuable.

My general outlook in terms of religious confession from now onwards is perhaps best summed up by Jean-Paul Sartre's phrase 'Life begins on the other side of despair'.[1] I have long given up trying to find any particular identity in Orthodoxy – it just happens to be the church that, for various reasons related to my own personal history, I find myself in. I am sceptical as to whether Russian Orthodoxy can continue much longer in its present modus vivendi (30 March 2017), but as I have zero say in the matter, I am not wasting time on this. It is much more important to live and witness as a mature Christian, regardless of which Christian confession I am in. I am concerned that we should not box ourselves into corners, especially with an insistence on 'traditional morality'. For me this marks a new split in Christianity which is potentially much more divisive than our current confessional differences (18 January 2015). While I hesitate to join the modernist camp, I sense that the old systems no longer work (18 February 2016. I sense new paradigms of Christianity on the horizon (13 January 2019) and am basically optimistic.

I know that what I write is followed and appreciated by a small group of people in Russia and elsewhere, many of whom I have visited and are happy to have a counterparty with a wider horizon than what they are accustomed to. Which is reason enough to continue to write.

On Christian unity

18 January 2015

Every year, as we go into the Week of Prayer for Christian Unity, I am less excited. Basically, and especially for people 40 years younger than me, and outside official church structures, the old confessional differences are largely irrelevant. What I fear rather is that by concentrating our 'ecumenical dialogue' on producing joint dogmatic statements, we may be missing the new splits which could bedevil Christianity for the next generation. I wonder if Christian disunity has not disappeared so much as mutated.

The main fault line which is opening up rapidly and catastrophically is between traditionalist and modernist. This fault line has always existed theologically, between liberal and Bible-literalist, but has taken on immediacy with the decisions of certain churches concerning homosexuality and women priests. Roughly speaking the divide runs between, on the one side: Orthodox, traditional Protestants and Third World Anglicans; on the other: most of Anglo-Saxon Anglicanism and Lutherans and Old Catholics. The Roman Catholics tend to the 'traditional', but have managed largely to keep out of the debate. It is along this fault line that I expect new alliances to be formed, including between the Russian Orthodox and some of the 'biblical morality' U.S. Protestant and ex-Episcopalian groups. And it is going to be the very devil to get some sort of unity here.

Episcopal liturgies

25 January 2015

Last Monday for the Feast of the Epiphany we did a full-blown episcopal liturgy in the attractive late-nineteenth-century church the Roman Catholics are letting us use in Mechelen, 30 km from Brussels and the historic centre of Roman Catholicism in Belgium.

Usually I don't much care for episcopal liturgies, with their complex choreography (I inevitably get dirty looks from the bishop for being in the wrong place), their constant changes of omophore (stole) and the centrality of the figure of the bishop.

Fortunately there are young men who seem to love all this and I leave them to get on with it. My preference has always been for small weekday liturgies with one priest, one deacon and perhaps ten people in church.

Yet at the same time, I am beginning to smell something important in these big liturgies. It ties into a primitive need for ritual, going back beyond Christianity into man's general religious past (*religio perennis* as some call it – I prefer the German term *religiöses Gemeingut*). Something you perhaps do not understand very well, but instinctively you know to be important to your humanity. Something which feels right when you have completed it properly. Something that, if the church does not provide, others will, starting with Freemasons. Also, in a Christian context, linking in to the permanent liturgy going on in heaven (even if I hope that, if and when I get there, the heavenly liturgy will be simpler than the Orthodox episcopal one, or that kindly angels will ensure I am always in the right place with my censer…).

The other thing that was right – and almost for the first time ever in my 20 years in Orthodoxy – was to hear the canon of the liturgy of St Basil (the very long one, now relegated to a few big festivals) read out aloud correctly, without being cut (as Fr X does) or gabbled at breakneck speed (Fr Y's manner) or said so quietly that only God hears (Fr Z). I am rarely laudatory of our bishop, but I thank him for that.

Two Orthodoxies

1 February 2015
It's like I'm trying to get two forms of Orthodoxy to meet. The first is that of a popular and 'national' Orthodoxy. The 'faces' it takes are of big ceremonies at major religious locations (Cathedral of Christ the Saviour in Moscow, major monasteries like St Sergius at Serguei Posad or the Monastery of the Caves in Pskov) with senior hierarchs in gaudy vestments, surrounded by candle-bearers and acolytes, of long religious marches (*krestni khodi*) though the countryside, and of 'spiritual-looking' priests, with flowing beards and gaunt faces in bright-coloured vestments, the sort of pictures that illustrate popular religious magazines. I would add, currently and less fortunately, that of

priests performing burials in the Ukraine war zone, surrounded by men in battledress, who clearly do not understand the ceremony, but sense the rite is important and to whom it gives some sort of meaning and closure to their comrades' deaths. It is a simple, folk religion, into which you enter by being essentially part of a crowd, without asking too many questions. It's what in bad moments I call 'priest and peasant' Orthodoxy.

The second is the Orthodoxy of the spiritual writers that Orthodox read: the church fathers, 'The Philokalia', and that of Mount Athos.

Right now, it is the first type of Orthodoxy that seems to have the wind in its sails, at least in the Russian church. This Orthodoxy, as part of a popular culture, appears to be pushed by the hierarchy, largely in step with the Russian political machine (which evidently wants to paint Western culture as disunited and morally depraved). This causes a problem in the diaspora, especially its more intellectual, non-Russian part, whose natural proclivity is very much towards the second type. This diaspora also lives within a wider Christian environment (Roman Catholic and Protestant) which has largely lost the first type, even if hankerings remain at the more 'integrist' end of the scale, and where the emphasis, especially in Catholicism, is very far from nationalist.

My instincts tell me not to jettison the first type of Orthodoxy. More for sociological than for theological reasons. Societies need some sort of glue to hold them together, and religion has traditionally provided it, including, paradoxically, giving identity to the liberal anti-clerical group in countries like France, who defined themselves as being 'not' church. My big worry with Europe, as it forgets Christianity, and with a Muslim population in cities of 25% and up, is that the remaining glue may not be strong enough. Therefore if, in countries like Russia, Christianity, or religion more generally, can indeed still provide part of that glue, so be it.

This first Orthodoxy reminds me more and more of the Old Testament, and particularly of later Judaism (very much the scene in which Christ Himself operated), with the popular rites which hold a people together and give identity, both in a physical country and in a wide diaspora. It is the religion of the big gatherings in Jerusalem to which people travelled long distances – remember Christ's repeated going up from Galilee to the feasts, first with His family, later with His disciples. There the people stood around for long periods, while priests performed rites in a language (classical Hebrew) poorly understood by the people. Religion was deeply woven into the political power structure – and the Gospels, particularly Luke, portraying Christ's death as His being removed for threatening the 'symphony' between the Jewish powers that be ('the high priests and chief citizens') and the Roman occupants. I am very tempted to label this as 'pre-Christianity' – basically one form of what Frithjof Schuon calls '*religio perennis*', or '*religiöses Gemeingut*'. I have also heard the term, unkind but not far off the mark, of 'updated Judaism'. It is religion, it is socially necessary, but it is not full Christianity. My concern right now, both in Russia and the diaspora, is that 'full Christianity' is being drowned in it.

A hundred years ago the situation was simple: 'full Christianity' was largely the preserve of the more educated part of monasticism, the people ('narod') lived 'pre-Christianity', and the secular priesthood hovered somewhere in between. This situation no longer holds, in particular, the more educated laity is no longer ready to accept this 'pre-Christianity' and is demanding 'full Christianity'. One senses the religious powers that be uneasy at this: one way around it (at least in the Orthodox diaspora) being to 'clergify' any more intelligent and pious male by putting him in a cassock and vestment and giving him a place in the liturgical dance. (This leaves open the question of intelligent women…).

How do you hold the two together theologically and practically? I am very tempted to borrow a solution from both Orthodoxy and Catholicism in talking of Christianity as a series of stages. I think of the 'Stages of Contemplation' of St Peter of Damaskos, one of the authors with the most pages in the 'Philokalia', and obviously of St Teresa of Avila, with her 'Interior Castle'. Both make a sharp distinction between a first level: basically 'keeping of the commandments and trying to be good' and a second level, where one is much more individually grasped by Christ, and, normally in a long process of spiritual struggle, comes into a deep personal relationship with the Trinity. For St Peter of Damaskos, the switch point lies between the fourth and fifth of his eight stages of contemplation, for St Teresa, after the third of the seven mansions, with the first two mansions bearing a striking resemblance to what I have called 'pre-Christianity'

Basically, what we are saying is that we are going to have to learn to cater for people at both stages: pre-switch and post-switch. For (Russian) Orthodoxy the big, and very big, problem here is that we have little experience (and sometimes, I fear, little interest) in handling post-switch Christianity at parish level. The Roman Catholics have got better at it, willy-nilly, since the 1970s, basically because, with the five-fold increase in university education in the 1950s and 1960s, it found itself with an educated *Fussvolk* which could think for itself, and wanted much more say in its own religious practice.

Both sides need each other. I am very far from sure that we can run a church in basically 'post-switch' or 'full Christianity' mode, even if 'full Christianity' must be both the locomotive and the goal. But we need to allow for a significant part of our more intelligent members, to go 'post-switch', on to full Christianity.

Businessman, clergyman

3 February 2015
I am right now travelling back on the high speed train from Paris, where I have been attending the management conference of a key division of a major Franco-Belgian multinational. My role is to write the message of the conference so that it can be passed down the line, or 'cascaded' in the company's internal jargon.

Listening to these senior executives brought home to me just how much a large multinational has, for many people, taken over the role of key place of meaning, a role previously taken by a mixture of local community, family and church. Or if you like, the physical village has been replaced by the corporate one. Certainly the language is distinctly religious: 'values', 'beliefs' and (for me a new one this time round, but it is clearly coming into the corporate vocabulary) the virtue of 'humility'.

Where I see a clash coming (or to use their terminology 'misalignment') is between those (mainly at the executive level) for whom the corporation is the main thing that gets them out of bed in the morning, and those for whom it is just one of many (getting up in the morning for the thing one does not do until the evening, when one's finished work) – or those of us with strong religious values who are not ready to give the corporation the role of value-definer in our own lives.

But yes, as a clergyman, I will admit that I rather like business. I like its crisp, no nonsense approach. If a person performs below par, they are told very clearly that they are, remedial action is tried, and if it does not work, they are fired. To a considerable extent, promotion is by competence, and you are expected to take calculated risks and to have the courage to say if you disagree, and then fight your corner. This does not bode me well in the church, where the dominant mentality is much closer to that of the civil service or academia, with the mentality of keep your nose clean, minimise personal risk and slowly work up through the ranks, and once someone is tenured, it is almost impossible to get rid of them other than for crass misconduct (and then not always…). Is this, incidentally, why the present Archbishop of Canterbury, Justin Welby, goes down so well (he is at heart much more a businessman than his predecessors, nearly all of them from the academic stable)?

Some incredible encounters

21 March 2015

It has been a rather incredible ten days, in France and Belgium, in terms of spiritual encounters. During this time I spent five days at Notre-Dame de Vie at Venasque, near Avignon, an *Institut séculier* of the Roman Catholic Church of Carmelite inspiration. The prospect of translating a major book for them required me to clearly understand certain key Carmelite concepts. In the process I crossed tracks with people of a deep spiritual life bearing the print of years of steady spiritual discipline. There was an extraordinary simplicity in our encounters, out of a common concern to plumb the truth and then express it across a major linguistic/cultural divide.

On my return I immediately had two very deep and open exchanges, with senior members of the Orthodox and Protestant communities here in Brussels. Apart from a confirmation of my own being on track (useful as the community I am part of is far from on track right now), these conversations enabled me to put words on something I sense to be increasingly important (in Protestant-talk, something I am 'burdened with'): the urgent need to teach a more advanced Christian spirituality. 'Entry-car' spirituality is everywhere: well-structured, more or less intellectually coherent, with masses of teaching material. But somewhere, 10, 20 or 30 years along the line, God kicks out a couple of lynchpins or supporting columns, the nice structure collapses, leaving you searching for something else to rely on. In fact leaving you having to rely more and more directly on Him, rather than any organizational or mental structure.

It is vitally important to recognise this stage, often accompanied by a lot of unease. It is a juncture at which many people leave the church, sensing that what they have had so far is not enough, but unable to find it in the weekly church round. But it is a critical passage towards really mature Christianity.

A curious parasitism

23 May 2015
Something is beginning to tell me that the whole Orthodox-Roman Catholic cooperation in Belgium (and possibly elsewhere) needs to be recalibrated. The relationship is curiously parasitic on both sides: the Roman Catholics have done a 'Constantinople 1204' on Orthodoxy, that is gone in and plundered what was useful to them, in particular music and iconography, to fill the post-Vatican II vacuum. They willingly invite Orthodox clerics to major functions to give them a sense of doing their 'ecumenism' duty, which in turn allows certain Orthodox clerics a place in the footlights (for me, in a country whose Christianity is 90% Catholic, ecumenism is a pastime rather than a necessity). In return, Orthodox communities are 'given' abandoned Catholic churches, which makes the Roman Catholics feel good, while solving the problem of unneeded premises.

What the Roman Catholics do not do, and I wish they would, is to hold certain parts of the Orthodox Church in Belgium to account. Sometimes I feel they are so dazzled by our 'uncreated light', that they seemingly fail to see the very 'created dark' which surrounds quite a bit of Orthodoxy in this country. A sharp word, for example, about the level of ordination candidates in certain parts of Orthodoxy, a demand that no one should be ordained priest in this country without speaking at least one local language correctly, and a reminder that a Christian's duty includes integration into the local (linguistic and tax-paying) community, would not, in my opinion, go amiss.

Definition of priest

24 May 2015 (Facebook)
What is a priest?

In Orthodoxy: someone somewhat trained to celebrate liturgy, who may or may not (incidentally) be a man of God.

In the rest of Christianity: someone trained to be a man of God, who may or may not (incidentally) be able to do liturgy correctly.

Yes, it's a simplification, and unfair on many good Orthodox priests I know who are also men of God, but I fear there is more truth in it than I would care for.

'Book Two Christianity'

6 June 2015 (Facebook)
A LiveJournal friend of mine asked me for my reactions to Fr Piotr Mesherinov's recent and widely-publicised Facebook posting entitled Расцерковление: протестантизм и Православие (Moving away from the Church: Protestantism and Orthodoxy). My reply was as as follows:

I have now found Fr Piotr's original article. I see what he is referring to with his term the 'asceticism of faith', what I more humbly call 'Book Two Christianity'. Simply Fr Piotr has hit a brick wall, and is honest enough to admit it. I have hit the same wall, and you may be coming close to. For me, he is absolutely right that Orthodoxy is almost unable, at the parish level, to teach a more advanced ('Book Two') spirituality.

A 'read your *pravilo* (daily prayer book), keep the fasts' Christianity, as he says, will take you only so far. Then you are stuck. Yes, there is a Christianity beyond this brick wall. But it involves a change of register, in particular a much greater surrendering to letting Christ work individually inside you, as Fr Piotr mentions. He is also right that there is precious little pedagogy of it in Orthodoxy, and certainly not at parish level. Reference to great saints on the 'heights of contemplation' (what I call 'Book Three') is not much use without having 'Book Two'.

Significantly, both Fr Piotr and I have had to go outside Orthodoxy to find language to map out the landscape at 'Book Two' level. He has used German Protestantism; I have used the Roman Catholic Carmelite tradition. What Fr Piotr would hesitate to say publicly is that, in my opinion, the Russian church cannot handle 'Book Two Christianity', because it challenges whole authority structure, from parish level (*batushka* has absolute control on who says what) up to senior hierarchy, where it calls for an alternative form of governance than a self-opted hierarchy with autocratic powers. The Protestantism that fascinates Fr Piotr is the result of the – necessary and inevitable – collapse of this type of feudalism.

For this reason I doubt whether you are going to find an Orthodox parish which is operating at 'Book Two' level. You can find individual priests to guide you, privately and discreetly. But you will have to do a lot of spade work yourself, both prayer and personal study. Don't be afraid of sharing with committed Catholics and Protestants, priest and lay. Don't fall into the temptation of playing 'Mr Orthodox' – it will cramp your style. I believe that it is critical, both for Orthodoxy and Christianity in general (and from 'Book Two' onwards, the confessional differences quickly blur) for there to be people at this level. The temptation to slam the door on the church is strong, but somehow one has to hang on. You will also make enemies, but as Winston Churchill said: 'You have enemies. Good. That means you have stood up for something, sometime in your life.'

'The Sacred Hill'

7 June 2015

It is rare that a novel keeps me spellbound. 'La Colline Inspirée' (The Sacred Hill), by French writer Maurice Barrès, published in 1913, did. I had picked it up accidentally off the bookshelf for something to read on the tram. I had bought it in 1972 and must have read it then, but totally forgotten it since. Suddenly I was immersed, in both the story, and the author's take on it.

The story is of the three brothers Baillard, all priests, who, led by their brother Léopold, with considerable energy revive a religious site in Lorraine, in eastern France, in the 1840s. They fall foul of the local bishop, scared that they are getting too big for their boots, who brutally cuts them back. They then go into league with a prophet-like figure, outside the church, with whom they rebuild their following, until the bishop again strangles them out of house and following. Then, after years of errance, there is a happy ending when Léopold comes back into the church in his eighties and on his deathbed, as a result of the bad conscience of the priest who was instrumental in throwing him out. 'At the depth of his long error, this unfortunate heretic had had an enthusiasm for the divine and an élan of adoration that the best faithful person ought to envy and wish to add to his own faith.'

The book is a carefully balanced play between what today we would call 'charismatic' versus 'structure', with both the author's sympathies (and mine) alternating between the two sides. Running through it is a deep sense of primitive spirituality and of 'sacred place' (the religious site they revive goes back to pagan days), which the official church has at times difficulty keeping up with. I admit to feeling very comfortable with this. Barrès has considerable religious sensitivity and the book rings true.

For me it is a fascinating dip into the French religious mind, which is rich and complex. The atmosphere is definitely right-of-centre, which is probably where much of the French Catholic Church still is, deep down, despite the slightly-to-the-left stance of its hierarchy. And yes, there are certain similarities with the Russian church today: a situation of restoration after the near-total shutdown of the church, with a church cautious and conservative, ready to clip the wings of its more charismatic elements. It was not a good time to be a charismatic figure in 1830s France, as probably it is not in the Russian church today.

Figures from my past – Canon Herbert Taylor

12 June 2015

Time filters memories of people – mercifully at times – sorting them into saints, villains, and those one quietly forgets. One figure who, surprisingly, emerges 50 years on in my memory as a near-saint, though I hardly ever spoke to him, was the vicar of the large unprepossessing Anglican Church in the unprepossessing London suburb in which I grew up: Canon Herbert Taylor.

I remember a lanky, rather gaunt 60-year-old, in a black suit worn day-in, day-out, struggling with his bicycle up the hill to the church from yet another visit to a parishioner. I remember the eucharists he celebrated in a side-chapel, north-facing with non-alcoholic wine – both signs of his very Evangelical Protestant background. I remember the church accounts telling us that Canon Taylor had been paid £440 that year (was it 1966?), or £9 a week, or a bit more than half my weekly wage on summer jobs. That figure summed it up: a man totally given to the Christian gospel, who took nothing for himself. Unmarried, in a part of the church where celibacy was not demanded.

An article in the church's magazine, two or three vicars later, tells me of him that 'with few pastimes apart from reading biographies, listening to music and playing the occasional game of Scrabble, he devoted his energy to visiting members of his congregation … The effectiveness of his ministry was borne out by more than 40 men and women from his congregations being called into the Anglican ministry or into overseas missionary work. These included two bishops and a dean.'

No, his Protestantism was not for me, as I moved away into Anglo-Catholicism and later Roman Catholicism and finally Orthodoxy. He would probably be horrified if I said a prayer for the repose of his soul. But his devotion to God and to God's people was real and exemplary. And that's what counts for me, especially in a priest.

Morality – Russian and Western

20 August 2015

On my recent journey through Russia I was questioned several times about 'morality' (нравственност) and moral behaviour in Europe. 'Is Europe really the Sodom people make it out to be?' asked one serious churchman. An aged journalist attacked me quite viciously on single-sex marriage. I tried to make it clear that the general approach in the West is that your behaviour, sexual or otherwise, is your own private business, providing you do not damage other people. I also insisted that the level of 'sin' is at least as high in Russia as in the West, but that each nation has its own vices – something my Russian counterparts pretty much accepted without my having to name them.

I have been turning this over in my mind a lot. Why is it that Russians talk of morality, while the word has almost gone out of currency in the West? What strikes me is that the Russian concept of morality seems to me to have more than a touch of idealism in it. Somewhere there is a concept of purity, of a high goal to reach, or high standards to maintain. Even if they are rarely attained, the concept is important. The Russian approach is to acknowledge the failure to attain this high norm, and to regret it with various degrees of breast-beating. Indeed it seems sometimes that salvation lies as much in the recognition of the failing as in the moving out of it – the hopeless alcoholic who recognises this in front of God is saved.

The Western approach is rather to 'normalise' or 'deculpabilise' such falling short. Pre-marital sex is normal, as is homosexual orientation and behaviour. To this we should perhaps add on the Russian side the concept of society as a whole having a moral purpose, a direction to go in, an idea largely abandoned in the West, and certainly in Europe.

Which position is preferable, the Russian or Western one? The Russian record on actual sinfulness, by all accounts, is hardly better than the Western record, possibly worse. In particular the Russian system seems to lack the checks and balances which prevent abuse of power (seen most dramatically in the Gulag system but still prevalent in levels of public corruption that are unacceptable in the West) and abuse of children and young adults. On the other hand, there is, curiously, a sense of 'hope':

the idea that there is space for moral change, that the longing for the really pure, beautiful, selfless is valid, and is attainable, albeit at great price. This also leaves open space for religious feeling, which intuits the importance of these. This 'hope' is, in Russian eyes, lost in the West, leaving it in a relatively comfortable but godless, ideal-less and dreary despair. Life may be materially better, but there is something badly missing.

St Stephen

25 September 2015 (Facebook)
I'm reading the Acts of the Apostles right now. I'm struck by the figure of Stephen. Not the late-nineteenth-century icon in our church sanctuary, where he is dressed liturgically as a deacon in a dalmatic much finer than I have ever worn, a bit stupid-innocent looking, and already putting on weight (professional hazard of full-time deacons). No, but the figure I read in the biblical account.

Clearly a very competent person, intellectually, spiritually and in terms of management/personal skills. As the first Greek-speaking Jew to be profiled as holding a serious position, he demonstrates – along with the Greek-speaking widows he served – that the Jerusalem church had quickly moved out of any Hebrew/Aramaic linguistic ghetto.

I suspect that, for the Sanhedrin, he was not an upcountry clodpoll to be looked down at like Peter and many of the other apostles, but a man with (probably) international experience, bi- or multilingual, someone who could cause serious damage in the diaspora that played an important part in the profiling of Jewry to the Romans. In short, he was a potential key figure of the Christian movement, and one who needed to be put out of the way. The rest of the story we know too well.

The icon painter's husband

23 October 2015
I'm not always bubbling with enthusiasm for icons. Perhaps I should be. I'm the husband of one of the best known and competent icon painters and theoreticians outside Russia. I helped a lot with the theological thinking process that will

sooner or later, God willing, put Leonid Ouspensky out of print. I have more good icons on the walls of my 'cell' at home than our local cathedral.

Yes, for those in the game, like my wife, icons are important, vitally important. But I guess that those for whom the artistic quality of the icons they have in church or in their homes is critically important in their spiritual lives, make up 5%, maximum 10% of our congregations. Most people, I suspect, could not care very much about quality, providing they have a half-way decent Mother of God and St Nicholas to whisper their prayers to. Often icons seem to be little more than markers of Orthodoxy, or vague 'providers of atmosphere', pretty much regardless of quality.

My practical experience is that icons are pretty incidental to our worship, except when either the priest or I, the deacon, cense them. Yes, on the Sunday of Orthodoxy we parade through the Greek Cathedral in Brussels with icons, though I and another senior cleric who shall remain nameless bring our own (the ones given to us being miserable). When did I last (or ever?) hear a priest preach seriously using an icon as a base, or more generally about what icons are all about?

So the question remains: for the faithful who are not aesthetically inclined, for whom beauty is not a primary path to God, those who react more to word (me) or music than to image, just how important are icons, and especially in a church setting? How do they work, how should they work?

My own approach to icons starts outside the Orthodox Church. Thirty-five years ago an American Episcopalian writer called Leanne Payne wrote a book called 'The Broken Image', aimed at restoring sexual wholeness to people who lacked it. 'Icon', as we know, is simply 'image' in Greek. The basic idea is that ingrained deep down in each of us is a natural 'icon' of what we are made to be. An icon that is either confirmed or infirmed by our subsequent upbringing. Ms Payne's contention, which I largely share, is that the process of deep Christian healing and wholeness lies in the re-finding and confirming of this 'deep image'.

I want to take this one step further and argue that a key role of the icon is as a tool in our reaching down into the depths of what we are supposed to be as Christians, first cleaned of the accumulated sin we are contaminated with though upbringing, surroundings and our own straight sin, and then on to the enlightened people of God. In other words, a key role of the icon is to help us sense our way through to the depths of what we are supposed to be in Christ, and to say yes to it.

How does this work? I don't know fully, nor am I sure how far one can/should investigate this. It is certainly not dependent on reverse perspective, the use of gilding or 'Byzantine' style and other such silliness. I know that very occasionally I have been struck by an icon (or a statue or painting) that puts me at a different, deeper level. I remember vividly as a monk 30 years ago being struck by a statue in a church in Rouen. I showed it to a colleague who said: 'Brother Michael, it's you.' Or another approach: when I feel low, the crucial thing has been able to keep looking at an icon of Christ I have in my cell. To look at it hard is to take the risk of Christ looking at me. Providing I can maintain that looking, I know I'm on track.

Avoiding arguments about 'canonicity', immediately begging an almost impossible question of what canonicity really is, simply I ask: 'does it work?' Does my being in the presence of a particular icon or series of icons deepen my prayer, make me any more holy?

Style for me is a very secondary consideration. Both 'Academic' and 'Byzantine' icons work equally well. Vitally important is the 'credibility' of the icon: a) can I get from the image in front of me to a real person of flesh and blood, and b) is this person then credible to me as an example for my Christian life? For me the 'conversion' fails in particular with icons done in a 'false-primitive' style, where I sense the painter has used a 'primitive' style either because he/she is incapable of better and/or because he/she is shying away from human reality. I have similar problems with icons in the 'Coptic' style (especially the modern Western ones with overtones of Georges Rouault) – they are too far from me. I cannot decode them. Credibility is lost also where the icon becomes 'everyone's favourite grandfather' and lacks a sense of deep, controlled, male energy. My favourite icons are the Serbian and Macedonian icons and frescos of the thirteenth and fourteenth century, in a late, 'realist' Byzantine style. Christ and the saints are totally credible there.

If I'm honest, where I look at icons the longest and most closely, especially those of the saints, is not in church at all: it is in monastery refectories, especially on Mount Athos, some of them (e.g. Dionysios, Xenofondas) going back centuries, others (e.g. Iveron) recently painted. There, we are all trying to be saints: just those on the walls seem to have made a better job of it.

The economics of God's favour

18 November 2015

I think I am hearing the sentiment in Orthodox circles that God specially favours Russia. The implication, hinted at or stated bluntly, is that He will favour it much more than Europe, whose people and churches many Russians see as wallowing in immorality. I ask simply whether this is good theology. I have my doubts.

At this junction it seems to me we have to talk of 'spiritual economics' – what spiritual action, behaviours and attitudes help a national or regional group gain God's favour, and what makes the same group lose it.

The key factor (accepted by both Eastern and Western Christianity) has, in my mind, to be the prayers of those people, who by personal sacrifice, abnegation, and faithfulness, have a special 'leaning power' on God. Many of them will be monastics, but many will also be lay people. I have no accurate figures, but what I see and hear around me suggests an equally strong presence in the West, as a percentage of the population, as in the East. I would suggest that the 'prayer pressure' on God is no less in the West than in the East.

A concomitant of this is that the prayer power of past saints may be equal again on both sides. That is if we include in the count not just canonised and venerated saints (a haphazard process at best), but those predecessors whose lives and death and ongoing prayers carry weight with God. It is also good to do a bit of historical smoothing here: in Russia's case balancing the twentieth century (heavy in martyrs) with the eighteenth and nineteenth centuries, not notorious for holiness. I suspect that it is this positive tally that counts much more with God than the negative tally of national sinfulness – the overall weight of which is probably very similar from one country to another, even if taking different forms.

For this reason I am guarded towards the approach 'the Mother of God puts her protecting veil over Russia', as expressed recently by Patriarch Kirill. We Brits thought God was on our side until the sun went down on our Empire, the French long saw themselves as the special daughter of the church, the Germans believed in 'One Kingdom, one People, one God' (until Hitler substituted himself for God), and Franco had Spain dedicated to the Virgin Mary. Why then Russia any more than anyone else?

I am treading carefully here: I am not out to bash Patriarch Kirill or the Russian church, just to suggest that a 'we are a holier nation than you are' approach is theologically dubious and possibly spiritually perilous.

Jean-Pierre, Leo, Vincent, Nino, Alex...

5 December 2015

... are some of the group of fifteen men and one woman with whom I've been doing carpentry classes for the past two years. A nice group, mostly between their late twenties and forty. A lot of jobs require two or three pairs of hands: pushing large planks through the planer, adjusting a door before clamping it tight and gluing it, and we work well together, with words and hand language.

How, if anything, to use traditional Christian language, am I to 'bring them the gospel'? And indeed what gospel am I to bring them? Certainly not to push them as fast as I can into a Christian church, whether this be my own rather exotic version (Russian Orthodox functioning in Slavonic) or the standard Roman Catholic variety. If I have any approach at all, it seems that it should be much more to attempt sensitively to understand them as persons, value and accept them as who they are, and at appropriate moments, nudge them in the direction of being more fully themselves, to have the courage to fight for the 'life in abundance' that I believe Christ wants for them and indeed for everybody. Whether they find it inside or outside the church or indeed Christianity at all is irrelevant at this stage. And if I do talk religion (which I rarely do), I present myself not as someone who has magically found the solution, but as someone who still fights with himself and with God and at times with the organised church.

One question often put in such contexts is: 'What is Christ for you?' I do not use it. I have problems with it myself. To be honest, I do not find Christ, as put across in the Gospels, an immediately attractive person. Indeed I'm not sure that the Gospel writers are trying to put across a personality as we understand it today. Rather there are certain words in the Scriptures, as much of St Paul or the Psalms as of Christ, that attract me, tease me, and will not let me go. What does 'newness of life' that Paul goes on about mean? What is this 'joy' which seems a constant theme? What is this 'glory' that St John the Evangelist constantly has Christ talk about? What is the purity of heart that Christ speaks of, which supposedly will allow me to 'see God'? It is these questions I ask over and over again when I cannot sleep, standing waiting for a tram, or planing wood in my workshop.

The family – a key Christian value?

12 December 2015

Am I the only Christian, I ask myself, to be unhappy about the continuous emphasis placed by our Roman Catholic brethren on the nuclear family as a key value, and about the Orthodox idea of the family as a 'little church' or 'family church'. Really I have two objections.

The first is that I suspect, but cannot prove it, that 'family' is, at least in part, a newly created value, that, in pre-contraception days, a family was more a practical and inevitable social arrangement, with a bit of romance at the front end. Simply: if you had sex, you had kids. With little social security, and most women tied to the home with more kids and less household gadgetry, the family was the natural social base, heavily supported by popular opinion ('if you get her pregnant, you marry her'). With divorce difficult and frowned on, and with the balance between 'duty' and 'self-fulfilment' weighted differently than today, an awful lot of couples (including my own parents) soldiered on where today they would have parted. At the same time this family was embedded within a larger social structure of extended family, village or church community, which could help take the pressure off at difficult moments. And again, 50 or 60 years ago, most children were out at work by 14, working long hours, the boys often with their fathers, and the whole disruptive stress on families of obstreperous teenagers (a word which dates back only to the late 1950s) did not exist. In other words, the family ideal of today, in both Roman Catholicism and Orthodoxy, is essentially a new invention.

My second objection is a curious sort of infantilising, when too much emphasis is placed on children, when they become centre stage. Sorry, the norm is adult life in wider society, childhood is no more than a preparation for it, to be completed as soon as possible.

2016

Cars, God, furniture

14 January 2016

Last week I read in 'The Financial Times', under a picture of Donald Trump, the saying of U.S.-German satirist H. L. Mencken 'Deep within the heart of every evangelist lies the wreck of a car salesman.' It immediately brought to mind Pieter J.

Pieter was an Afrikaner evangelist who crossed my path in the early 1990s in a Protestant charismatic church in Brussels. He was exactly that, car salesman turned evangelist. He had been top VW salesman of South Africa some time in the 1980s before coming to Belgium as a missionary, where he would try to 'clinch' people to Christ (including my first wife) like he was closing on the sale of a Golf or Passat. A man of simple tastes (a good meal, a good beer), utterly sincere and deeply devout (the pages fell out of his Afrikaans Bible through being read so much) but no theologian.

I sent the quote to a rare surviving friend from that church, now Roman Catholic, who came back with the rest of the story. Returning to South Africa, Pieter took a pastorship that went wrong. He quit, and is now running a very successful business importing European furniture, which wealthy South Africans like, and showing his Christianity by treating his employees better than the norm.

God, furniture, cars – all part of the same business?

The dead language of icon painting

16 January 2016

I could lead my private life with God entirely in 'dead' languages – Latin, Greek, Slavonic, with the occasional help of the appropriate dictionary. Once you have command of them, especially Greek, they are tidier and more concise than English. All three give me a sense of being part of a long church tradition. Outside of my *hortus conclusus* (walled garden) which I share with God, they are, however, useless to the communication of the gospel, which I do mainly by word – spoken and written – to those around me.

I sometimes have the same feeling with Orthodox iconography in the traditional 'Byzantine' style. Yes, I buy the argument that image can serve the gospel as an alternative to word. Yes, I am also ready to see beauty as a way to God, at least for some, and more importantly, an increasing sensitivity to beauty as being 'of God' as a sign of the deeper penetration of the Spirit of Christ into a person. And certainly such icons work for some.

But when I look at the 'standard' 'Byzantine' Christ with a mane of hair and thick neck which are well outside my canon of beauty or refinement, or the sack-like dresses of our Lady and the female saints, I ask whether this is not in danger of being a sort of language for the initiated which is unable to stretch to the edges of Christianity. Does, I ask, the Christ depicted in this way work effectively as a 'soul picture', attracting to Christ and providing healing through gazing at Him, to a Western non- or just-about Christian? Does a woman dressed like a nun or a Muslim woman provide a Western twenty-first century man or woman with a deep sense of what femininity is in God's eyes? To use the language of the Seventh Ecumenical Council, do such images still really 'take us to the prototype', at least in our part of the world?

I remain to be convinced, either for those at the edge and also for many of us – including myself – closer to the centre. Many times I feel that icons in the traditional style serve mainly as markers, saying that we are either Orthodox or ecumenical, just as the stray bits of Latin which crop up in the Catholic Church – including those horrible one liners sung over and over again to Taizé chants – tell others they are Roman Catholic with Latin somewhere in their past.

I don't want to discontinue reading the New Testament in Greek, nor do I suggest that my wife should stop icon painting in a traditional form. But I have to question just how far they work as languages to proclaim the gospel on the so-vital border between the Christian and non-Christian world, and at times, well into the Christian hinterland. And to ask whether, just as we have added modern English to our biblical languages to make God's Word accessible to the *hoi polloi* (the people we meet on the street), we are not going to have to look for other ways of depicting the human face and figure and other media

– starting with photography – that put across the prototype to a broader base.

Unchaste celibacy

18 February 2016

For the last few weeks the edifice has been fissuring and crumbling. A large chunk of it came away last week at Mount Athos in conversations with a monk friend. 'It' is the traditional church teaching on family and sexuality, which I find increasingly unrealistic and *realitätsfremd*.

I sense a terrible vacuum forming as an old order is passing, whether we want it or not, and a new order has still to be developed. A suspicion that much of the population – and probably quite a few serious church people – sense that truth, deep truth, is not always to be found in traditional family and sexual patterns as promulgated by the official churches. That there are deeper truths and integrities we have to reach out for.

The traditional pattern, which some still hold to, was a simple one: you aspired, or felt called to, something 'higher' than marriage, leading you to be celibate, generally in a specified vocation with other persons, or you were committed lifelong to an opposite sex partner, and open to children, preferably at least three in order to have a real family life. This two-way choice is still the pattern promulgated by the official Catholic press in Europe, and is the pattern that Orthodox clergy (who are generally married) are expected to promote.

Historically this was, I suspect, more necessity than choice. Unless you felt a clear vocation to something 'higher' before your early twenties and were ready to be celibate to achieve it, your natural drives led you to marry, have sex, have kids (hopefully in that order). Contraception smashed this paradigm, making it possible to both aim for something 'higher' and still be sexually active. 'Unchaste celibacy' if you like.

My guess is that this desire for something 'higher' than family life as experienced heretofore runs deeper than we in the churches like to admit. We praise the family, but memories of the inadequacies of generations of nuclear families live deep: intelligent women housebound with kids, or shacked up with the wrong partner. If raising families is all that God put us here on this earth to do, then He was a mean creator!

Where does this lead us? Possibly to a three-way pattern:

1. Celibacy for (quasi-)religious purposes.

2. Family life as a specific (Christian) vocation, with large numbers of kids to make it really meaningful. But like the celibacy vocation, this entails considerable financial and cultural sacrifices.

3. A huge in-between space, inhabited by sexually active couples, often childless, or with one or two kids, not always from the same partnership. It is this in-between space that we as theologians have to have the courage to address in the church. Accepting that family life is not the be-all-and-end-all of Christian existence. Finding a morality for this that puts integrity and meaning higher than sexual and family conformity in our judgements on the world around us, and in what we teach our kids, and whom we give communion to in church.

As I said to my monk friend: we are in for a turbulent 20 or 30 years ahead here, but we need to face the challenge.

Any fool…

12 March 2016 (Facebook)

… can look pious on Facebook by posting articles full of religious quotations, pictures of monks and startsi and the like. I call it dressing in borrowed clothes.

The only people I give time to are those who write themselves, out of their own experience of God, or sense of lack of it. People who have the courage to admit that the Christian life is difficult, that they don't understand things, that they go up the wrong street sometimes, that they are not particularly holy. It is together with such people that I can go forward in my own Christian life, and we can together form (part of) the body of Christ.

(Un)holy noise

25 March 2016 (Facebook)

Needing something more sophisticated after a day of translating bank statements, I watched on YouTube a version of Charpentier's Tenebrae, recorded and filmed in the Royal Chapel in Versailles.

I'm fairly certain the singers did not know what they were singing, and if they did, I'm far from sure they were committed to the words they were singing. I don't know how important they were to Charpentier, as it is nearly impossible, even with reasonable church Latin, which I have, to disentangle word from musical complexity. Put a bawdy Latin ditty, the sort of thing medieval students delighted in, to the same music, and I'm not sure many people would know the difference…

This brings me to a pet hate: where the Word of God gets lost to become 'holy noise', through loss of language competence, and a desire for musical sophistication. You sense this loss of Word content generally in Western church music with the rise of polyphony in the Middle Ages. This Word which was largely rescued by the Protestant churches.

The Protestants rescued it, not only with the Word in the vernacular, but also with music where the Word is not totally crushed and subservient to performance: large parts of Bach's Passions are immediately understandable if the acoustics of the building or recording studio are good.

In Orthodoxy it's a bit knife-edge: yes, you can just about understand the language with an effort, at least if properly educated, the singing is normally not too complex. The killer is rather readers' desire to show off: either by reading at breakneck speed or 'tarting up' the epistle and Gospel readings, with 'performance' drawing attention to the reader and away from the Word.

Parles-tu français, monsieur le missionaire? Spreek je nederlands, mijnheer missionaris? (Do you speak French/Dutch, Mr Missionary?)

12 May 2016

I learnt today that 2,000 missionaries are coming to Europe this autumn from an American organization called Antioch Ministries. Five-hundred are coming to Belgium, 200 to Brussels. Not all at once, but in waves. In response, I was told, to the refugee crisis. They are leaning heavily on the Protestant ministries in Belgium to help them. I asked their representative today a silly question: do they speak French? No. Dutch, I presume not. Any idea of the religious history of Belgium? No, I assume. Then: what leads you to think that you have the right to be here, preaching a gospel reeking of a culture alien to ours? Every time you go out onto the street, you will need a local interpreter. Why can't he or she give the message direct, him or herself?

Yes, we Europeans need to sort ourselves out with God. But we need to do it with our cultural background and values, in our languages. Sort out rather your own mess: a culture that breeds a Donald Trump, that has made havoc of most of the Middle East, where health care costs twice as much as in Europe, where social security has gaping holes ... If you really want to respond to the refugee crisis, to which your country is a major contributor, then persuade Congress to take half a million of them – including 80% Muslims – to the USA.

St Catherine's, Brussels

18 May 2016 (Facebook)
Between visiting Le Lion (the last old-fashioned chemist in Brussels) for woodworking oils and the Chinese supermarket for green tea, I slipped into St Catherine's. This downtown parish, after several years' rather miserable existence in what is now a non-residential area, and slated for closure, suddenly sprung back to life when the previous Archbishop installed the rather traditionalist Fraternité des Saints-Apôtres there, allowed them to do a rather traditionalist style Catholic mass (black cassocks and cotta) and the municipality (responsible for the building) cleaned the outside stonework.

Yes, the paint is gently peeling off the inside walls and ceiling, but the place feels loved. The notices explaining what is what are neatly worded and printed. There is a priest there in a small glass-walled office, available to talk or confess. The sacrament was on display, with a dozen people kneeling in front of it when I went in, and they started saying the rosary.

They are not certain what to do with the place. There is a permanent threat of closure, not least because the parish's traditional style, against the trend, is something of a fly in the ointment. But they tell me it is full on Sundays.

But it may be giving a message: that a more traditional way of doing things, with full liturgies, and processions, and a certain strictness, can draw people and keep them. Though not a Roman Catholic, on coming out, I was very glad that they were there, with a praying presence in the centre of the city. Long may it stay open.

My hermit side

9 June 2016

As much by accident as design I have found myself reading one book after another on the (semi-) hermit life: an American book on modern eremitic life, a bit short on the spirituality but long on practical details and the variety of forms the search for God in silence takes; fascinating lectures from a novice-master to Carthusian novices; two books with a Calmoldese setting, including a modern one from Poland; and a 30-year-old English classic from the former head of an enclosed Anglican women's order.

While I don't think it is time to seclude myself totally from the world, the eremitic life is an area of spirituality which has fascinated me ever since my monastic novitiate 30 years ago. It is territory I feel comfortable in. With few rules there is room for manoeuvre and hard theological thinking – there is quite a bit of territory where the maps are not fixed. How does becoming one with Christ really work; how does prayer work in greater proximity to God, and especially prayer for healing (can one ask for healing for others only to the degree one has been healed oneself?); what is the dynamic of entering into Christ's death and resurrection; how does one reconcile 'annihilation' and 'passionless-ness' in God with 'desire' (*coincidentia voluntatum*); how do hermits 'carry the world to God in prayer'? And so on. I note the fact that many hermits are quite cultured people.

As an Orthodox one faces the fact that there is very little modern writing from one's own camp that covers this area. At best the occasional biography of a modern starets, or letters from one, and one rather dryly written book on the 'theological legacy of Archimandrite Sophrony (Sakharov)'. One senses it is not an area of spirituality particularly encouraged: the Russian church in particular seems to fight scared of personal callings outside of recognised structures, and indeed of 'advanced spirituality' in general.

A Russian puzzle

12 June 2016

I reckon to have a pretty good feel for religious history. If asked to, and with a little research to fill in the gaps, I could comfortably lecture on the history of Christian spirituality in most European countries: certainly England, France, Belgium, Germany, Sweden and the Netherlands. But Russia's spiritual history baffles me. Yes, I know the main dates and names, strung out on a timeline, from my theology student days: Saints Anthony and Theodosius – St Sergius of Radonezh – St Nil Sorsky – Metropolitan Nikon – St Paisius Velichkovsky – St Seraphim of Sarov – the Optina fathers. But it is getting from one to another, developing any sense of continuum, of how Christianity was passed from one generation to another, which is all the problem. Great saints arise, but within two generations, their inspiration has petered out. Yes, monasteries and parish churches have been open continuously since the conversion of Russia, but one suspects that their spirituality was often pretty superficial, the whole organization kept afloat by the constant repeating of a complex, very 'sacred' but often poorly understood (linguistically and theologically) liturgy and people's need for rites of passage. I note also that, unlike in Europe, most spiritual reform in Russian has been imported from outside (Nil Sorsky, Nikon, Paisius Velichkovsky), rather than developing endogenously as an internal necessity. So much so that one asks: is Russia able to maintain a lively spiritual tradition under its own steam, or is it vitally dependent on the rest of Christianity to keep it afloat?

The question of tradition is eased slightly if one is ready to accept that the passage of the Spirit of God from one generation to another has often gone outside the 'official' church – which means *inter alia*, Old Believers, Baptists, the Underground Church (and perhaps even the much-maligned-because-much-misused Renovationist movement of the 1920s and 1930s).

The situation clears slightly if we accept 'Russian spirituality' is wider than any one Russian confession.

I also ask: is the problem compounded by a sort of schizophrenia of the Russian religious mind which has existed since Peter the Great (and perhaps already since Nikon and Avvakum)? Whatever the merits or demerits of his 'great step forward', pulling Russian out of medievalism, one senses that somehow the resulting church is 'not quite Russian' or 'not the whole Russian truth'. Like the great churches of St Petersburg, built by imperial dictate: missing something, curiously unrooted. To complete the picture we have to include an unwashed, uneducated popular piety, with considerable energy (human beings being naturally religious animals) but discarded by the elite and historically prey to chiliastic preachers and, since 1988, to loud-mouthed, self-appointed, anti-ecumenical 'elders' (*mladostartsi*) who use them to build their own petty power bases.

Catechumens

20 June 2016 (Facebook)
The Orthodox liturgy is long, and for this reason the full set of prayers between the gospel and the entrance with the bread and wine to consecrate is often shortened. This includes cutting the prayers for the catechumens (after which, in the early centuries, they left the church and only the baptised remained for the liturgy).

We have received instructions to omit these prayers. Because, they tell me, we don't have catechumens, that is people preparing for baptism. I find this fallacious. If we are a properly functioning Christian community, we ought to have catechumens, and say the prayer. If we do not, we ought to say it penitentially, asking ourselves if their absence is not a reproach to us for failing in our duty to preach and be the gospel. If our self-elected limitation to Russian-speakers is justification for not having them, at least we should pray for them in other parishes and other Christian communities.

Catechumens are a nuisance: someone has to instruct them, which takes time and commitment, and to curb neophyte excesses. They ask the questions we prefer to avoid and challenge

us to put our own faith into words. I ask myself: do I really want
to make new Christians? The answer is – just about – yes. Often
a rather small yes. My own Christian path has been a messy one,
at times painful. The investment has, I believe, been worth it,
though I still ask whether, with some better guidance, or my
being a bit smarter (or humbler), I could not have got where I
think I am now 10 or 20 years sooner.

Where I remain stuck is that to make new Christians, you
need some sort of reception structure, a Christian 'family'
which pulls together and which can take in a catechumen,
and train him or her. Yes, I have in mind two or three friends
whom I sense it is time to push a bit towards serious Christian
commitment. Yes, theoretically, I can train them myself, but
I have to be able to bring them in to a properly functioning
Christian community, ready to accept, integrate, nourish them
and take them further in the faith. I wish I could be more sure
my own community is able or willing to do so.

The Brexit debate: a problem of method

23 June 2016

By the time many of you read this we will know whether the
UK is set to remain in the European Union or not. For me
the Brexit debate and its ultimate resolution are a problem of
method. Let me start with a quote from an opinion column
by Philip Stephens in today's 'Financial Times' (Stephens is an
acute commentator whom I respect): 'Modern democracies
operate within a framework of rationalism. Dismantle it and
the space is filled by prejudice. Fear counts above reason;
anger above evidence. Lies claim equal status with facts. Soon
enough, migrants – and Muslims especially – replace heretics
and witches as the targets of public rage.'

This is precisely where the problem of method lies: we
have told ourselves for the past 200 years or so that we are
rational beings and that we guide our societies by rationality,
expressed in democracy. But as any Christian theologian worth
his or her salt will tell you, that is not how humans – individuals
and society – work, or are made to work. Real decisions – love,
marriage, whether and where to buy a house – are taken at
another level: when people are working properly, at a level of

knowledge/sensing of what is deeply right and wrong which
is more intuitive, but no less real. It is the level at which
religious people work, where 'faith' becomes 'knowledge'. But
as religious people will also tell you, it is a level that requires
discipline to use successfully: to get down to it you have to get
beyond a thick layer of confusing emotions, the 'prejudice …
fear … anger' that Stephens fears. These are certainly there. But
rationalism will not save us from them; many times it will serve
to offer excuses for them.

Questions to Russian monasticism

7 August 2016

There will always, I suppose, be a bit of the monk in me. In
the 50 years since reading Thomas Merton's *The Silent Life* at
age 17, I must have visited/stayed in at least 60 monasteries,
both Catholic and Orthodox, including a two-year novitiate in
France in my thirties.

I was again in a monastery for ten days in Russia last month.
Founded about 15 years ago, two hours' rough driving from the
next main city, six kilometres from the nearest village. Newly
built, half-finished, with space for a dozen monks, perhaps 20 if
and when completed. Now that the former abbot has decamped
to a warmer climate, it is operating on two monks plus one very
new novice, with a priest sent out from the main town once
a week. I don't want to knock anyone, not least my very kind
hosts, but this remains for me a strange situation, and part of
what is for me the far from convincing story of monasticism in
Russia since the end of communism.

Put simply: in Russia my impression is that the desire for
monasteries outstrips the desire of individual men and women
to become monastics. Monasteries play multiple roles, including
being places for the pious wealthy to expend their largesse,
something that every bishop feels he needs to have in his diocese,
and a key component of the lives of many ordinary believers
– I think of the crowds of people making the long pilgrimage
to Solovki, or the number of people working there as summer
volunteers (perhaps 150) out of all proportion to the number
of monks in residence (about 25), or the people making long

'cross processions' lasting several days, in the summer heat, to other monasteries.

Take it from another angle: if we assume that the cornerstones of the monastic system need to be men who are sufficiently developed spiritually so as to be able to be real spiritual guides, I have to ask: is the Russian monastic system able to develop these men internally? It takes a long time, and very often involves going off for a period 'into the wild', into a silence a normal monastery cannot give. My impression, but I am happy to be corrected, is that many men do not get that far, simply because either they get talent-spotted and siphoned off into bishoprics or because they are too essential a part of the daily machine to be given the freedom and time they need. Or a bishop takes them out to fill gaps in the parish structure.

And I ask: if a young Russian-speaking man senses a call to dedicate himself to God in silence, prayer and deep conversion, is a monastery necessarily the right place today? What he needs is three things: a spiritually competent man to guide him, a certain amount of rough-and-tumble with other people to get rid of his pride, and some serious silence and aloneness. Rough-and-tumble he will get, serious aloneness I doubt. Good guidance I am also less sure about. Possibly in a skete, if there is a good spiritual father, but in a major monastery, where everyone is queuing for the starets, I'm less certain.

And does the whole thing have to be so expensive? I don't know what the monastery I was at cost to build, but it can't be far off seven figures in dollars or euros. My back-of-an-envelope calculation is that Panteleimon (Athos), Valaam and Solovki have cost between one and ten million euros per monk to restore. At a time when country priests are struggling to survive on 300 euros a month, is this a correct use of funds?

In Catholic Europe we have seen an interesting phenomenon. After a huge revival movement between 1830 and 1880 (the French Revolution had dissolved all monasteries), paid for by a nouveaux-riche industrial class and often manned by their excess sons and daughters, traditional monasteries went into free fall in the 1960s through lack of vocations But at the same time, a whole new wave of 'new monasticism' came into being: people sensing the need to answer a call to God in community, but something more in keeping with the time. Progress has been bumpy, and there have been serious casualties, but the 'new monastics' now outnumber the traditional ones. There are also quite large numbers of people sensing a call to hermit and quasi-hermit lives, especially in the Anglo-Saxon countries.

I wonder whether Russian monasticism does not have to go through a similar pattern: a realization that traditional monasticism is not necessarily the best or only pattern for people to devote themselves in silence and conversion to God, and to the constant bringing of humankind to God in prayer that is so desperately important, and a readiness to test other paths.

St Nil Sorsky and judgement

16 August 2016 (Facebook)
I'm rereading the monastic rule of St Nil Sorksy (1433–1508). Nil, an educated monk who had spent some considerable time on Mount Athos, moved out of a large Russian monastery to found a skete in Northern Russia. He collected quite a following and several sketes were founded, all very much on the Athonite model. This was not always to the liking of the church powers that be, who wanted monasteries to be and do other things, and in the next generation his movement was quashed.

It is pretty standard Athonite stuff, but with little comments which suggest that it had been tested and tried by Nil himself. But reading it, I come up again against one approach, widely found in monastic writing and which I have difficulty with: the call for a constant memory of death. One is supposed to picture oneself in the throes of death and facing the torment of judgement, in the hope that this will force one to repentance.

It does not work very well with me. Yes, there is judgement, but is not judgement ultimately, providing we have lived reasonably honest Christian lives, a liberating experience: 'then [we] shall know fully, just as [we are] fully known' (1 Corinthians 13:12, NIV)? When the sin and pain that block and damage our relations with God and with our fellow-men are revealed, then we will know what is really primary and what is rather secondary. Providing we can stand this truth, we can only rejoice. Indeed what we should want to do is to 'bring forward' this judgement, not wait for this last judgement and, like the psalmist, ask God to show me my secret sins (cf. Psalm 19.12).

The concern must surely be already now, and as far as possible to pass 'from death to life' (John 5:24, 1 John 3:14), so that when we meet Christ in judgement, this is no more than the completion and perfection of an exercise of purification and entry into the life of the Trinity begun long before. Or am I missing something?

Entry into the (clergy) tribe

2 September 2016

I was talking last night with a friend about clergy training in Russia, where I am right now. Does a young man really need to spend five years in seminary in order to become a priest? An educated person can learn the essentials of Christian theology in a few weeks of a summer course and with intelligent reading. A bit longer if he wants to learn Greek and/or Hebrew. The answer hit me in the taxi on the way home: 'Entry into the tribe.'

My working hypothesis right now is that, in sociological terms, the Russian clergy operates within the church and society like a separate tribe, very much like the Levites of biblical Israel.

And like any tribe, it has its initiation processes, into its own particular ways of thinking and acting. And for those who do not come from priestly families (probably 40% of new entrants nowadays), seminary is this place of initiation. Which also means that those who, like myself, have not gone through this initiation process, will always be somewhat on the edges.

This tribal aspect was obvious yesterday morning, when I took part in a full-flung cathedral liturgy in a larger Russian city: senior bishop, a dozen priests, five deacons, and another dozen or so young men, mostly seminarians, in the minor roles, candle-holders in processions, passing censers, laying the 'eagle' (the special little round carpet a bishop stands on). All of us were in the attractive light blue vestments for the Octave of the Dormition of the Virgin, spread across a huge sanctuary. There were two liturgies: an 'outer' liturgy for the people and a second, inner and quite complex one, in the sanctuary, a ritual for the 'tribe' (a 'tribal dance' if you wish), coordinated largely by the bishop's proto-deacon.

I'm not knocking it: I can see its value – increasingly I am recognising the importance of 'rite' in the Russian Orthodox tradition (that's for another posting) – and I know the choreography well enough to join in meaningfully. But yes, like much of Russian church and clergy life, it is very much a world on its own, in constant danger of losing contact with, and being unable to serve the changing spiritual needs of the everyday world around it.

On the Jesus Prayer

7 September 2016

Am I pushing things too far by suggesting that the Jesus Prayer – the constant repeating in the heart of 'Lord Jesus Christ, Son of God, have mercy on me' – is very much the prayer of the road to the kingdom, but it is not the prayer of the kingdom? That it is a temporary prayer, serving perhaps in particular to position our prayer in the heart, which has to give way to something else, especially adoration. We pray the prayer when we lose God, when we sense ourselves far from Him, but it is not a prayer of proximity. Maybe its reduction to the words 'Jesus, Jesus' express proximity better. But even then is there not a time when we are simply 'there' with God? We know it in the depths of our being, God knows that we know it, and that is enough…

The bases of Christian life – questions to Fr Nikon Vorobyev

25 September 2016 (Facebook)
A kind priest in Russia gave me as a present the collection of writings of Father Nikon Vorobyev (1894–1963) entitled 'О началах жизни' (On the Bases of Life).

As Father Nikon's dates suggest, he was a Russian who was priested in the early years of the Communist regime, went inevitably through the camps, was posted in out-of-the-way villages, but still attracted a large following. He is one of those figures the older Christian generation of today look back to, including A.I. Osipov, one of Russia's most popular theology teachers, who edited the book.

The book is published in a 180,000 copy edition by the Publishing House of the Moscow Patriarch. It is nicely made with two CDs. All this tells me that it is a book the powers that be want the faithful to read.

I have little quibble with the basic message of the book, that of the importance of deep and continuous repentance on the Christian journey. Yes, it is a basis, as the title suggests. What I do ask though is: is this the sole message one can base a Christian life on over a period of 20, 30, 40 or more years? Repentance is certainly necessary, and yes, it is continual, as we go deeper and deeper into our own hearts (and possibly into the collective heart). But at the same time this repentance has to open out onto both joy and a sense of responsible freedom, a spiritual maturity as 'brothers and sisters of Christ', including, it seems to me, an increasing ability for spiritual discernment and taking our own decisions, as we move towards the 'perfect Man, unto the measure of … the fullness of Christ' (Ephesians 4:13, KJV) that many of the church fathers see as the goal of the Christian path.

It is this 'opening out' that I miss in this book. The Christian profile that it seems to presume is that of 'permanent beginner', with the clergy as permanent moral guides, and with very little concept of a process of maturity and growing spiritual discernment. Or am I being unfair…?

On political argument

1 October 2016 (Facebook)
One rule I insist on in political argument: it is easy to throw stones, or bombs, but don't smash people's houses until you can offer alternative accommodation. Revolt is valid ultimately only if one can offer a viable (and not an 'if only people were good' idealistic) solution.

The systems we use

24 October 2016
A young man in his late teens whom I know is crashing into a wall for lack of a system to take him into adulthood. This has focused my mind on the systems we build and use to make sense of life and make it worth living. Despite all the fine talk they give us at school about individuality and freedom of choice and 'doing one's own thing', only a very few manage to really develop individual systems which work. The lucky ones inherit systems from family, school and social clan that are strong enough to see them into adult life.

For those less lucky – my young friend today and myself 50 years ago – one is almost forced to take an 'off the shelf' system: that is an existing set of values and a context provided by other people, which one plugs into.

These off-the-shelf solutions come in a variety of forms. They include:

- Traditional Christianity.
- The business corporation.
- The army.
- Monastic life.
- Seminary and priesthood (at least in Russia).
- Street gangs.
- Scouts (if properly run by credible people).

- Certain sports, especially martial arts.

- Certain trades and art forms which involve a considerable level of discipline to do correctly.

Each of these has in common a strong basic framework and a strong internal discipline – you know exactly what you can and cannot do. Its members operate corporately like a clan or tribe, each with its own jargon and shibboleths. Almost all have their downsides: some are tighter than is perhaps psychologically good for a person long term (the strict mores of traditional Christianity and seminary and priesthood can result in hurried marriages to avoid pre-marital sex or qualify for ordination). Others require you to surrender much of your judgement and conscience to others (in the army, your commanding officer and the ministry of defence). Some, once you are in, are extraordinarily difficult to get out of.

I know very few people who have developed truly individual systems from scratch. One ended up a multi-millionaire, another two as hermits. Looking back, I have borrowed systems (various forms of Christianity mainly) to get me around some tight corners, but in each time with a certain pulling away once I was back into clear water.

To a young friend (male, early twenties)

9 December 2016
Dear X,
Our latest Facebook exchanges, where you were suggesting biblical support (Leviticus 20:13) for killing gay people and your citing of St Joseph of Volotsky in order to say 'Roman Catholics' are not Christians, are the most recent of several of your postings which worry me.

It is as if over the past several months you have been trying out one 'fundamentalist' position after another – strict Orthodox, Daesh, proto-Fascism (Evola, Dugin) with a dash of mysticism (Sufi, Boehme…), in and out of Orthodoxy and Islam and (possibly) Donbass and the Middle East. Rather like trying on different jackets in a clothing store.

The simple fact is that ultimately none of these jackets will fit. That Christ calls us to something beyond fundamentalism.

Fundamentalism can match the psyche of the young adult male of your age, looking for a 'pure' cause. But very quickly it can lead us in directions which are life-destroying (stoning people) and running against the evidence of the Holy Spirit (denying the presence of God in Roman Catholics). The classic example is St Paul, whose fundamentalism led him to approve a stoning party. You know the rest of the story.

All these fundamentalisms are surrogates. Sooner or later we have to move beyond, like Paul, meet Christ, direct, outside of neat systems, and with the Spirit taking over from the rules of structures. And it is out of this meeting – direct, and without hiding behind the authority of other people – that real Christian writing and discourse (and you are potentially a good writer) comes.

It is uncomfortable, it is also liberating.

This is my wish and my prayer for you.

With love in Christ,

d.M.

2017

In your presence is fullness of joy...

15 February 2017

Should I shout out 'Smile, Jesus loves you', or put a sticker with that message on my censer, I thought to myself as I censed two rows of glum faces during yesterday evening's Vespers and Matins for the Feast of the Presentation.

The feast (often known as Candlemas in the West) has a marvellous story: Jesus is brought into the Temple at 40 days, and this old man Simeon, who has been waiting all his life for the person who will be 'the glory of thy people Israel', who knows instinctively that there is something more to life, to religion, to temple worship, that he has to wait for, finally has the baby in his arms. The promise to him is fulfilled, and he can 'depart in peace'. It is the story of those of us who have held out, and still insist on holding out, for something more in Christ and religion than the lukewarm pottage that is too often served up.

OK, Russians can look serious on occasions, and I've learnt to handle and get past it. But here it was too deep. Duty yes –

and I suspect it was duty ('Feast of Obligation' as our Catholic friends say) more than anything else that had brought most of them into church – but Christianity is also about love and joy. The troparion (short hymn) for the feast has the word 'rejoice' in it twice. Sorry, but last night was joyless. To be fair, Sundays are generally better…

After the service I went down to the woodworking class to pick up my Italian friend Leo. And there were Nick, Fulvio, Luc and others. There was more joy and laughter in ten minutes together there than in the two hours in church.

As my wife said: where's your church?

At the start of Lent – Mary the Egyptian and Zosimas

26 February 2017
Mary the Egyptian, on her conversion from life of flagrant sin, fled straight to the desert, where she spent 47 years. Zosimas – who found her and gave her communion before her death – along with his fellow-monks, left church on the first Sunday of every Lent to be alone with God in the desert, returning on Palm Sunday to the monastery.

None of them went through the Great Penitential Canon of St Andrew of Crete, which is said at prolonged Compline services during the first four days of the first week of Lent and again in one very long haul towards the end. Good breast-beating stuff, as we accuse ourselves of passion, lust, self-will and the like, comparing ourselves with Adam, Lamech, David, Abimelech and other Old Testament characters. But every year I ask whether this really reaches the jugular, whether it really cleans and purifies us and brings us closer to God.

My own experience of sin – and I suspect that of Mary the Egyptian's – is not this. It is first and foremost of 'soul wounds', the fact that somewhere, deep down, an inner equilibrium has been broken, which leads to behaviour patterns – especially in my case a rather silent inner anger – which do me and others no good. The reasons are mixed: my own family's (which goes back at least three generations) life-inhibiting belief systems, inside and outside church, that I was brought up with; and yes, at times later, but ultimately rather secondarily, my own stupidity or cowardice. These are things which are difficult to put into words, which hit me at four in the morning rather than during church service times, and need silence and openness to God's mercy, to place myself 'soul-naked' and sometimes in pre-verbal pain (rather than breast-beating contrition) in front of God for long periods of time and ask much more for healing than for forgiveness.

I rather suspect it was the same for Mary the Egyptian: the story I tell myself is of a woman whose sexuality was damaged at an early age and in reaction to the wound lived a life of considerable depravity. When she realised what was wrong, knowing instinctively perhaps that this would confuse the issue rather than solve it, she did not go to a church in Alexandria or Jerusalem and stand in the confession queue, and allow herself to be 'in-churched' but threw herself into the desert, alone and on God's mercy, where she had time and solitude to allow God, slowly and mercifully, to take her apart and put her together again, restoring what was damaged deep down, and 're-virginifying her', ready (apart from the barriers of age) to either take up a celibate life or marry and have a sexual life honestly as God intended most of us to do.

So, do I go to church for the Great Canon this year or not...?

Beware of religious wishful thinking

17 March 2017 (Facebook)
The 'Agrippina' story (or scandal), as related to me (see below) has caused me, and no doubt others in the Russian church, quite a bit of soul-searching. Slowly, it is looking to be part of a larger pattern: where the attraction of deep spiritual purity – something I think Russians are particularly sensitive to – has produced narratives which are either pure imagination or conflations of real situations into what they were not. Wishful thinking, with often negative spiritual consequences.

The Agrippina story is that of Fr Pavel Troitsky, a starets (holy man), interned in a Gulag, supposedly sending messages of spiritual guidance to and from his spiritual children in the 1970s and early 1980s through Agrippina, a parishioner of a well-known Moscow church still open at the time. Many of these spiritual children were young men considering becoming priests. Only with the opening of the records after *perestroika* (restructuring) did we learn that Fr Pavel had died a couple of decades earlier. Simply, the messages were the fabrication of the KGB, and their message: the need for absolute humility and obedience to one's superiors, suited the religious politics of the day. Pointedly, several of Fr Pavel's correspondents went on to be ordained and some still hold senior positions in prominent Moscow churches.

Other possible imaginations/conflations are the stories of 'Father Arseni', highly popular in the 1990s both in Russia and in translation into several languages. These are stories from the life of a priest who led an underground existence and went through the camps between the 1930s and 1960s, and of several of his spiritual children. The stories are an excellent read. But both the just-too-miraculous and the unwillingness or inability of people to put a name to him is worrying – was it just because he remained in the underground church and never came back into the Russian Orthodox Church, or was he too much of a free spirit to be canonised? Also people who read Russian better than I do say that the testimonies of his spiritual children are all written in the same style. At least one senior priest I know believes they are a fabrication. If ever it were proved to be false, the general feeling would be 'if only it were true'.

Widening the circle there is the Russian pilgrim (*Strannik*), the account of a wandering pilgrim's introduction to the Jesus Prayer at the end of the nineteenth century, which is hugely popular both inside and outside Russia. Again, very difficult to put a boundary between truth and fancy: I have difficulties of quite believing the speed with which the pilgrim picks up the prayer. I do wonder how many people who really do practise the Jesus Prayer or something similar recognise themselves in this book.

I do not want to be too harsh. They say the devil never pays his own taxi: he takes an impetus that is fundamentally good – here a desire for saintliness and purity – and perverts it to his own ends. The perversion here is triple, first that of vicarious sainthood: the constant reading about first class saints (and inventing them if need be) distracts us from the need to set out ourselves to be at least fourth-class saints. Second: of misreading the authoritarianism of certain startsi (essentially a temporary

tool in specific and closely controlled discipleship situations)
into a duty of obedience to any clergyman who demands it.
Third: of the thirst for the spiritually spectacular/miraculous
blunting the important spiritual gift of discernment.

My father

25 March 2017
My father was born 100 years ago today. Christened William, a
bit strangely for someone born in the middle of World War I, he
was known to everyone by his second name of Sydney.

His marriage was not a good one – his best friend snatched
his fiancée from him during his five-year absence from England
during the war – and he married my mother, a pretty, highly
intelligent but emotionally damaged young woman two years
after his return. He remained doggedly faithful to her and us
four children, more out of duty than of joy, clinging I suspect,
to the rest of the Methodist faith he had had as a young man,
and which was then strong enough for him to register as a
conscientious objector (pacifist) during the war, most of which
he spent in China mending trucks for a Quaker relief agency
and later teaching carpentry in an orphanage.

In a way I 'lost' my father when I was 11. I won a scholarship
to an elite London school and from it went on to the University
of Cambridge. Both were beyond my father's social range (his
family was 'professional tradesman') but within my mother's
(aspiring London suburban bourgeoisie), and from then on
I was 'mother's boy'. At age 13 I moved from Methodism to
Church of England, my mother's church and that of my school,
a socially 'higher' church. I was a 'good' boy, and my father was
more concerned keeping my mother operational and a younger
brother from going off the rails to worry too much about me.

Dad was a good, decent man, honest, hardworking, respected
at work, head of the local primary school parents' committee
and in his retirement a school governor. But he never really
inspired me. Something, I sense, either went missing, or never
had the chance to flourish. I think he could appreciate good
music, art and literature, but rather hid this side of himself
which my mother was unable to appreciate. How much of all
this blocking was due to the British class system, still pretty

vicious when I was a young man, or to the caesura of the war, I do not know. I remember Dad saying how on the return from the war, all his generation wanted to do was to return to 'normalcy': to marry, start a family, buy a house, settle down … Maybe it was this normalcy that blunted him.

A big regret is that he did not pass on to me the 'male' things fathers often pass to sons and which provide bonding: he did not teach me to drive or mend a car (he could pull a truck or a car to pieces and rebuild it), nor woodworking, which he did well. What little I learnt about sex and women came from my mother (badly – she was too messed up in this area to teach me well). He almost never spoke about religion, which I was into deeply. He could not understand my entering a monastery, and was rather glad when they asked me to leave.

After my mother's early death he remarried to a woman I did not much care for. Thankfully she looked after him through to the end, when his mind started to go. Perhaps paradoxically it was me, not she, nor my fellow-siblings, all closer to him, who saw him out when he died in hospital, a few days before his eightieth birthday.

Restorations (political and religious)

30 March 2017

The English Restoration (of the Stuart monarchy after Oliver Cromwell's Commonwealth) lasted 28 years, from 1660 to 1688.

The French Restoration (of its monarchy) lasted 33 years, from 1815 to 1848.

How long will the Russian (church) restoration, of the religious system as it existed pre-1917, last?

The first two restorations fell apart because they became increasingly out of sync with the spirit of the time, and because people who thought they stood to gain from them found themselves increasingly short-changed.

A restoration is always a stopgap: an old system has collapsed, no forward-moving alternative is yet available, so one grasps back to something earlier. Once a credible alternative exists, the stopgap becomes redundant. When will that be?

On evangelism

10 April 2017

Evangelization has never come easy to me. God has always been there in my life, never away long since I started Sunday school at age three in a wooden hut behind the local Methodist Church, heated with a paraffin stove in front of Holman Hunt's 'Light of the World'. But it has been a constant fight, since my mid-teens, to shape out of what was being preached to me a message that I really believe in, let alone might want to pass on to others.

I think I have puzzled out the Christian message, as it impacts me. It is a message of a God who remains faithful, working at a level of truth and integrity which is deeper than what the 'world' offers. It is of a God who, if you let Him, enters deep into the human psyche and heals and slowly turns pain into joy. It is of a God who desperately wants human beings to come to the fullness of their potential. Of a God who gives the strength to look at oneself and the world in the face. But the working out of this in my own life has been an intensely personal experience, something to be shared with people I really trust, but not to be preached Billy Graham style from a pulpit or soapbox.

It is also an experience in which church plays a very ambiguous role. In theory church or Christian community teaches us to listen to God and one another and discern and put into practice what God deep down wants for us. A place of unconditional, disinterested love out of which worship becomes possible. My church experience has too often been of a 'love' concerned not for what God wanted for me, but what the leaders wanted me for: whether to swell their score of conquered souls, to be an audience for their bad sermons, generous donor or a good-looking young man to try to entice into bed. No, I'm being a bit harsh: the Methodist minister stepped in vitally in a serious crisis when I was a boy. A couple of Christian schoolmasters were good to me in my teens. My Bible class teacher was one of the most Christian men I have met. A Protestant pastor kept me afloat when I was going through the mill 25 years ago. But they have been rare beacons in a sea of grey.

Is this the church I want to bring people into? Right now there are perhaps five or six people I know and love, for whom

I think Christ, experienced deep down as I know Him, would make sense. Would make them fuller, more human people. But in which church do I place them? Perhaps I just have to try to put across the message and leave the rest to God.

God bless LiveJournal

23 April 2017

Where do I express myself as a Christian? Not in my parish. Yes, I am allowed to 'speak': the standard prayers that a deacon reads every Sunday, sometimes the gospel if the first deacon is absent, the epistle if we have no ordained reader in church. But talk about my faith: share what matters to me in it, no that's pretty much for priests only: other people are not encouraged to speak about faith, much less to think about it creatively, except to 'toe the party line'.

The solution: to join the increasingly large crowd of people who are moving from parish to the Internet, looking there for a spirituality maturity and Christian fellowship they cannot find in the parish structure. The exiting people are especially those with the educational level to read the Scriptures and the Christian classical writers themselves, and often with a spiritual maturity well above the one at which the official church runs and which most priests preach to. Educated people, accustomed in the rest of their daily lives to think for themselves, to draw conclusions and act on them, and for whom the near-monopoly of the priesthood on 'word' within the church is oppressive. For me, and for an increasingly large percentage of the Orthodox intelligentsia, the Internet is a life-saver. Nearly all my serious Christian conversation happens online. It is here I fight my way through to what is really important and what is secondary in the Christian life, including dialoguing at times with 'tax-gatherers and prostitutes' who might not be welcome in church. The 'friends only' button also allows me to take the risk of saying things which are necessarily not for the ears of neophytes.

Some of us continue to go to church most Sundays, others have reduced their attendance to the minimum they feel to be necessary – essentially to take communion and experience liturgy, of which the official church retains the monopoly – in order to continue to be Christian. But for both groups the parish is no longer the place of the *koinonia*, the common Christian life. The informal and protean Internet groups with whom we share have largely replaced it.

This new form of 'inner immigration' bodes ill for the church: when a spiritual head of steam develops on the edge of the official church, as is happening in these groups, a reformation is near. But till this reformation comes, God bless Facebook, God bless LiveJournal.

Why I am not 'Western Orthodox'

17 May 2017

A Belgian Orthodox convert friend of mine wrote in reply to another posting: 'Here are my roots – Western Orthodoxy, from Alps to Scotland ... Not Romanian Orthodox, Greek, Russian, certainly not the lately arrived Roman Catholicism of course.'

My question to him – and without wanting to impugn in any way his sincerity or godliness –: 'Can one have "roots" in "Western Orthodoxy"?' I admit I have my doubts on at least five counts...

It seems to me that we cannot choose our religious roots: they are the ones we were born with: for him Roman Catholic as practised in Belgium, for me a mixture of English Methodism and Anglicanism. It is these that have (sub-)consciously formed us. We may not like them, we may feel that they have constrained or even betrayed us, and we may feel the need to widen our horizons and decide to make our religious lives in another context (for both of us Orthodoxy). But they remain our roots.

I am scared of 'broken traditions'. If a tradition broke, there was a reason, not necessarily of the devil. To want to 'jump back' over a 1,000-year gap is somehow to deny God's presence during the intervening period. In my case, I refuse to accept that God was 'absent' or 'less present' in England or Belgium between from whenever you date the break with Orthodoxy (664 (Council of Whitby), 794 (Council of Frankfurt), 1054 (the official split date between the Roman Catholic and Orthodox churches) or the mid-fourteenth century (when the Eastern and Western artistic traditions separate) until its 're-establishment' in the mid-twentieth century.

Given this gap and the paucity of remaining material, 'Western Orthodoxy' is very much whatever you want to put into it – theologically, liturgically, artistically, spiritually – and what you want to leave out. It lacks the restraining fences that are an essential part of a coherent religious system. With all the perils of 'religious romanticism'.

Also, religious systems are intimately linked with the social and power structures that they are part of and/or respond to. Without this reference, they are inherently inconsistent. That of historical Western Orthodoxy is (pre-)feudal, which does not marry with the modern Western mind. (The same logic explains why Russian Orthodoxy is a no-no in Western Europe: the despotic-authoritarian background it both answers to and to a large extent incorporates, are unacceptable to a Western psyche.)

'For the kingdom of God is not in word, but in power' (1 Corinthians 4:20, KJV). My experience – perhaps one-sided – of Western Orthodoxy is of a lot of word and not much power. I am not convinced of its deep salvific power. Deep Christian conversion and its power are very much tied up with purifying one's own internal roots and through this purification bringing into God's field of grace the others, alive and dead, that are part of this. I don't want to cast aspersions, and the exceptions prove the rule, but most of what I have seen, in Belgium during the past 25 years, feels 'not-rooted' and leaves me unconvinced.

This being said, I recognise fully that my correspondent, I myself and others, have needed to move away from our 'birth' church backgrounds, which became too contaminated, for one reason or another, often personal to us, for us to survive in. Thank God these alternatives were available. But to justify this as being part of a 'return to roots' is for me, sorry, one step too far.

Humility and glory

20 May 2017

'Glory' is a word we are a little reticent about. Yet it is clearly fundamental to our Christian vocation. The writer of Hebrews speaks of God 'bringing many sons and daughters to glory' (Hebrews 2:10, NIV). St Paul to the Corinthians talks of God's

hidden purpose of our coming to glory (1 Corinthians 2:7). And indeed, Christ speaks in the High Priestly prayer in John 17 of having already given the glory to His disciples: 'The glory that thou gavest me I have given to them' ($\delta\acute{\epsilon}\delta\omega\kappa\alpha$ $\alpha\mathring{v}\tau o\tilde{\iota}\varsigma$ – perfect tense) (John 17:22, KJV).

This why I feel uneasy with a constant breast-beating 'I'm a sinner, I'm a pig' attitude, which I find for example in some LiveJournal postings. Yes, we may certainly have behaved sinfully, 'swinefully', in our lives. And further on in our spiritual development we may be acutely aware both of the sinfulness around us and of the structures of sin which remain deep inside us. But we must not define ourselves by sin, but rather by glory. Sin is by essence a stranger to the human race, an intrusion from outside. It is something we are not made for, whereas for glory we are made.

St Paul tells his Roman readers 'not to be conceited or think too highly of themselves, but to come to a sober estimate of themselves' Romans 12:3, NEB). I wonder whether 'to think too lowly of oneself' is not an equal sin, and indeed may be rooted rather perversely in the same pride: both can be ways of setting oneself aside from humanity, making oneself someone 'special'. Not to mention, in the latter case, as an excuse for not pulling one's weight in the Christian and wider community. It can also be an excuse for not opening ourselves up to the painfulness of conversion and inner cleansing. Sin can be mediocre, but it can be perversely comfortable.

Someone will bring up here the argument of the importance of humility, often closely connected in the Russian mind with sense of sin and need for repentance. Dare I suggest humility is ultimately not about sin at all, but about our absolute dependency on God, a dependency not predicated on our sinfulness ('we need God because we are sinners'), but simply because God made us to be 'partakers of the divine nature' (2 Peter 1:4, KJV)?

And when repentance is necessary, it is not grovelling *pokayanie*,[1] 'I'm a swine, I'm a swine', that God wants, but truth, and the courage to look honestly at what we are, to accept the fullness, the 'glory' that God wants for us, to say 'no, in fact, with your help, I am not a swine', and saying this to take up our beds and walk.

Two very English religious books

3 June 2017 (Facebook)
Two books have accompanied me in spare hours during the past two weeks. The first is 'Revelations of Divine Love', written in the opening years of the fifteenth century by English anchorite and mystic Julian of Norwich. Really I should have read it long ago.

Much of it I like and warmed to. The book is an account of a series of 16 revelations Julian had, as a young woman at the point of death, meditated repeatedly and finally recounted twenty or so years later. It has an attractive positiveness about it: the importance of humankind for God, which is the subject of His constant love and concern. Yes there is sin, as much the result of ambient surroundings (original sin) than of personal guilt. God can be hurt by His creatures, but is never really angry. It is a story much more of God's mercy than of man's ascetic struggle, of God's love more than human guilt. This is very much in the English spiritual tradition, which has never taken kindly to 'sin-binning'. Also the account is pretty much free of 'bride/bridegroom' language borrowed from the Song of Songs, and the inevitable sexual overtones, of Continental Catholicism, which the English religious mind has never been comfortable with. Yes, like many, I baulk at her making Christ a male/female figure ('our mother Christ'), though I doubt any specifically feminist intent. In so doing she de facto evacuates Christ as a male role model (with the Mother of God as the female pendant), which I regret. While I like her stress on the fact that the birth of the Son before all ages and the plan for the creation of the world and humankind are basically a single act of the Father, her theology of the Trinity I find confusing (possibly not helped by the *filioque*), but for the main narrative not damaging.

The second book, which I finished in a single sitting, is the biography of medieval historian and exclaustrated Benedictine monk Dom David Knowles (1896–1974) by his near-contemporary Dom Adrian Moray. Knowles, a Roman Catholic, had entered Downside Abbey in 1914, straight out of the secondary school run by the Abbey. An outstanding scholar, he rose rapidly up the monastic ladder, under a couple of excellent abbots. All goes well until his mid-thirties: then he gets increasingly uncomfortable with Downside, wants something stricter, finds himself heading a group of 'rebel' monks, all under a new, less competent abbot. 'Exiled' to a priory in the London suburbs he meets Swedish medical student and Catholic convert Elizabeth Kornerup. A close relationship evolves, though with nothing sexually untoward. Five years later, at the start of the war, he quits the priory to live close to her, clearly in a very disturbed state (then diagnosed as 'nervous breakdown and a mild case of schizophrenia'). Nursed by her, he refuses to return to the ranks, de facto excommunicating himself.

A year later his first major work 'The Monastic Order' is published, which is a scholarly success. He is invited to Cambridge in 1944 to fill an empty teaching position. At Cambridge he flowers, becoming Professor of Medieval History and later Regius Professor of Modern History, and publishing his mammoth 'The Religious Orders in Medieval England' – a masterpiece which I remember perusing in a fellow student's study. In the meantime the monastery has generously had the excommunication moved and officially exclaustrated him.

Dom Adrian's book is beautifully written, with a quintessentially English sense of balance and concern for fairness and a slight dash of cultural elitism that typified 'better Catholicism' (i.e. recusant aristocratic families and intelligent converts rather than Irish labourers) for most of the twentieth century.

Dom Adrian and many of his fellow monks are clearly a little mystified by Knowles. I am less so: while I have questions, the pattern is clear. Until his mid-thirties, Knowles is carried by a well-structured, coherent 'system', strict but caring, a respectable distance along the Christian path, with ample room for his academic bent. At some stage this is not enough – he starts looking for alternative models, Cistercian and Carthusian. No surprise: St Bernard and William of St Thierry were there eight centuries before him. Under a not so good religious superior (a periodical but damaging inevitability) he is sent packing and a period of exile begins and a long period in the wilderness. Again, nothing terribly surprising. For me this is essentially the 'Dark Night of the Spirit', that often frightening and at times lonesome stage later in the spiritual life when one has to cast off previous supports and rely on Christ and His grace alone, possibly including periods outside of official church structures. Knowles knew St John of the Cross's writings well, and they probably provided a vital guide. The involvement of a deeply spiritual woman follows a pattern too: Benedict and Scholastica, Francis and Clare, John of the Cross and Teresa of Avila, which Dom Adrian rightly refers to (he could have added Popes Pius XII and John-Paul II). Once out of the 'system', Knowles flowered. And yes, I have no doubt that God was happier with him (and he with God) in Cambridge than in Downside. To apply Julian's often quoted phrase: 'All will be well.'

Pentecost has left me a little foxed (confused)...

7 June 2017

Having just gone through the (nearly) full cycle of the Pentecost liturgy (in Orthodoxy we run Pentecost Sunday and Trinity Sunday together on the Sunday and Monday) I remain a little foxed. Basically, taking the main liturgical texts (the Bible readings and the special 'kneeling prayers' of the Vesper

service tacked onto the Sunday liturgy), the reference to the
Holy Spirit, which is what Pentecost is all about, appears, at
first sight, distinctly understated and one-sided.

In particular the biblical readings: the absence in the gospel
of either day to Christ's promise of the sending of the Holy
Spirit in John 14 and 16 (the main Sunday gospel is from John
7, around the one-liner: (v. 39): 'By this he meant the Spirit,
whom those who believed in him were later to receive. Up to
that time the Spirit had not been given, since Jesus had not
yet been glorified' (John 7:39, NIV). The same applies to the
epistle reading. Of course we have the descent of the Spirit
(Acts 2) on Sunday, but for Monday I would have taken the
long passage in 1 Corinthians 12 on the various gifts given by
the Spirit (word of wisdom, word of knowledge, faith, gifts of
healing, working of miracles, prophecy, discerning of spirits,
glossolalia and the interpretation thereof). Instead we get the
passage from Ephesians: 'Do not get drunk on wine ... Instead,
be filled with the Spirit, speaking to one another with psalms,
hymns, and songs from the Spirit. Sing and make music from
your heart to the Lord' (Ephesians 5:18–19, NIV).

I could say the same of the long 'kneeling prayers' we say
during the Vespers. Beautiful and more than all-encompassing,
but there is very little in them which tells that they are specific
to Pentecost. The main purpose of the Spirit as expressed in
them is very much 'ad intra', that is purification and consolation,
but nothing 'ad extra' in terms of building up the church and
the fellowship of Christ.

In particular, prophecy has gone by the board – which in
the New Testament tends to mean as much 'strong, conversion-
related preaching' as much as it does future-telling. It is almost
as if 'speaking out' (the word of wisdom ... the word of
knowledge ... prophecy, as mentioned in 1 Corinthians 12:8–
10) is considered unnecessary, or a gift limited only to the very
few. Discernment – for me a vital gift (1 Corinthians 12:10),
the gift which allows a community to discern which way to
go, where to place its efforts, what the role of its individual
members is – is similarly hushed. The 'church of the Holy Spirit'
which the Orthodox liturgy seems to give us is a very much
controlled body, with 'speaking out' and the right to participate

in deciding which way the community should go, limited at best to the selected few. Certainly not that rather messy, noisy body that the New Testament churches, and perhaps particularly that at Corinth, were.

Yes, probably we don't want Corinth-style churches anymore – anyone who has experience of a 'primitive charismatic' style church (I have) knows just how chaotic it can become. And yes, a set liturgy saves us from constant exposure to a worship leader's personal fads and 'flavour of the month'. But nor do we want – I hope – what the church often became in the Eastern Roman Empire and later the Russian one: a place where you kept your mouth shut, did exactly what the emperor and the episcopal class told you to do, and no more.

I have good friends in the charismatic part of the Catholic Church, and while their overall style is not mine, I do envy them sometimes the considerably wider space they give for a creative and building-up word than we perhaps do in Orthodoxy.

Ramblings around, but not about, homosexuality

9 June 2017

Often, for easy reading in the tram, I look at my bookshelf, and take out what stares at me. In this way I reread last week 'Washed and Waiting – Reactions on Christian Faithfulness and Homosexuality' by U.S. Christian writer Wesley Hill.[2] Hill makes a good case for persons who, like himself, are faced with SSA (same-sex attraction) to remain celibate and sexually unattached. I for one, hesitate to pontificate in this area: I dare to suspect that the result, salvation-wise, of the choices taken by persons in this situation depends as much on the honesty and integrity with which they make them as on the direction ultimately chosen.

But it was a number of ancillary issues which Hill touches on that really set me thinking. Hill takes a strong indirect swipe at the great emphasis on family of modern-day Catholicism and Orthodoxy. He quotes to great effect a letter from a friend to him (pp. 112–113):

We must call into question any notion that the supreme expression of human love is found in marriage. The ancients did not contend this ... and neither does the Bible. The Old

Testament suggests that there is love between men that is stronger than that found in marriage (2 Samuel 1:26) [The reference is to David's lament over Jonathan.] But so does the New Testament. According to Jesus, there is not greater love than the sacrificial love of one friend for another (John 15:13). Is it not peculiar that in writing the greatest discourse on love found in the New Testament, Paul chooses to put it, not in his discussion of marriage in 1 Corinthians 7 (here love is not even mentioned), but in the context of spiritual gifts in 1 Corinthians 13! And even when agape love is discussed in the marital context of Ephesians 5, it is *sacrificial* love that is the model for marital love, and not the other way round. Marriage is a venue for expressing love which, in its purest form, exists first and foremost outside of it. The greatest joys and experiences God has for us are not found in marriage, for if they were, surely God would not do away with marriage in heaven. But since he has already told us he is doing away with it, we, too, can realise that the greatest things God has to give are not to be found in marriage at all.

While I hesitate to give this text full marks for theological logic, I like its thrust. For me this takes love out of the closet, not into gay sexual relationships, but vitally into something beyond sex, including into areas which many, especially of my generation, are scared of. How do I honestly and deeply love in Christ a person of either sex who is not my covenanted life partner? And without damaging the relationship with the latter?

The more a church really does its work, it inevitably attracts broken people, many of whom have made a mess of their sexuality and family lives. One urgently needs another definition of love which gives value and meaning to human interaction outside of family relationships.

Hill also points to the issue of solitude, as a problem for celibate and fully sexed gays. This again is something we are not good at in my part of the church: if the church is going to play an evangelistic hospital role, it has to offer real community, an alternative to both family and work, with honest love and as little manipulation and using of people as possible.

That being said, it seems to me, someone along the Christian path, that many of us have to face sooner or later a position of solitude, which we cannot – and vitally must not – drown with friends, work, alcohol or whatever. Hill quotes (p. 119) fourteenth-century Persian poet Hafiz:

> Don't
> Surrender
> Your loneliness so quickly.
> Let it cut more
> Deep.
> Let it ferment and season you
> As few human
> Or even divine ingredients can.

Other than loneliness, apparently unchangeable situations like SSA, if faced courageously, can also open up new levels. I've not worked this one through yet, but sense there is something very important here. A spiritual law which may indeed go beyond Christianity. It is somehow St Paul's 'strength in weakness'. But not 'weakness' as false humility or disguised cowardliness, or a Thoreau-like gentle despair, but something which demands great spiritual courage, and pays high spiritual dividends. Something which indeed would not be demanded by God of someone unless He was reasonably sure that that person had a spiritual stamina to convert it, with grace, into something very positive.

'The Cloud of Unknowing'

18 June 2017 (Facebook)
I've just finished the fourteenth-century English religious classic 'The Cloud of Unknowing'. Written almost at the same time as the last great Orthodox classical writers, Gregory of Sinai, Palamas and Callistus and Ignatius, it is in many ways an English equivalent of the latter's 'Directions to Hesychasts'.

Reading it blows out of the water any notions that the Roman Church of the time was totally in thrall to Scholasticism. While the methodology of direct meeting with God is slightly different to the Jesus Prayer, which I think its author would have found too wordy, it stresses the recognition of and giving space to the fundamental desire for God in the soul, the need of purity of heart and an inner nakedness for the dynamics of a contemplative relationship with God to work. Like Julian of Norwich, the author in no way denies sin, both personally caused and 'picked up' from one's environment, but does not concentrate on it, does not want his pupil to spend hours dissecting its different components (he speaks of it as a 'lump'), but rather on the 'thrust towards God' and on the cleansing and burning away of the lump of sin that comes out of a continuing relationship with Him.

Is there a female version of the starets in the Russian Orthodox Church?

2 July 2017

'Is there a female version of the starets ('staritsa', plural 'staritsi') in the Russian Orthodox Church?' I was asked this by an American friend in response to an earlier posting of mine.

The answer is, I think, yes, to a certain extent. There have been and are spiritually deep and wise women in the Orthodox Church, whose advice has been and is sought. These include the abbesses of certain women's monasteries, who are able to guide the women in their own monasteries and pious women close to these monasteries, and who also assist senior clerics, often very discreetly, on key decisions. I have two in mind, Mother Olga, the former abbess of the monastery of Bussy-en-Othe in France, and the former abbess of Pühtitsa monastery in Estonia. (I use the qualifier 'certain' advisedly: the recent Maria Kikot scandal in Russia and my own observations cast doubts on the quality of leadership in a number of Russian women's monasteries.)

Two of the three figures listed as equivalents by another female correspondent (Hildegard of Bingen, and Teresa of Avila) fall into this category. (Catherine of Siena defies any neat classification!) Outside of this there have always been women in Orthodoxy known to be persons of prayer, sometimes with healing powers. (...) There are also figures like St Ksenia of St Petersburg and St Matrona of Moscow (the former more in the 'fool for Christ' category), both supposed to have powers of prophecy. (...)

What sits particularly uneasily with Orthodox (male) clergy (which includes me) is the desire to have staritsi for sexual equality reasons. A case in point about 15 years ago was 'Mother' Rachel Goettman, wife of Fr Alphonse Goettman. The latter, an Orthodox priest, ran with his wife a monastery/spiritual centre in the French Vosges mountains, popular with a certain profile of Orthodox convert – intelligent, bourgeois, very often in the alternative medicine/psychology movement and with a penchant to 'New Age'. They set up Mme Goettmann as a spiritual counsellor in her own right. This did not go down well with the local Orthodox bishops and was a main reason for the monastery to be disowned by the mainstream Orthodox Church. And where is God in all this? This second 'charismatic' strand in my model (prophet-starets) is essentially God-appointed, and God is sovereignly free. If God raises up staritsi, it is not for the Church to put them down. But equally, it is not for man or woman to create them for reason of sexual politics.

Lurking somewhere behind this is another question, of the very nature of the call of starets/staritsa. It seems to me that the fundamental call, which is equal to both sexes, is not to be a 'starets/staritsa', nor indeed even a hermit or anchorite. It is one of deep prayer and intimacy with God, the very hiddenness of which often precludes it taking a publicly recognisable form. That this hidden prayer, by men and women alike, exists in Orthodoxy as much as in Catholicism or Anglicanism, I am pretty much convinced. Indeed, by the very nature of the way God seems to work, I cannot conceive it being otherwise.

'Things that cause people to stumble are bound to come'

5 July 2017
Church is like fabric: certain smells it picks up (tobacco, diesel etc.) can be extraordinarily difficult to get out, however many times you send the garment to the cleaners.

I sense this in my own life. Deep down, 50 years on, I battle with the negative smells which cling to my early Christian memories, the middle-class smugness of 1950s suburban London Methodism, the sexual repression/perversion of Cambridge Anglicanism of my university days. And perhaps, in a sort of

Jungian 'group subconscious' way, that incredible negative of World War I, the killing fields of Christian Europe, which so deeply affected my grandfather's and my father's generations. Such negatives easily take three generations to clear out of the system.

I see the same thing in the Catholic Church in Belgium. A folk memory of a Catholic Church abusing its socially omnipotent position – spiteful nuns in girls' boarding schools or priests prying into young men's sex lives in the confessional – is only just starting to die out, two or three generations after the deeds in question, and after doing immense damage.

If we in the Russian church offend an inherent sense of integrity and justice of the millennial generation, it is going to take till at least 2070, when I shall be long dead, to shake free the results. Yes, there will, by the mercy of God, be individual people who will fight free of this and maintain deeply spiritual lives despite it, but the prospect of two 'lost generations' is indeed a frightening one.

As Christ said: 'Things that cause people to stumble are bound to come, but woe to anyone through whom they come' (Luke 17:1, NIV).

'La vie commence de l'autre côté du désespoir' (Life begins on the other side of despair)

7 August 2017

This sentence by Jean-Paul Sartre pretty much encapsulates my experience of Russian Orthodoxy right now.

The negatives stack up pretty quickly: an official discourse which seems to place morality and nationalism higher than the gospel; too many bishops who are either spiritually immature or managerially incompetent; an effective near-blanket censorship which has forced free thinking out of the official church press and onto the Internet and replaced it with glossy propaganda; a deadening pall of *Mittelmässigkeit* (the 'neither hot nor cold' of the church in Laodicea – Rev. 3:14ff) and sucking up to authority. It is difficult not to be pessimistic, and cynicism is a constant enemy.

Yet I do not despair. God is there, and He loves and wants His people. And if He cannot get to them, and they to Him, through 'official' channels, He will get to them through others. Church history tells us that God works as much on the edges of the official church as in the centre of it: the names we remember and commemorate as saints are rarely those of the official figures of authority. In all cases they have been men and women with a deep and direct experience of Him, with intense prayer lives that made them largely independent of church structures and able to withstand the weaknesses and contingencies of these.

It is essentially these people I seek out right now, both inside and outside official structures. They are there, I am convinced. Perhaps it is good that they are hidden, so as not to be vampirised by too many people looking for salvation through the prayers of others.

'Nomad' by Brandan Robertson, thoughts on and around…

27 August 2017

It proved a good book. I had hesitated: the publisher's guff sounded good, but made much of the author having been turned down by his first publisher for refusing to sign an 'anti-gay' declaration, and I feared the worst.

In fact, it is a fine account of a young man moving beyond an initial conversion experience at age 12 in a very narrow American Protestant environment (megachurch, Bible only, penal substitution) into a much wider approach to Christianity in early manhood. While this initial conversion was essential in seeing him through an awful adolescence (living with an alcoholic father in a mobile home), it was unsuited to carry him through into productive Christian adulthood, and a major shift was necessary.

I too moved much the same way as a young man and sympathise, though it seems to have taken the author seven years (he is just 25) to do what it took me 40 years to do! But otherwise I sense that the author has something to say to the next generation. His Christianity is fresh and moves beyond false barriers, and out of the holes we have often dug for ourselves. I would be happy for my sons, of the author's age, to read it.

Yes, the pro-LGBT line, which seems almost de rigueur in any 'modern' Anglo-Saxon Christianity, and which raises so many hackles in Russia, grates on me. But it is not enough to invalidate the book.

That being said, I admit to having a problem with pro-LGBT discourse in general. But method is everything, and Jesus' method is radically different from both Pharisee and megachurch pastor: Jesus 'converts' or changes people not by throwing the book at them (Leviticus 18:22, Romans 1:27) but by living with them in a way that brings out the best in them, the deep desire for fullness of life which is in all of us, even if we refuse to listen to it. This is what happened to the woman who sobbed over Christ's feet and wiped them with her hair. There was something about what Jesus was, what He said, the way he handled people, and her, that struck her so deeply that she could do little else than yield to Him.

But having this Jesus touch is difficult, very difficult, and I know few people who have it. Also the way forward ('conversion') for people in 'fallen' life situations demands courage and integrity, not only of the 'sinner', but equally of the 'guide' or 'witness', and much more than most people show in their daily lives. Such courage and integrity are a grace, a gift of God.

Reply to a young friend

8 October 2017

A young friend came back at me on my recent posting about priests in Russia. He said that I was too concerned about priests' educational levels and too negative about their spiritual competence. This is part of my reply:

You say: 'Our priests are like treasures given to us by God. They love us and guide towards the kingdom of heaven.' With respect, this is the language of someone fairly young in years and young in the faith. It is that of someone who is in love as much with the church as system as with Christ Himself. There is nothing wrong in this, and it is part of a normal system of spiritual growing up. Most of us need systems from outside to grow up in, with a strong faith element, and which provide a structure in which to contain and constrain our wayward emotions and impulses. (Others find it in the army, in political parties, in a large business company with a strong culture, in social organizations etc.)

However, sooner or later this structure breaks down: church fails us. And fail us it must, if we are ever to become spiritually mature. There comes a time, sooner or later, if we are serious with God, when we have to move on beyond structure, naked, towards Christ alone. This, as far as I can make out, is a pattern common to more 'advanced' spirituality (what I call 'Book Two Christianity') in most Christian churches. My own experience tells me it is a slow and messy process, and painful, in particular as we come to face all the demons of our psychological inheritance and try to move towards the inner purity which gives Christ real room to work. It is for this reason, I think, that the Athos tradition says that people should not talk or write publicly about Christianity until 14 years after their conversion (this is the time St Paul went silent between his conversion and his first missionary journeys). Until then they can paste pretty pictures of icons and bearded startsi on their Facebook pages, but they do not and cannot speak with the authority of real spiritual experience.

Maybe I am a particularly desperate case, but my own experience has not been always of priests as 'treasures'. Yes, I have met good priests and pastors, and am chastened by their examples. I owe my life spiritually to a Roman Catholic abbot, a Roman Catholic psychiatrist-monk, and a Protestant pastor, who helped me through a couple of major crises, and my present Orthodox *dukhovnik* (spiritual director) who has insisted on my being spiritually adult and mature. At the same time there is certainly one priest who caused me serious spiritual damage as a university student, and possibly a second at the monastery, where I leave judgement to God.

Most priests I find somewhere in between. Too often in Russia, I find priests worn out morally and physically by an exhausting round of services, the large families that are de rigueur for priests, constant financial worry and the need to stay on the right side of the bishop, and without the time and space to develop spiritually.

Where I am personally particularly sensitive, and this may be a particular feature of diaspora Orthodoxy, is to finding myself playing a role in someone else's psychodrama. There are, unfortunately, men who seem to need priesthood as part of their identity kit. For this they need us as willing and stupid sheep, bleating '*batushka, batushka*', whistled in my constant calls of '*pokayaniye, pokayaniye*' (repentance, repentance) to allow them to play the shepherd role they aspire to. Our spiritual advance and maturity, and our ability to shepherd ourselves, is a threat to this position.

Don't be put off by me. Run your course as a young man must, become well educated in God's Word (and if you are serious about it, learn Greek), but if and when the time comes to move beyond structure, do not be frightened. Then your Christian life is really beginning.

Send your wife to a monastery...

21 October 2017

'Send your wife to a monastery and you could still become a bishop,' a senior cleric friend from another part of the Orthodox Church said to me earlier this week. Joking yes, but not without a gentle reproach 'do not complain at being on the edges of the church, if you refuse to play the system'.

That stung, and still does. I have said to myself many times that, if I had played the system – ecclesiastic and social – right, starting from my very Anglican Cambridge college, I would probably now be a minor bishop in the Anglican Church, Hereford, say, or Ripon. The same later from my Catholic monastery days, if I had not been obstreperous and critical – my very pagan brother said: 'He'll either become abbot or leave' and I left; and even in the Orthodox Church: by honing up my Russian and playing to the local archbishop and Moscow, I could probably have gotten a decent priest position. And yes, today, being 'just' a deacon, with a lot of less qualified men as priests above me, hurts at times.

But then the verse from the Psalms hits me: 'If I had said, "I will speak thus," behold, I would have betrayed the generation of your children' (Psalm 73:15 – The Liturgical Psalter). There is a deep-rooted 'no' inside me to playing systems and a loathing of sucking up to people, which runs deep, and which I cannot reconcile with the Christian gospel as I understand it. I can trace it through my family's Nonconformist tradition...

In the 150 years of so between around 1630 and 1780 the English established church haemorrhaged about half its population. A trickle at first of people who did not want to be herded into Anglican churches and fined for non-attendance at dreary moralising sermons; who could read their Bibles and judged the established church severely against what they read in them. A trickle that became a flood when the church, despite being far better financed (and a spate of church building, in London especially after the Great Fire of 1666), failed to respond to the social changes of the nascent Industrial Revolution and the Methodist movement gathered momentum in the mid-1750s in the new working classes (which is why Great Britain never had an anti-clerical working class). Somewhere back then a distant forbear 'got the Spirit' and signed up ... And while I eschewed Methodism in the rather sterile 'low-middle class respectability' mould it had got itself into by the 1950s and find its churches drear (though some early ones have beautiful woodwork), non-conformity remains deeply – and at times uncomfortably – in my genes.

The spiritual life cannot be made suburban

21 December 2017

'The spiritual life cannot be made suburban. It is always frontier and we who live in it must accept and even rejoice that it remains untamed.' This quote by Howard Macey starts John Eldredge's bestselling book *Wild at Heart* (Thomas Nelson, 2001), in which he berates Christianity for emasculating its men, making them dutiful and obedient and destroying any sense of vision or heroism or desire for adventure which, for him, is essential to maleness as God made it.

While Eldredge's very Protestant American 'frontier spirit' and the constant military references tire at times, he makes for me three very good points...

First, that spiritual life at any depth does not work unless we, both men and women, accept the desires – adventure, heroism, sex, (wo)men, God – that are deep-wired into our

psyches. The late Arnaud Desjardins, in one of his books tells
that, when a young man presented himself to a monastery to
test a vocation, one of the first questions was: do you have good
erections? If the answer was a straight yes, he was allowed in.
If not, he was refused. I'm not sure he is referring to Christian
monasteries – Desjardins was an expert on Eastern religions and
I have not found the story in any other Christian source – but it
makes sense. Trying to develop a Christian life when the inner
structure of desire in not in place – or better, is repressed, with
religion too often part of the repression process – is like trying
to build a house on sand. Any pastor will tell you that it is easier
to work with a man who has ventured too far in the wrong
direction – whether with a woman, with a criminal gang or
whatever – realises it and is sincerely penitent, than with a man
or woman who has been too scared of what God made them
to be and has stayed around at home. In the same category is
chastity born of fear rather than generosity.

Second, that Christianity is an adventure, which should take
us to our frontiers, a calling to a *dépassement* (going beyond)
into God. No, it does not always feel like an adventure, there
is a miserable hard slog sometimes in the cold and dark, but
like any adventure, there is this 'call from beyond', which we
cannot but follow if we are to be honest to ourselves (and
hence by definition, to God) in the very centre of our being. To
frame the Christian message in a language of duty, which still
happens too often, is to miss the point, and not to have made
the fundamental shift out of Judaism (St Paul's 'law') to the
new life which Christ offers.

Third, that many people – perhaps men more than women
– are deeply hurt inside, and it is only in recognising this pain,
living with it and standing in front of God with it, that we will
find the joy that is the Christian promise. This is particularly
important, again, for people in pastoral positions: until they
have recognised their own pain they are ineffective at best and
a menace at worst.

I thank God that I did not become a priest in my twenties, as
I originally intended. Much of my early Christianity, I realised
later in a couple of mid-life crises, was a painkiller, necessary
at the time for me to survive a difficult family situation as an

adolescent. But it was only, on the wrong side of 50, when I started to get hold of the pain and accept the resulting hurt and wounds, that my Christian life really started to make sense.

Copes, cottas and blue shoes

25 December 2017 (Facebook)
Christmas is still 13 days off for us Russian Orthodox, who with Mount Athos and schismatic Greek Old Calendarists, cling to the Julian calendar, now 13 days out of sync with the rest of Christianity. This is uncomfortable, Christmas is 'in the air', and if your Christian identity is not padlocked to Orthodox idiosyncrasies, you want to go with the trend.

So this year I sneaked again incognito with my wife into the back of a Roman Catholic Church for midnight mass (to tell the whole truth: to the schismatic SSPX, who maintain the old-fashioned Latin mass).

There is a lot I don't like in this mass: that nearly the entire canon is said *in secreto* by the priest up at the altar, with tinkling bells telling us when the consecration is done. Their priests tend to act like a race apart, often adopting a rather 'O sweet Jesus style'. And, like any dissident and schismatic sect, they can be so tied up with perfecting the externals of their distinctiveness as to forget that 'one greater than the temple is here'.

But I do like their processions: thurifer in front, with the long, heavy Roman censer, cross bearer with metal cross carried high, flanked by acolytes, then boy acolytes, adolescent and adult acolytes, candle-holders (with protective caps so they can't go out in a crosswind), and priest. All in black or red cassocks and white cottas (like a nightshirt cut off a few centimetres below the waist). The priest at the back in well-cut cope. Walking in step, palms flat together. All (except a couple of the small boys) in black shoes, cassocks the right length, sober haircuts.

To be honest, it was not their best ever – one rehearsal too few – one of the candles was at a tilt, and they were not perfectly in step. But it's a far cry from our sanctuary party. One acolyte arrived yesterday with dark blue cloth shoes, laces open, ten centimetres of blue jeans to the bottom of his now too short cassock, another ten centimetres to the bottom of his cheap poly-something badly falling sticharion (dalmatic), shaven head. (Actually he's a lovely kid, in the middle of the late-puberty identity-seeking process they all go through.)

I like our schismatics' music too: the priest sang both epistle and gospel well in Latin, and the rest was done by a small schola of cantors in the back gallery. Practised and accurate, and no more singers than needed. Far better than too many modern Roman masses with a gesticulating woman up front trying to get an unwilling congregation to sing to an accompaniment of guitars and recorders. Church music is like icons: either it is very good or it's horrible, and there's no middle ground.

Truth is that as a young man, 50 years back, I lost my heart to Anglo-Catholicism. The best of the old Roman mass plus the entire canon read or sung distinctly, proper choir, only the priest, deacon and subdeacon in well-made vestments, the rest in cassock and cottas. And all of course in black shoes.

2018

The pilot's son

25 February 2018

He is the son of a Luftwaffe pilot who went right through the war and survived. I'm the son of an English conscientious objector. We met at business school: we both went parachuting. He broke his ankle on his first jump. We have remained friends ever since.

We spoke on the phone today: he has had a rather unpleasant operation which requires some very unpleasant after-treatment, starting next week.

He is of Protestant origin but is non-believing himself. Yet with him I am able to talk about religion, and how I stand with God, and with the church, almost better than I can with any religious friend. There's no hiding behind pious phrases. I insist that Christ is about freedom, and about truth – deep truth about ourselves and one another. That church is the company of those who have met Christ and want to move forward together in Him. That until we have experienced Christ deep inside, including facing with Him the mess inside ourselves, we are not much use to man or beast. Why can't I say this in church on Sunday?

The harvest is past...

3 March 2018

'The harvest is past, the summer is ended, and we are not saved' *(Jeremiah 8:20, NIV)*.

'Do you Orthodox have a healing ministry?' My Catholic friend looked at me across our kitchen table this lunchtime: 'Er, hmm, to be honest, no.'

This is the third time I have had a similar conversation in the space of a week. And this 'no' answer hurts. It is wrong. I believe that the Christian gospel of salvation is fundamentally about healing. Much more than about being morally good, keeping fasts or being socially respectable. It is about allowing Christ to come so deep inside us, and to allow His Spirit to sweep through us that we become 'new creations', no longer constrained and constricted in our lives by the psycho-social messes we were born into or which we created ourselves. Able

finally to act with the freedom and joy God has intended for us
to have. 'Come and dwell in us, cleanse us of all impurity, and
save our souls, O good one' we pray at the start of every liturgy
and in the small hours.

For me this includes deep healing of the traumas of childhood
and abuse. I do not know what percentage of the population
falls into this category – almost certainly an increasing one as
traditional family and social structures break down – but it is
clear that a lot of people come to the church looking for inner
healing. In principle they are right to do so. This is what they
flocked to Christ for. I do not believe that Christ wants anyone
to carry for the rest of their lives the psychological blockages
from parental separation or sexual abuse or unhealthy schooling.
A message of 'patience and longsuffering' may be necessary in
outer situations we cannot change, but not inner situations,
where with Christ's help and proper spiritual guidance, change
is possible.

Yes, this healing is a painful process. It starts with full
acknowledgement of the depth of pain, and it is only in facing
this pain ('taking up our cross') that we move to resurrection
and salvation. It is also a slow process; if we are not to create
empty spaces into which seven worse spirits can enter.

And yes, the process of healing in Christ involves accepting a
terrible nakedness: Christ can and does accept my nakedness. I
have to throw away the social fig-leaves of degrees from two of
Europe's most prestigious universities or an ability to translate
out of ten languages; accepting a void inside which only God
can fill.

Is this the message of the church I am a member of? Does
it allow place for it? As far as I can see, no. Should it be? Yes.
Why is it not? For two basic reasons: because we lack guides
who have gone through the process themselves; and because it
would blow to smithereens all the false structures of power and
influence which we Orthodox use the church for.

In particular our clericalism precludes it. We have to replace
clergy who 'know it' and have the answers from the book,
by spiritual leaders, chosen by their flocks for being perhaps
one step ahead of them, and able to lead their flocks into a
'place of freedom', and, if this is their gift, to plead for them in

front of God in private. Leaders who know themselves to be as vulnerable and sinful as their flocks and do not hide behind their 'dignity'. Flocks who have the right to call their clergy and fellow-believers to account when their behaviour does not seem to mirror the gospel, and who also hopefully also have the discreet stamina to provide support when clergy run into trouble – yes priests, and bishops too, if elevated to that rank too young, have mid-life crises also.

And once we are redeemed, we need a language to thank God for our salvation communally. Yes, we have praise services, good ones actually – providing you have fluent Slavonic. But that's another posting.

Dead words

4 May 2018

Three words commonly used in Christian-speak have gone dead on me. I avoid them and find alternatives...

The first is love. It is a word debased through over-use. For me it went wrong from the start, as my mother was psychologically too damaged to give me good love. Later, being a father myself, and feeling the very primitive, gut love a parent has for his offspring, repaired some of this. But when talking of and with God, I feel safer with 'faithfulness' (*fidélité*), as in the chorus: 'Great is Thy faithfulness, Lord unto to me.'

The second is church. Dented by the 'primness' of my suburban Methodist Sunday school, damaged by the Anglican

establishment ('the Tory party at prayer') of my Cambridge
college, and nearly destroyed in the Russian church, where
clearly 'church' is not coterminous with 'those being saved' or
'people of God'. My alternative: people of God.

The third and last is judgement. A word which seems to vary
in meaning between 'interpret correctly' and 'condemn' at the
speaker's convenience. Especially when 'Judge not, that you be
not judged', intended in the latter meaning, is used by clerics to
place themselves above criticism. My alternatives: 'interpret' or
'condemn' as the situation demands.

Male mystery

9 May 2018 (Facebook)
Poets have sung, lovers tried to untangle, and painters capture,
the mystery of the female.

Much less described and sung is the mystery – and sensitivity
to mystery – of the male. Mystery directed at and revealed in the
encounter and relationship with the female, mystery directed
at and revealed in the relationship with God-Trinity, and – I
suspect – mystery revealed in deep male-male relationships.
Three-fold mystery that a man must learn to understand, guard
as precious and God-given, and not reveal to all and sundry
(pearls before swine).

Mystery that can be complex and frightening, in particular
in its third component. I suspect that we have lost a sense of
male-male love, scared to death of being slotted as gay. I believe
increasingly that male-male love is vital to spiritual development,
and that if we men take the risk, we carry a wealth of sensitivity
we ignore to our peril. This includes, for those of us who are
Christian, our relationship with Christ. While women's love for
Christ can parallel normal female sexual love, male love for
Christ has to work at a level that is beyond sexuality, more that
of the soul-friend (*anam cara*) of the Celtic tradition.

Yes, it was the devil … but

13 May 2018
One of our parishioners gave a talk today on the persecution of
the Russian church under the Communists. Her conclusion: the

persecution of the church was the devil at work. For me this is too easy. If it's the devil's fault, it's not ours.

The devil is always at work. Any situation that becomes unstable and where with a small push on the right people he can create havoc, he will use to do just this. To me this does not relieve us of our responsibility to sense this type of situation and do what we can to avoid it.

I have to ask whether the Russian church was not severely co-responsible for the post-1917 situation. Read the biographies of nineteenth-century clergy,[1] especially the country ones, and you sense a church system rotten to the core – a hereditary clergy, performing semi-magic rites for an uninstructed peasantry, subject to the whims of local landlords and their bishops, and caught in the complex paying for favours system. Could nobody see what was happening and have the wisdom or courage to stop it? Before the Bolsheviks did.

On the religious dimension in Europe

17 June 2018

The Christian representative offices to the European Institutions are pressing for recognition, in the Institutions' thinking, of the acceptability of an anthropology that includes a religious dimension. That is, to avoid the imposition, in European legislation, of an anthropology that leaves no room for reference to the transcendent. I spent quite a bit of time last week helping lick a key document into shape.

So far so good. The problem becomes then to find representatives of this religious dimension. Not as easy as it may seem. To explain, I take a parallel: trade unions. For decades, the Institutions have seen it important to listen to the 'worker' category of society. This means finding representatives of workers. The answer: the trade unions. The result: considerable funding made available for certain activities, including a major research institute in Brussels (my brother and I have, over the years, earned a small fortune translating for them!). The problem: representativeness: trade unions represent a relatively small (more or less 20%) and declining part of the dependent workforce.

There is a similar problem if you want to encourage the religious element in society. Who represents it? Who is your contact point? The official representatives of the Christian churches, mosques, synagogues? Dangerous from two viewpoints: one – spirituality in Europe, especially among the younger generation, is often a *'spiritualité sauvage'*, diffuse, multifaceted, not always fitting into the traditional confessional patterns of expression; and two – the official representatives of church (and mosque and synagogue) do not necessarily reflect the actual opinions of practising believers on the ground, who are often much less negative towards divorce, abortion and homosexuality than their leaders are.

On not being a priest

7 July 2018
My nephew, an intelligent and sensitive man in his thirties, outside of the church, asked me: 'Would you have liked to be priested? Do I hear a certain disappointment that you have not been? Who decides whether you can become a priest?' Here is my reply, slightly shortened...

Priesthood is a complicated matter. Yes, I am deeply committed in my Christian faith, and certainly have the training level and (hopefully) the spiritual level to be a priest. That being said, priesthood involves not just you, but the Christian community, the bishop and, of course, God. Yes, one part of me would have liked to be a priest, and people regularly ask why I am not. From my side I insist that one should become a priest only if asked to by the community, speaking through the bishop. I am not sure I am a natural fit in most of our parishes: what I consider primary and what I consider secondary in the spiritual life, what I am prepared to give people time for, and what not, do not always fit what people are looking for. (...)

For me at the present stage, it is more important to be a 'man of God', with a deep proximity to Him, than to be priested. No, I cannot preach, which perhaps leaves gifts of mine 'under a bushel' (Matthew 5:15). But I can and do blog – a bit irregularly – on Facebook and on another site read mainly by Russians, and what I write seems to be appreciated. No, I do not confess people, but the way confession is organised in our church (hurried three-minute confessions to be allowed to take communion) strikes me as too often a waste of both priest's and penitent's time. But, again a bit irregularly, I do have very meaningful, longer conversations with other people, who are struggling towards real Christian maturity, and where my being perhaps a couple of steps further down the road is helpful.

And yes, the deacon's role in the liturgy is a pretty important one – and a tiring one: I'm half-dead after a long liturgy – as he is effectively the link-man between the people and the altar, and it has to be done properly.

OK, if God wants me to be priested – if there are things for His kingdom that I am needed for and others cannot do, then it will not be for me to say no. But then, I believe, He will give the message to other people who will set things moving. This would involve jumping over a certain number of hurdles (…): historically in the Russian church, priests have been seen as fairly lower class: qualified worker, rather than university educated. Our bishop's selection of priests has certainly confirmed this. While a certificate in woodworking includes me in the qualified worker category, my instincts remain largely bourgeois. Also, the Russian church is rather enclosed on itself, with more than a streak of nationalism and is not very open – put mildly – to the rest of the Christian world. I horrify some by my quoting also Roman Catholic or Protestant theologians. (…) In true Russian tradition, a priest is expected to 'toe the party line', and preferably not think for himself, something I am pathologically incapable of doing.

There is another thing I had a difficult childhood and adolescence, which left damage. This is why, I believe, God thwarted my initial plans to be priested in the Anglican Church (deacon at 23, priest at 24, bishop by…). To be priested without being very clear with God and oneself about one's deep inside is a recipe for disaster. I have seen it too often, in every church. Handling this damage has been the hardest – and most meaningful part – of my Christian experience. The rest I leave to God.

'A spiritual but not religious age'

22 August 2018

It was a light read and I finished it in an evening: Professor Jane Shaw's 'Pioneers of Modern Spirituality', subtitled 'The neglected Anglican innovators of a spiritual but not religious age'.

(...) Professor Shaw, a leading figure in the Anglican-Episcopalian world, has a message to give: the need to be innovative in an age that is spiritual but not religious. She has gone looking for historical examples to support this message. Fascinating as a couple of these portraits (out of four) are, in particular – and new to me –, those of Reginald Somerset Ward, a sort of Anglican starets in the inter-war period, and of liturgicist Percy Dearmer, they are at least two generations old, and how far they can serve as examples today I doubt. Much more interesting and challenging is the final chapter 'Spirituality and the Church today', with examples she gives of current Anglican sharp-edge priests and parishes: St Gregory of Nyssa in San Francisco with Fr Paul Fromberg or St James in West Hampstead, London, with Fr Andrew Foreshew-Cain.

She does face head-on the question of Christianity in a 'spiritual but not religious age'. To ask this question is already to accept that traditional style Christianity, with its particular worship patterns and moral emphases may be excluding many people looking for God, or not serving optimally those who remain within its structures, and that it is right and proper to allow space and time for those who want to try to do things differently, with different patterns and emphases.

I admit to being slowly converted towards an acceptance of this, and sense that the Anglicans and Lutherans may be way ahead of us Orthodox here. Perhaps we Orthodox are wasting our ammunition shooting at women priests and gay marriage, and need to be looking much harder at how to link in to the religious expressed in non-traditional language, to providing guidance to (and also learning from) those on non-confessional meditation paths, and facing the demands of the gospel in terms of social justice.

Dutch interlude

3 September 2018 (Facebook)
Last Saturday I travelled north into the Netherlands. In a high speed train you hardly notice the border, except that suddenly there is a lot more water around. In fact you are crossing a major cultural border: from Catholicism to Protestantism. It was these large stretches of water which enabled the Dutch, in the late sixteenth century, to defend their Protestant faith, in protracted wars against the Spaniards, hated for their despotic and brutally imposed Catholicism, ending up with the recognition of the independent state of the Netherlands.

I had gone for my friend Bert's seventieth birthday. Bert and I were in the same work group at business school in France 45 years ago. Bert typifies for me the best in the Dutch character: clear-sightedness and rugged determination, and a deep sense of democracy, fairness and service to the community. He has done well in both business and local politics.

The afternoon included a concert in the local Dutch Reformed Church, in the Protestant Calvinist tradition. The simple brick church, once serving a rural parish, now part of a leafy better-class suburb, spoke to me of generations of people of simple, but deep faith, rooted in the Word of God, constantly preached and read in understandable language, distrustful of enforced hierarchy and power structures, and with a sense of strong individual responsibility to God. I find its theology a bit harsh and its services liturgically unsatisfying, but for me it is a vital part of an overall picture of Christianity in Europe, and an important balancing factor.

Orbán and co

14 September 2018 (Facebook)
I'm not sure I would like to spend an evening with either Viktor Orbán, who has brought Hungary close to expulsion from the EU for refusing to play ball on migration, or Marion Le Pen, or the leaders of other far-right European parties who oppose the type of society the EU establishment seems to want to move us towards.

Their popularity with many, cloaked in Viktor Orbán's case with calls for a 'Christian Europe' (essentially 'stop migration of Muslims, and end gay marriage') points to a fundamental problem in the European mindset that will not and, in my opinion, cannot go away.

'Christian', for Mr Orbán and his ilk, is, I suspect, shorthand for something else: a sense that the world is governed by other rationales than the pure reason celebrated ever since the Age of the Enlightenment by the EU establishment. And a demand to be allowed to conceive the world, and to base one's actions in it, on gut, intuition and emotion as much as pure reason (i.e. heart as much as head). However much one may denounce their discourse as illogical and not for really civilised people, concerns for national identity and a dislike of 'deviant' sexuality lie deeply buried in the human psyche, especially the group psyche, and are ignored at one's risk. I tend to believe that the pure rationality of the society that the EU establishment proposes, with its sexual and gender equality, and de facto openness to anyone who can cross into its territory, legally or otherwise, and its studied avoidance of any reference to religion (or at least to Christianity) covers an aching spiritual void, which Orbán and his friends in Germany, Sweden and Italy rush to fill.

This is the void of the Weimar republic that Joseph Goebbels recognised and filled with his quasi-religious rhetoric of racial purity in the 1930s.

While we in the church must surely decry the excesses of the far right, we must equally call to task the European establishment, which by refusing to acknowledge the existence and validity of rationales other than its own Enlightenment-based one, has created a spiritual gap and a hunger for other value patterns, that Orbán and others want to fill with their very bastardised 'Christianity'.

A time to ... be silent and a time to speak

25 September 2018 (Facebook)
I have been a rare visitor to the blogosphere over recent months. As the preacher said, there is a time 'to be silent and a time to speak' (Ecclesiastes 3:7, NIV). The last three or four months

have been a time to keep silent: old certainties have wobbled; doubts have refused to be quiet.

Much of this has been occasioned by my view on the Russian church to which I belong, both at national level and in my own community. I believe increasingly that we are seriously delinquent: that instead of pointing to the freedom that Christ promises, we have created an oppressive structure, which serves little more than its senior hierarchy.

However, blaming the 'church' and the 'structure' for everything very quickly becomes a futile and depressing exercise. One is forced, sooner or later, to face oneself and God in a naked, stripping exercise, uncovering one's own blockages, fears, wounds; working free of oppression. In the process priorities change, old certainties ('traditional morality') dissolve. One also learns to recognise the workings of the Spirit outside of the church, too often in a search for freedom that the church lacks the courage to offer. One hopefully becomes human, and becoming fully human as God intended us to be, is surely what Christianity is basically all about. I have still some way to go.

I have a lot of sympathy for the Reformers, who in conscience broke with the structures, even if I believe that they threw the baby out with the bathwater, leaving us with often cold and cerebral religion and losing touch with a certain primitive religiosity which is hardwired deep in the human psyche, and which Orthodoxy caters for. I am not sure I am ready to break ranks – and any Mayflower leaving a Russian port will be torpedoed within a nautical mile of the harbour wall – but I increasingly question the right of a self-appointed and self-perpetuating church oligarchy to maintain a monopoly on the sacraments, and ask whether in extremis one could not be justified in front of God in breaking this monopoly.

Someone wrote that theologians are no longer necessary

3 October 2018 (Facebook)
My reply to this…

This depends very much on what you see a theologian's task to be today. If it is to be simply a commentator, describing what has already happened, yes, he or she is largely irrelevant, other than perhaps putting system into the unsystematic writing of certain great figures (Maximus the Confessor, Meister Eckhart, Thérèse of Lisieux). And indeed most university/seminary theology is in fact the history of the development of doctrine, or the development of structures, often in excruciating detail.

But that for me is to miss the real purpose of the theologian: to be able to assess situations, to say whether a particular approach to the gospel – individual or pan-church – is valid, whether it brings one nearer to God or takes us away from Him, to sense where the Spirit of God is moving, and not moving. Using the different tools and methods available to him or her, some more 'scientifically logical', others the 'logic of faith', and with a sense of what is genuine revelation and what is not.

If we believe that Christianity is a religion of immutable patterns, revealed once and for all, then this role is pretty limited. If, however, we have some sense of ongoing revelation, that God continues to reveal Himself more and more, with outward circumstances also changing the way we think of God, then this role becomes crucial, and indeed the theologian can be part of this going forward into God.

I sense that the Orthodox mindset is one of immutability, unchangeability, of moral patterns valid once and for all ('traditional morality'), and indeed in this system one has little need for theologians, and indeed theological debate, other than on the description and interpretation of past history, is pretty dead. Theology is neither challenging nor exciting. Orthodoxy has a long way to go before it can produce a Teilhard de Chardin or a Bonhoeffer.

Taste of heaven

4 October 2018

As a spiritual exercise, try thinking hard on what heaven really means for you. Chase all the angels with harps on a cloud into a corner, and try to work out what is really the hope that one longs for, and believes will be realised in the 'second life', however one conceives it. In your own words and your own images. Because if we are unable to express that hope, to sense this promise awaiting us, our spiritual and church world becomes constricted and suffocating, and we die spiritually.

The fly on the hermit's wall

20 October 2018
If I were in the cell of a hermit, witness to him or her speaking directly with God, and God speaking to him or her about the current rupture between two significant parts of the Orthodox Church, what would I see and hear? Tears, I suspect foremost, hours of them, prostrate on the ground, with a searing sense of something gone very deeply wrong. Neither the man or woman of God or God Himself will be pointing fingers at particular people, dates or events – they will be taking the long view, though floating in the background will be the question of how a church should be led and the adequacy of the current key players: Bartholomew, Kirill, Hilarion, Onufri, Filaret and those supporting them. An awareness, I suspect, of a need for deep prayer, lots and lots of it, without which a church is built on sand and not on rock, and the need for silent waiting on God, including the readiness to hear Him say that structures and forms deemed immutable are inappropriate today and will have to be discarded.

This secret prayer builds up spiritual capital and good things happen – almost certainly such an accumulation of prayer and the sufferings of the Russian church permitted the breaking free in 1988, but it is a capital that does not last, and I sense that is right now nearly exhausted, and will need to be rebuilt in a long and silent process.

Much of this prayer is going, I suspect, to be very hidden, often by people with no official labels ('hermit') or uniforms or vows. It is they as much as Bartholomew, Kirill, Hilarion, Onufri, Filaret and their successors, who will carry our church for the next several years.

Cold beauty

24 October 2018
'Dour' was the word that came to mind as I sat in the Anglican pro-cathedral last night, with its bare brick walls, simple wood

beams and patterned tiling built at the end of the nineteenth century. Waiting for a special two-hundredth anniversary Choral Evensong to start, I saw in my mind's eye stern women from around 1900 in heavy high-buttoned dresses and hats arriving of a Sunday morning for an hour's very Protestant religion to keep them on the path of propriety and rectitude. My heart sank further as the choir entered, the women in light peach-red coveralls which could have been made by a hospital garment company, preceded by a female crucifer carrying a plain wood cross too low and at a slight tilt.

But then they struck up the 'Lord open thou our lips', and my mood changed. This was real cathedral style and it was good. Good, yes, but still bitterly lacking something. As if music was the only thing that, for 300 years from the Reformation to the Anglo-Catholic Revival, raised English cathedral Christianity out of a slough of morally impeccable despond. We went through the traditional Anglican short evensong: hymn, Old Testament lesson, Magnificat, New Testament lesson, Nunc Dimittis, Anthem, concluding prayers, hymn blessing. Cold beauty, the hymns and prayers speaking, it seemed to me, less of profound hope and a deep sense of joying in God's presence, and more of patiently bearing with moral rectitude the hardships of life till the last trumpet sounds.

A religion I fled 50 years ago…

Go down to the water's edge

2 November 2018
Wagt euch zu den Ufern,
Stellt euch gegen den Strom,
Brecht aus euren Bahnen,
Vergebt ohne Zorn.
Geht auf Gottes Spuren,
Geht, beginnt von vorn,
Wagt euch zu den Ufern,
Stellt euch gegen den Strom.

'Courage, Go down to the water's edge, set yourself against the current. Break out of your ruts, forgive without anger. Follow God's tracks, Go, start again from the beginning. Courage, Go down to the water's edge, set yourself against the current.'

I read these words yesterday in a modern hymnbook in the Castle Church in Wittenberg, where 501 years ago Martin Luther nailed his 95 Theses to the church door, unwittingly setting off a process which led to the implosion of the Catholic Church in this part of the world, seen as having strayed too far from Christ's message. In fact a slow and messy process, now known as the Reformation, which lasted about 30 years before becoming permanent.

As my readers know, I am not, theologically, a Protestant. For me Protestantism has become too intellectual and too focused on morality, both public and private, and – perhaps especially in its German form – out of a concern to be inclusive and bless everyone, weakens the striving towards any idea of perfection, of excellence.

That being said, the call to courage and readiness to go against the current (or the 'party line') seems more than ever essential in our church at the moment. Just as in early sixteenth-century Germany, there is an obvious groundswell of discontent, which the senior hierarchy seems unable or unwilling to recognise, whether in respect of a fasting and confession practice which appears to bring little real spiritual gain, of the emergence of a clerical caste with a sense of its importance not shared by the laity, of financial exactions on parishes forced to pay for a large number of new bishops of dubious real use, or an unhealthy closeness of the senior clergy with the political powers that be.

Will history repeat itself 500 and some years later?

Priesthood under threat

10 November 2018
As I read things, priesthood is under threat in two major parts of the Christian church: in the Roman Catholic Church from the increasing shortage of vocations; in the Orthodox Church, from growing resistance to the manners of a priestly caste and the monopoly it assumes of Christian teaching and sacraments.

I ask myself: are we moving inexorably towards a much more radical – and frightening – re-think? How should Christian community operate in today's social-educational structures; how can the traditional priest-based structure, and its monopoly of the Eucharist, be changed without ensuing chaos? What is the position of the non-priest holy (wo)man, elder/ eldress, prophet(ess) in all this? Is the traditional patriarchal/ nuclear-family-as-little-church model that underlies much of the existing model sustainable in a post-contraception, gender-equality, world? It is not a debate I particularly relish – religion is a subtle thing and babies quickly get thrown out with the bathwater in reform movements. In particular people have a need for rite and mystery and if the church walks away from it, God knows which other force will fill the gap. But I fear we cannot avoid it either.

Perhaps *horror horrorum*, for all the bad press it gets in the Orthodox world, I am starting to quietly respect parts of the Anglican communion for their readiness to face the challenge of changing situations, in the persons of Archbishop Justin Welby, Michael Curry and their like.

As I said to my son...

14 November 2018
If Christianity is not about freedom and joy, I'm on the wrong train...

The unity of the Spirit

18 November 2018 (Facebook)
Today's epistle talks of 'endeavouring to keep the unity of the spirit in the bond of peace' (Ephesians 4:3, KJV).

Against the recent breaking of communion between the Ecumenical and Moscow Patriarchates this sounds harsh. Except that: the wording tells us that the unity/oneness is that of the Spirit. Perhaps the split tells us simply that we are not travelling in a direction that the Spirit wants. That trying to get a 'unity of Orthodox' is not God's priority right now: He is looking further, in particular for the various Orthodox churches to get back into communion with Rome. And perhaps not necessarily all together...

Dukhovnik

25 November 2018 (Facebook)

A nice woman comes to our church today for the first time. Russian speaking, but with near-perfect French. She has travelled for an hour and a half, across a national border, arriving slightly late and after cut-off time for confession. Why: because we are the closest Moscow Patriarchate church to her home. Until now she has gone to a local church, under the Ecumenical Patriarch, in the country where she lives. Her *dukhovnik* (spiritual guide) has advised that with the split, she should come to us. At a cost, I estimate, for her and her daughter, of at least 40 euros (cheap weekend fares do not work cross-border) a time. Our priest played fair, confessed her and gave her communion after the service. She was happy.

I kept my mouth shut. Maybe I have misread the situation, but a priest who insists that a woman who has been in one church for several years should uproot and go to another, at considerable expense, just because of a split which has absolutely nothing to do with her, is not worthy of the title of *dukhovnik*.

Ex opere operato

27 November 2018

There is a running discussion in the Russian part of LiveJournal on the official doctrine of the Orthodox Church (shared with the Roman Catholic Church) that a sacrament is valid regardless of the personal worthiness of the priest (in Roman Catholic language '*ex opere operato*'). There is evident unhappiness at this teaching, which is seen by many as serving to justify and excuse priests behaving in ways that are socially unacceptable, and episcopal tardiness in intervening. 'The sacrament is still valid, so what are you complaining about?'

In this context, major sins, like alcohol abuse, paedophilia and stealing church funds are cited as examples, but I suspect that most of the time, the problem lies elsewhere: that of priests considering themselves entitled, because of their office, to impose themselves. 'Clumsy, uncouth, overbearing, phallocratic, unable to argue their positions rationally' and 'being the sort of person I would never invite to my house' might be closer to the mark. Some would suggest that manners and attitudes learnt in seminary do little to help here.

For me one can usefully distinguish between 'validity' and 'effectiveness'. If I take the sacrament from an 'unworthy' priest, who is alcoholic, a paedophile or stealing church funds, it is a valid sacrament, and grace-giving to me. On the other hand, the 'effectiveness' of the priest's ministry, his duty to lead the people of God forward, is severely compromised by inappropriate behaviour, especially when people stay away from the sacraments as a result. And, as I said above, probably much more because of uncouth and insensitive behaviour than because of flagrant sin.

I suspect the question of validity conceals a second area which needs urgent attention: the far-too-common practice of priests being forced on a parish which has no choice in their appointment, and the slowness of the hierarchy to intervene when things go wrong. It seems to me that there is a reasonable case to be made for the validity of a priest's orders to be dependent, not just on a bishop having laid hands on him sometime in the past, but on the people of God accepting him by means of their being part of the appointment decision process – well before any cry of *(an)axios*.[2] And by extension, one could argue that a parish has the right to withdraw its acceptance of a priest, thereby suspending him *a divinis*, in the same way as a bishop can.

All of which is simply a variation on the question: is the correct situation that of the people of God speaking through the bishop, or the bishop speaking (without consultation) on behalf of the people of God?

Bulwarks and buffers

21 December 2018
I have not been a very good LiveJournal correspondent in recent months. Yes, time is at a premium and I read Russian only slowly.

It is also as if I sense a deep turning of the tide inside me, including moving away from traditional Orthodox discourse, both in terms of methodology and on individual points. I have tried three times this week to get this into writing. It refuses to gel, and sounds too much like another jeremiad among many. But two paragraphs sound right, which I offer here...

In most Orthodox discourse, and certainly in Russia, 'unchangingness' seems to feature large: we are an immovable bulwark, a sure reference point, with unchanging values in a surging sea of change. I challenge this assumption: nothing tells me that God created the world once and for all to work in a certain way, and that His Spirit cannot or should not move to change the way we view the world and our place in it.

For me, post-1988 Russian Orthodoxy has hit the buffers, and is beginning to turn around in circles and lose energy and adherents. A quantum leap forward is needed, and we cannot find it. The road or roads are not signposted. I believe such roads exist, and indeed I dare to believe I have found one such road, but I have had to go outside Orthodoxy into the wider Christian world to find it.

'Christ in the church is not needed'

23 December 2018

I was struck by a recent comment by a competent icon painter in my blog: 'I have long been convinced as an icon painter that Christ in the church is not needed.'

This seemed to echo with an observation I made at the current exhibition in Brussels (BOZAR) of the early seventeenth-century religious painter Theodoor van Loon, that the only Christs that van Loon paints well are either infant Christs ('Adoration of the Magi') or dead ones ('Pietà', 'Descent from the Cross'). His adult Christs, whether 'The Woman Taken in Adultery' or the 'Supper on the Road to Emmaus' fail to convince and one senses a difficulty in 'capturing' them. Indeed the most convincing male figure in his work is Joseph, much younger than the old man of Orthodox tradition or pre-Reformation Roman Catholic tradition. And it's not just van Loon, many religious painters from the Counter-Reformation onwards seem to do a much better adult Joseph than an adult Christ.

I would suggest the following logic which underlines both situations...

First, that religion (as distinct from faith), in order to play its social role, needs basic role models, good male, good female, preferably sexually active and in a family context, and that Christ (despite being on the right hand of the royal doors on the iconostasis, with the Mother of the God on the left) does not really fill this role very well. St Joseph does it much better – he is also the 'good handworker', the honest artisan and family man, beloved both of those in power (and the Counter-Reform church that van Loon was working for was very much a political instrument) and of Romantics.

Second, that in one sense, Christ does not want to serve as prototype, someone to be modelled on: He has gone up to heaven, and left us in His church, with the Spirit of God sent from the Father at His request, who are to stand as witnesses and models, especially in the form of the saints. Indeed one can go further and ask how far prototypes, for Christians to pattern themselves on, are useful at all, and how far at a critical stage along the Christian path they do not limit the freedom of the Spirit to take us into that critical area where we have to go blind, naked and beyond models and patterns.

2019

The English God

6 January 2019 (Facebook)

The English God is gentle, merciful and very patient with our foibles and failings. Perhaps this has something to do with our climate. In our ascetic theology and practice one senses none of the torrid heat of a Roman or Greek or the biting cold of a Moscow winter. Some more of it may have to do with a key spiritual figure, Julian of Norwich, the late fourteenth-century anchorite whose *Revelations of Divine Love*, essentially meditations following a series of 'shewings' of Christ to her in a deep sickness, have been an essential and continuous part of the English spiritual heritage ever since.

For Julian 'God is that goodness which cannot be angry, for God is nothing but goodness' and any 'wrath' of God is more the effect of our 'perversity and opposition to peace and love' crashing against it. Elsewhere she writes that 'Peace and love are always alive in us, but we are not always alive to peace and love'. She insists that God's love rests upon us, and goes on resting upon us in spite of anything we in our blindness or perversity or ignorance may do.

Accepting this love of God, and not letting our readiness to love and be loved be blocked by memories of impure love or the abuse of love, or fears of loss of love, which too many of us have experienced, is surely one of the keys to advance towards God in Christ.

Full circle

13 January 2019

I am where I was 55 years ago: in the crypt of Canterbury Cathedral. This time round at an Anglican liturgy followed by the blessing of an icon painted by a good friend of ours.

In the 1960s, my father, a travelling salesman, would bring me as a teenager to Canterbury and leave me to wander around the cathedral on my own. I was fascinated by medieval architecture, and Canterbury has a full range of styles from Norman Romanesque to late Gothic. There was also a sort of numinous presence, especially in the crypt, which helped mould a sense of Christian vocation – at the time, I thought, via Oxford or Cambridge, to the Anglican priesthood.

It did not turn out that way. Fortunately, and in God's grace, I suspect. While I admit to musing at unguarded moments that if I had played my cards better, I would now be a minor bishop or a cathedral dean, there is an equal likelihood that I would have become unstuck, either theologically or psychologically, as more than one of my future priest colleagues in my Cambridge college did.

Instead, my Christian life has ended up a roller coaster existence, lived largely outside my home country, in three different churches (Anglican, Roman Catholic and Orthodox, plus temporary stays with Quakers and Protestant charismatics) and in very different cultures (English, European, Russian, with occasional dashes of American). Outwardly I am Orthodox, and a deacon in the Russian church. Whether, deep down, I can really brand myself any longer as anything other than plain Christian, I don't know. I love the simple beauty of an Anglican service with the word spoken well, the Catholics have given me most of my ascetic theology (Orthodox ascetic theology is still too monastery-oriented), and the Orthodox a glimpse into the power of ritual. I have little love for 'establishments' and have successively run foul of (or failed to play properly) the Anglican, Roman Catholic and Orthodox structures.

In a sense it is a Christianity beyond confessional identity, an area where I suspect a lot more mature Christians of all confessions really are. For us, confessional barriers – whether 'educated' ones of the *filioque* or, increasingly populist ones of railings against gay people and women priests – feel increasingly artificial and leaky, needed by some to maintain identities which, it seems to me, have to give way if we are ever to meet the risen Christ in His full power and glory.

On conversion

26 January 2019 (Facebook)
Christian conversion is a remaking, a recreation. It is letting God remould the original materials one is made of into a new form, able to communicate with Him and with one's fellow men in the way He intended. This presupposes two things: one,

not throwing away any materials and two, making sure that all the materials are available to be remade.

I am increasingly convinced that there is nothing fundamentally wrong in the energies that God gave us initially, even if they may run down wrong channels owing to blocks that we or others (in most cases others) have placed to prevent their natural flow. If we are afraid or embarrassed of these energies – in particular if they reveal themselves as hunger for power or as sexual urges in forms not normally acceptable in church confines – and if for this reason we either discard them, or refuse to use them, any new building we try to build (I say 'we' as I'm sure that God will not build anything without having all the materials to hand) will be lop-sided and liable to subsidence.

For your joy

20 February 2019 (Facebook)

A little phrase stared at me from the page of my morning Bible reading: συνεργοί ἐσμεν τῆς χαρᾶς ὑμῶν (we work with you for your joy – 1 Corinthians 1:24).

These words of St Paul remind us of two things: that joy is the sign of the gospel working fruitfully in a Christian, and that the task of any priest, pastor or teacher is to work with the persons entrusted to him or her to increase this joy. If the outcome is anything else, something is wrong.

Moving beyond guilt

3 March 2019

What happens, I surmise, if we in the church simply throw our condemnation of pre-marriage sex (where it still exists), same-sex activity and solo sex out of the window? The only rules being that everything be genuinely consensual, and that the proper measures be taken to avoid unwanted pregnancies and AIDS/STIs. And change the thrust of our teaching to insist that our task as Christians is to learn to use our entire God-given energy – physical, sexual, emotional – in a positive and guilt-free manner. Two possible advantages...

One, it could do away with a guilt culture that (still) pervades the sexual area. Fostering a sense of guilt can be a way of maintaining control of people, especially in churches which insist on sacramental confession.

Two, it could stop the huge wastage of spiritual energy in the LGBT debate. I suspect that, in many ways, this is a non-issue which the evil one blows up to prevent us from concentrating on the real spiritual battles of our day.

A terrible beauty...

17 March 2019
How do I tell a young man – a serious Christian and a university graduate – that the statement by certain startsi ('the startsi tell us') that 'in the last days the number of faithful will reduce' does not justify his view that it will be only rigidly observing Orthodox, who reject the possibility of Christ's presence outside of Orthodoxy, and who 'endure to the end' (Matthew 23:13) who will be saved?

My knowledge of the 'startsi' universe is limited, but somehow I suspect that much of the responsibility for this sort of attitude lies with a kind of 'second-tier *starchestvo*', living totally in its own self-referential world, already with limited contact with 'normal' people in their own countries and with no contact at all with other Christian cultures and confessions.

The people these startsi attract are often young men, and perhaps women, who, with a different background and creed, could have become jihadi fighters. Yes, there is an attraction in the type of Christianity they offer: it is the 'terrible beauty' of which Yeats spoke of in his 'Easter 1916'. It is this attraction which keeps these startsi in bread and computers. But unless the ascetic rigidity which their systems entail can burst out of its enclosedness into love and prayer for the whole of humankind, and express the love of the Father who 'makes his sun to shine on good and bad alike', it is ultimately sterile, reducing rather than increasing the Christian population.

We are going to dedicate an altar to St John of Shanghai and San Francisco in our Antwerp church. St John seems to have got the balance right – an asceticism which is beyond nearly all of us, a strictness that frightens, but under it an overwhelming love – the love of God – for everyone.

Breaking of systems

20 March 2019 (Facebook)
A fellow cleric's system has broken apart over the past 12 months. A nasty but necessary divorce has forced him to withdraw from the Christian community in which he has had a prominent position.

Thank God. This is how He works, when He gets serious with us. Forcing us to junk the systems, the 'church' structures we use for the sense of worth they give us, and confront naked the Christ behind them (*nudus nudum Christum sequens*). It is an act of His love, and even if we feel precisely the opposite at the time, a sign that He has not abandoned us. Indeed of a certain preference – if I can use the term – over those whom He has left to gently rot.

I have been through this. It takes time. Five years at a guess till he is back fully on track, quite likely elsewhere in the church.

The children in the Temple

22 April 2019
It is the children who carry the day in the story of Christ's entry into Jerusalem. The ones who so irritated the chief priests and scribes by continuing the shout 'Hosanna to the Son of David' into the Temple. Children who had caught a sense of festival and expectancy, without knowing too well what it was all about. Too young and innocent to be caught up in the mixed and confused expectations of the crowd that followed Christ into Jerusalem and then seems to have dispersed pretty quickly. Innocent and unknowing.

And certainly, the children were too young and innocent to know that the Jewish system of which they are physically at the epicentre is on its last legs. Run by an inner circle family-related people ('the high-priestly family', religiously out of date, Sadducees acknowledging only the Torah as a source of law and very centred on ritual) involved in power politics with the Romans ('If we let him go on like this, everyone will believe in him, and then the Romans will come and take away both our temple and our nation' John 11:48, NIV), inimical to the prophetic side ('Zechariah son of Barachiah whom you murdered between the sanctuary and the altar' Matthew 23:35) and increasingly distant from the common people ('This crowd, which knows nothing about the Law – they are accursed' John 7:49; 'we have the people to fear, for they all hold that John was a prophet' Matthew 21:26). It is also tied to a hideously expensive building campaign. Yes, there is the more popular and more 'modern' movement of the Pharisees, who believe in the resurrection and post-Torah tradition; but this group too is paralysed by its fundamentalism, unable to see God in broader terms than in strict obedience to law and ritualist purity.

Christ is innocent and knowing. He is under absolutely no illusions as to His own fate and that of the Jewish idea in its then form, which has had its day and has lost God's favour. 'If you too had only recognised on this day the way to peace' (Luke 19:42).

But within two months, after Christ's crucifixion, resurrection and in particular after Pentecost, the whole system is upended. Yes it continues outwardly, the Temple is completed, but it is a dead duck, which limps on for another 40 years, even finishing its building campaign a few years before the Romans finally kill it off in AD 70. God has moved on, into Christianity and (depending on your take as to whether God's promise to the Jews remains valid outside of the Christian church) into a radically recast Judaism.

Consummatum est – Es ist vollbracht

29 April 2019
These words ('It is finished/done' – Christ's last words on the cross, in Latin and German) came across my lips, out of season (four days late) as I boarded the train back to Brussels from our annual Easter Monday liturgy of all clergy of the diocese with our archbishop.

Finally I am through the long set of Easter services starting on Maundy Thursday with the commemoration of the Last Supper, through the Burial Services on Friday, the beautiful Vespers and liturgy of Saturday morning with the first announcement of the resurrection ahead of the Easter Vigil itself, the Easter Vigil, Easter Sunday Vespers (bishop, priest and me), and our Easter Monday bash (mentioned above).

In one sense it went pretty well. As senior deacon I read the long composite gospels of Thursday and Friday pretty cleanly (Slavonic read in a very 'Anglican' manner); on the Saturday we (just about) avoided mishaps with the inevitable 'force-feeding' of struggling kids brought to communion once a year; on Easter night I'm not sure whether it was the altar or the choir which was in command, I suspect the latter; on Monday the archbishop blew a fuse as every year because none of us has the archiepiscopal liturgy off pat, but this year I just let it blow over.

In the next few days, as the tension goes out of my body and I start sleeping regular hours, and recover the balance between church and private prayer, Easter will catch up on me: with an increasing sense of having touched something incredibly deep, something which is beyond theology, something which is almost beyond Christianity as an expression of God in action in humankind and creation; with an almost pagan sense of the importance for the salvation of the world of doing the rite and doing it properly; of an area where shaman and priest/person of God merge.

Battering God?

12 May 2019
A couple of days ago my priest host in a small Russian town and I were invited at the last minute by the local bishop to serve liturgy with him the next morning. Normally, in Russia, to take communion at the liturgy one is supposed to be present at Vespers the previous night. It was too late. My host asked the bishop how we should prepare. 'Just read the usual evening prayers, triple akathist[1] and the usual preparation prayers.' My friend read the lot in Slavonic; it lasted nearly an hour as we asked forgiveness and help variously from God the Father, Christ, the Mother of God, and our guardian angels, presenting ourselves as wretched, worthless sinners perhaps 20 times.

Parallel with this I am reading Catherine De Bar, one of the great French Catholic mystics in the seventeenth-century flowering of French Catholicism before Louis XIV heavy-handedly put down 'Quietists' and Protestants. Her idea is of being aware, in silence and trustingly, of the presence of God, already in us. Minimum words.

I recently read Norwegian Protestant pastor Ole Hallesby's classic 'Prayer'. His line is that we simply tell God what we need, and then leave our requests in trust with Him, not anxiously presenting them to Him over and over again.

Which is the right approach – the Orthodox, Catholic or Protestant one? If I am a member of the household of God (Ephesians 2:19) and a brother of Christ (Matthew 28:10), is it really necessary for me to batter God, and His mother and my guardian angel like this for an hour? For me, this is essentially the language of someone 'outside', whereas I hope that I am, by now, 'inside'.

Paganism and Russian Orthodoxy

16 May 2019
I looked out of my bedroom window last week in the Russian city where I was staying. In front of me was a large, square building, recognisable as a church by its onion dome and some traditional ornamentation, and the people going in and out for Radonitsa: the service at which prayers for the dead are permitted liturgically again for the first time after Easter, and including visits to cemeteries. On this occasion, and on other occasions during my stay in Russia, the dividing line between Christianity and pre-Christian paganism seemed particularly thin. The Slavs, like many ancient peoples, had a tradition of visiting family members' graves during the springtime and feasting together with them, and I sensed that this was a direct follow-on.

There is a lot of the 'pagan' in Russian Orthodoxy, in particular among the less well-educated. Chanting in half-understood ('mystical') languages, walking around in complex configurations in coloured vestments, with incense and candles in dark churches, plays to a sense of the numinous, as does the sense of 'particularly holy space' accorded to the sanctuary, often hidden from the common people and accessible only to a selected few. Certain icons, especially of the Mother of God, seem to reach back into pagan idol practice. Priests can become slightly magical figures, the continuation of the 'shaman'. In ritual, message and medium become inextricably entangled.

I hesitate to condemn this: increasingly I suspect that Russian Orthodoxy, at least in its public worship aspect, is around 80% general religion (*religiöses Allgemeinsgut*) and human beings' inherent sense of the numinous and of the interplay of our tangible world with other, less tangible ones. As a celebrant, especially in country/small-town settings, I sensed that what I was doing rooted well back before the conversion of Russia in the tenth century. Pagan, if you like, but something that one shuts out of one's public and private life at one's peril.

These are roots that we need to keep. Protestantism has done itself a disservice by cutting them away, and I believe it is no accident that psychotherapy started largely in Protestant countries and in Judaism, where these roots are absent. Roman Catholicism after Vatican II, pruned too hard, and had to backtrack, finally reintroducing the more 'ritualist' Latin mass.

But at the same time Christianity has to be more than this. Paganism unites to the world around, but it has no *telos*, that is, it lacks forward movement towards any sense of perfection or higher goal.

Moving beyond

25 May 2019 (Facebook)
I sense though that, however uncomfortable it is, I and others have to move beyond 'clergy comfort zone' and party line. I have to move to dialogue, not preach, allowing people to put God into their own words and not mine, to respect their value systems and attempts to construct systems of meaning, even where I do not share them. I have to suggest that there may be alternative (sexual) morality and lifestyle and organizational systems – neither paternalistic or 'family values' nor late-capitalistic – which are viable under the banner of Christianity. I have to suggest that ascetic theology has to integrate the body rather than fear it as a place of the devil. It is a scary call, one which can take me to not-too-respectable places, but I fear it may be of Christ.

Strangely unbothered

26 May 2019 (Facebook)
Today's gospel reading in the Orthodox lectionary relates the episode of the woman – who Jesus meets at the well (John 4) – who had had five husbands.

If indeed she is a woman of loose morals (the troparia in the canons for Mattins refer to her directly as a 'harlot') and the five husbands are not – as some suggest – simply a reference to the five groups of the Samarians (see 2 Kings 17:24–41), it is perhaps not irrelevant that Christ seems to be strangely unbothered by her sinful status. Yes, He names the situation, but, it seems to me, in order to identify Himself as a prophet and not as a reproach. He continues talking as with any other woman. We see a similar situation with the woman taken in adultery (John 8) ('I do not condemn') and with the woman who washed Christ's feet with her tears.

I sense a pastoral principle in this: to 'speak past' the doubtful and poisoned areas in a person's soul, not mentioning them, to the very core of a person's being, which generally is pretty intact and has guarded a sort of primal innocence. It is from this inner depth, with the 'water springing up to eternal life', that the poison is brought to the surface and flushed out of the system.

Speaking the wonderful works of God

21 June 2019
'And they began to speak in other tongues, as the Spirit gave them utterance … we do hear them speak in our tongues the wonderful works of God.' (Acts 2, 4-11, KJV)

Perhaps we've got it wrong in seeing these 'tongues' primarily in terms of different languages like French, German, Greek or Russian. Perhaps we should see them more in terms of speaking to different mentalities, speaking (and being) the gospel in the words that bring it closest to our own and other people's hearts, words that vary greatly even within a single language group.

This makes me question the way the Orthodox Church (and to a certain extent the Roman Catholics too) wraps the gospel in a single 'language' – one particular form of service, one particular ritual form, one (half-dead) language per patriarchate, one particular form of building (expensive to build, run and heat, and easy to blow up in a revolution) and a single (paternalistic, oligarchic) power structure.

Perhaps the multiplicity of forms of Christianity that Orthodoxy rails at ('Protestantism divided into a thousand sects') is in fact a blessing, providing different 'languages' in which each can hear the gospel as best suits him or her.

On bad days I'm tempted at times to compare the Orthodox Church to an IBM 360 mainframe: long outdated and replaced by PCs, and with IBM out of computer-building altogether. And perhaps the Christianity of the future has nothing to do with large church buildings at all. A string of home churches, and people sharing God via the Internet, could do most of the job equally well.

Bodiness and dance

28 June 2019
I like watching 'good' dance. For me it is the body being used as a means of expression in a very full way. Dance speaks to me of the fundamental beauty that God has placed in me, and of the energy He has placed inside me in order to express it. Even as my energy wanes and I am not as supple as I was, the way I walk and bear myself are critical
Yes, the body has its limits. Ballet dancers age quickly, in particular the men, as outer bodily beauty makes way for inner soul beauty. And the temptations of the dance milieu need no describing, but neither should they scare us away from the medium.

I note here St Paul's teaching that 'if the Spirit of him who raised Jesus from the dead is living in you, he who raised Christ from the dead will also give life to your mortal bodies because of his Spirit who lives in you' (Romans 8:11, NIV). For me this means that, as we progress towards *theosis* (divinization), we throw off the sense of shame that, for many of us, clings to our bodiness and in particular our sexuality. We can stand in front of God stark naked and not ashamed. Indeed, as long as we are ashamed of our bodies, we cannot really do the dance of the liturgy properly.

I do believe that God made humankind originally fundamentally beautiful, and it is our job to find this beauty in ourselves and in others. This beauty is our identity in God. Yes, sin may temporarily have clouded the picture – not least by making us ill at ease with our bodiness – but in heaven we will walk, dance, sing this beauty (naked, or clothed in a special way by God). And why wait for heaven?

Stealing God

1 October 2019
There is a nasty, nagging suspicion that I have had all my life that organised Christianity is, for quite a bit of the time, about something else than God.
In my worst moments I ask whether a self-co-opted group has not 'stolen God'. That is, it has grabbed a monopoly on supplying a basic human need, that of religion and ritual, and is milking this monopoly, with the complicity of other powers that be, for its own benefit: in the same way as a drug company patents a medicine to maximise its gain from dependent people.

The monopoly takes the form essentially of exclusivity on the celebration of the Eucharist, the right to pronounce absolution of sins in God's name, and to speak publicly about Him. The benefit in the form of respect ('the uppermost rooms in feasts, and the chief seats in the synagogues') is due to office, rather than holiness. Monopolies ultimately impede progress. I have to ask whether, like all monopolies, it does not, sooner or later, have to be broken.

Freedom and freedom

9 October 2019
There is something thrilling in Christ's words to the paralytic 'Your sins are forgiven' – the Greek word being the same as remission of debt. Christ pinpoints that deeply buried inner knot that 'paralyses' a person, and breaks it. You are no longer bound. You are free. Christ's healing miracles are essentially this: a freeing up, a breaking of bonds, to walk, run, dance, sing, clap one's hands, to be fully human.

I suspect the difficult bit comes later: the immediate environment. It is no use opening a person's prison cell if he then hits an outer prison wall. This wall also has to be broken for the freedom/healing to be really effective. This wall has many forms, internal or external, and interconnecting: mental (a false understanding and practice of humility and 'knowing one's place', which opens one up to abuse); theological/anthropological (bad versions which trap us in a castrating world of duty, with no room for desire or joy); and physical (bodies which are overfed/badly fed, over-caffeinated, overworked, under-exercised and under-aerated in order to maintain that slight depressive state needed in order to survive in an oppressive atmosphere, bodies which cannot 'dance and clap their hands').

I've certainly hit all three types in my time. Hopefully the Spirit of God will give the wisdom and strength to get over or break down these outer walls. But be prepared also for a hard fight with some warders (including internalised ones) in the process.

Remember your first love

17 October 2019

I am reading again 'Remember Thy First Love' by Archimandrite Zacharias Zacharou, who comments on the teaching of Fr Sophrony Sakharov, his predecessor as head of the stavropegic Monastery of St John the Theologian at Maldon in Essex.

I have difficulty with Fr Sophrony's teaching on 'self-condemnation' and 'self-hatred'. Yes, it seems to me, to the realization that the 'self' we have built up for ourselves can be a false construction, and get in the way of God, especially where the bricks we have used include comparison with others and an implied 'being better than'. But no to the demeaning of what God created as good. It seems to me that, once all the rubbish is removed, once the desire to centre the world around myself goes, there must remain something – a me – which is good, through the very fact of God's having ordained that I come into being – though under the condition that I do not possess myself selfishly, and recognise this being as something given to me.

The goal of an ascetic endeavour seems not to whip myself into a frenzy of self-deprecation, not strike myself with stones like St Jerome (and, an unfortunate parallel, the possessed man whose devils ended up in the Gadarene swine), but to arrive, very soberly, at a sort of inner emptiness, a freeing space in which God can speak and act, in which I can recognise the voice of the bridegroom (and also that of the false pretenders) and react, unencumbered by my own preferences and desire for status and security.

To a devout Roman Catholic friend

18 November 2019

I certainly count myself fortunate to have, like you, started my Christian life in Protestantism. It is easier to start from a bare-bones gospel, and then bolt on and integrate the valuable additions of Catholicism and Orthodoxy, than it is to start in Catholicism or Orthodoxy – especially when enveloped in the paraphernalia of popular piety and distorted by their appropriation to guard public morality as dictated by the powers that be – and then try to sort out what is primary and what is secondary.

COMPARATIVE THEOLOGY:
THE NEED FOR A PARADIGM SHIFT

This essay, the earliest in this collection (April 2010), is intended as a critique of the way comparative theology is taught in the Russian church. If I had to rewrite it today, I would probably be kinder to Roman Catholics, whose Carmelite tradition in particular I have learnt to respect.

Comparative theology in the Russian academic mould has traditionally consisted of mapping out one's theology in certain critical areas of dogmatics – Trinitarian theology, soteriology, Mariology, ecclesiology and others – and comparing it with that of the other main Christian families. For those who see it as important to restore visible communion between these families, the task is to narrow or fill in the gap between them, on the premise that once this theological gap has been bridged, Christian unity is achievable. I have my doubts about this method. Can I suggest that there is another way, as we say in English, 'to skin a cat'.

Ultimately, I would argue, our willingness to ally with one or the other part of the Christian family in presenting the Christian message to the non-Christian world should be based, not so much on its conformity to one or the other set of theological criteria – whether *sola scriptura* (Protestant), the seven ecumenical councils (Orthodox) or the documents of Vatican II (Roman Catholic) – but rather on its products, that is on the depth and strength of the spiritual life and witness, individual and corporate, of its confessing members. This is the criterion that Christ Himself applies: 'you will recognise them by the fruits they bear … a good tree cannot bear bad fruit, or a poor tree good fruit' (Matthew 7:16–18, NEB).

I do wonder if there isn't in fact a tendency in both Protestant and Orthodox theology to define oneself at least in part by 'what one is not'. The very word Protestant speaks of drawing theological distinctions ('we protest against certain doctrines and practices of the Church of Rome'). The Orthodox Church has picked up this practice: it has taken on the identity of purists who have not allowed themselves to be led astray by papal doctrines. And if suddenly these doctrines were to be invalidated (and de facto they are pretty much invalidated by having very little real influence on the spiritual life of Roman Catholic Christians), I rather fear that Orthodox would desperately search around for others in order to retain a difference by which to define an identity.

Let me immediately express a couple of caveats, before going any further.

The first caveat is to bear in mind, in particular in relation to the Roman Catholic Church, is that while its dogmatic pronouncements are as a rule clearly stated and irrevocable, there is considerable stretch as to both their interpretation and their degree of reception at any one particular time. The doctrine of papal infallibility, in as far as it has ever really been received by the people, is interpreted quite differently today, with a much greater emphasis on the corporate consciousness of the church, than when the doctrine was first promulgated in 1870. Once we make allowances for this 'stretch', we find that the bases on which Orthodox and Roman Catholic spirituality are built are in fact quite a bit closer than we might have thought.[1]

The second caveat, when judging the situation in Western Europe, is to make a clear distinction between 'de-Christianization' and 'de-institutionalization'. Do near-empty churches mean that people do not feel they need Christ, or does it mean that they do not need the church as an institution in the particular historical form it has come down to them?

After three years of fairly intense contacts with Roman Catholics and Protestants in the context of my church work, I seem to be arriving at two slightly contradictory observations…

On the one hand, those of us with a solid Christian experience seem to be able to put our doctrinal differences behind us fairly quickly when we start to speak from the heart, from our own yearning for and experience of God. Certainly we recognise each other as honestly engaged in the same search for the living Christ, and the same desire to reflect Him in our lives.

Yet at the same time one often has a sense when observing Roman Catholics, and even more so Protestants, of a sort of flatness – to use a very Belgian simile: weak beer at 4° proof, instead of the strong stuff at 12° proof (Jupiler rather than Duvel!). I would also talk of people wanting to change their lives, rather than having them changed, or if changed, only to a certain depth, and indeed an unawareness of just how far Christ can enter into, change and take over someone. I hear little of a real spiritual outlook on life, of spiritual battle, of tears of the heart and the like. Notably both Roman Catholics and Protestants seem to have lost grip of a Christian science of the soul, and are too ready, when things get difficult, to refer people to the psychiatric profession, which is in fact rarely competent to handle the inevitable interplay of the spiritual in this area.

And this is where the rub comes: even if we resolve all the outstanding theological creedal questions between us, I am not sure that we strengthen the beer. It is this strong beer that people are looking for. What this is rapidly coming to is saying: how do we together brew this 'strong beer' Christianity.

My own contention is that we should be redirecting our view away from comparative dogmatics towards ascetic theology and practice. Are we indeed attaining and living out the depths of Christian conversion and the presence of God, individually in our hearts and corporately, that we believe to be possible and indeed necessary? This refocusing would reduce dogmatic theology to its real role, that of guarding the area in which this deep experience of God can take place, instead of at times replacing it.[2] My own limited experience is that I can talk ascetic theology pretty much across the entire creedal spectrum, and indeed often more easily with the new-generation Protestantism than with traditional Protestantism or Roman Catholicism.

Obviously this approach faces us with a problem of method. It requires not the intellectual exercise of comparing creedal statements but a more instinctive approach of being in contact over time with people of other confessions, sensing where their strengths and weaknesses lie; trying to discern how much these are individual and how much they are typical of their particular confession. From this vantage point we can see how we can incorporate any particular strengths into our own system in weak areas. Structurally it is the approach that, within the Orthodox tradition, any spiritual guide uses with an individual believer. And like individual counselling, it demands that the counsellor not only know his or her counselee and be able to correctly connect words, gestures and deeds to spiritual conditions but also that he/she have a strong spiritual life him/herself which can serve as a reference and anchoring point. Dare I suggest that the number of people

able to do this, within the Russian Orthodox Church, is pretty
limited? How many of us have enough contact with Roman
Catholics to really sense the ways they structure their spiritual
lives and to assess the results, also against the backcloths of
cultures which are not our own? The same with Protestants,
both of the more traditional episcopal confessions (Anglican
and Lutheran), but also the new Protestants of the US/Korean/
Chinese ilk?[3]

With no pretensions to expertise, let me put down on paper
a few observations from experience in this area. These are what
seem to me to be the real areas of concern that need addressing.
They are in two sections: where Orthodox have problems with
non-Orthodox Christianity, and areas where non-Orthodox
spiritualities may have examples to give the Orthodox Church.

Orthodox difficulties with non-Orthodox Christianity

- A failure to present a clear road map of spiritual development.
  In particular a tendency to interpret the key Christian virtues
  of love, joy and other virtues on too emotional and superficial
  a level and a failure to preach the fact that the Christian life
  is cross and resurrection.

- The absence of certain (to us Orthodox) basic concepts of
  spiritual hygiene. These include the belief, prevalent in the
  Russian church, that if you have seriously sinned (adultery,
  abortion, sodomy etc.) there will be a price to be paid in terms
  of a personal cross to bear, equally the spiritual experience
  that sin in one generation can affect following ones.

- A weakening of the concept of metanoia and spiritual
  growth as an ongoing practice. This goes hand in hand with
  a de-emphasising of sacramental confession (though it is still
  practised and may be experiencing a comeback, in slightly
  adapted forms).

- The evacuation of Christ towards either Deism, or an overly
  large place to the Mother of God, sometimes both at once,
  leaving no room for a real doctrine of divinization, or to use
  the more Catholic term, realised eschatology.

- (In particular but not only, in Protestantism) an overemphasis on the spoken and written word as the only means of communication of sacrality, to the detriment of the image (Christian art and iconography), music and dance (liturgy). The current state of religious art in the Western church is, in my opinion, little short of catastrophic.

- A certain Protestantism, certainly the rather old-fashioned, slightly fundamentalist type I was brought up in, seems to have lost the second gift of the Spirit, that of joy, from its vocabulary.

- The unconvincing showing of priestly celibacy. While it would be wrong to cast celibacy as the primary culprit for a lack of priestly vocations among the native Belgian population, it is common knowledge that many of the Congolese and other African clergy imported to fill the gap do not adhere to the church's rules in this area.

- A certain legal stiffness, coupled with a lack of *oeconomia*.[4] The blatant example of this is the continuing refusal of the Roman Catholic Church to give communion to divorced and remarried Christians. While a degree of stiffness is necessary in order to preserve the sacrament of marriage from abuse, most Orthodox priests consider this approach overly harsh and not necessarily spiritually expedient.

- A fear of excellence. The Roman Catholic Church has since Vatican II been keen to show itself as siding with the poor and the oppressed and the socially marginalised (*la préférence des pauvres*). This is not wrong in itself, but it does come with the danger of producing a misplaced egalitarianism in which the gifted and more intelligent – the potential sources of leadership – feel out of place. My impression is that such people, in so far as they remain in the church, tend to cluster in places like Opus Dei and around the Jesuits and Dominicans, and out of normal parish life. We must be careful here as Orthodox not to throw stones: an awful lot of Western Orthodoxy is very unattractively second-class.

- To this I would add a lack, ultimately, of a credible Christian image, that of the whole man, a strong man, who is heroic rather than 'cissy'. I am pretty certain that this more heroic 'icon', the one which will encourage a young man to make the sacrifices that priesthood demands, used to exist. In both France and Belgium, this was certainly white, professional class and slightly elitist, the product of the upper forms of Catholic grammar schools, but seems to have got badly tarnished and abandoned in the post-1968 whirlpool. It appears, thankfully, to be coming back, but much more in the new communities than in parish life.

- The existence of a sort of *génération maudite* (cursed generation) in the Roman Catholic Church, in the clergy and more particularly in religious teaching in schools, of what I would call the failed remnants of the 1968 crisis – people preaching and living a Christianity which seems little more than enhanced humanism, many of whom have more or less given up on their church, very often on their vows of celibacy, but are chugging along on their state salaries.

- A danger of *enféodation* (becoming prisoner of) to the worldly consensus of the day and an inability to enunciate a Christian view of humans and society that clearly differentiates itself from the 'general consensus' in which our societies operate. This is particularly noticeable in the backing certain churches give to the desire of the European powers-that-be to absolutise as social dogma certain ideas like 'democracy', 'rule of law' and 'equality of opportunity', confusing means with ends (is democracy the only way to achieve the definitely Christian virtue of justice?).

- A similar *enféodation* may exist in terms of psychology: that Western Christianity has adopted too quickly the psychic categories of Freud, Jung and company, abandoning its own 2,000-year tradition of spiritual healing, and its understanding of the interplay of the spiritual, physical and emotional found in its ascetic theology.

Where we Orthodox can learn from the non-Orthodox Western church

- To overcome the 'iconostasis barrier'. An Orthodox liturgy is de facto two liturgies: one going on behind the iconostasis in the sanctuary, and one going on in front of it, with the deacon as the link factor. While it may have been historically justified, and has become entrenched practice, it seems to me theologically wrong and an incorrect approach in a society of relatively well-educated people.

- An underuse of the 'word' element. While I appreciate that the word is not the only vector of the faith – that art (icons) and music, incense and the dance of the liturgy are important – non-Orthodox could well point to the fact remaining that we severely underuse the 'word' element available to us, underestimating the power of the word, spoken clearly in a the language of the people, to convict and elevate.

- A certain practical cumbersomeness. There are times in Christianity where you have to be able to operate light. All Orthodox services are heavy and slow, and heavily dependent on having a suitable building and a choir. It is instructive that the fast spread of Christianity in China in the past two decades has worked largely on the house-church principle, one which also works when evangelising Muslim communities.

While the above list is certainly not complete, it does suggest two important conclusions. The first is that real differences between churches lie less in dogma and more in attitude and mindset. The second is the message, however unwelcome it may be to certain purists, that Orthodoxy has lessons to learn from other parts of the Christian family.

ORTHODOXY IN BELGIUM: TOWARDS WHAT FUTURE?

This is a translation of an article originally published in 2012 in Russian in 'Alpha&Omega', perhaps the most serious journal in the Russian Orthodox Church of its day. As such it is aimed at intelligent Russian readers within the Russian Orthodox Church. Its genesis is my angry reaction to a 'praise-singer' trying to twist my remarks into yet another 'how wonderful is our church' article. How it got through the church censors remains a miracle I don't try to explain. I remain eternally grateful to the late Marina Dzhirinskaya, a great Russian lady, for facilitating its publication. I have added explanatory footnotes to help non-Orthodox Western friends in reading between the lines.

In this essay, I share my observations on the life and development of the Orthodox diaspora in Belgium over the last 20 years. The analytical conclusions from these observations are, I stress, my own and do not represent any official point of view.

Currently, Russian Orthodoxy in Belgium looks to be doing really quite well. In 1992, when I entered the Orthodox Church, the Russian Orthodox Church (Patriarchate of Moscow) had just two fully-functioning parishes, one in Brussels and another in Louvain-la-Neuve, plus a small monastery.[1] Today we have churches in Antwerp, Liège, Louvain, Mons, Charleroi, Namur, Libramont and Ostend, we have a full-time Russian-speaking prison chaplain, and have purchased a second, more spacious church in the centre of Brussels after the original church, which dates back to the 1880s, proved way too small. In 1992, besides the archbishop, there was just one Russian-speaking priest in the entire country – now there are nine. On a typical Sunday we have a total of perhaps 500 people in our churches, a figure that swells to 4,000 to 5,000 for the Easter Vigil. All of which enabled us to celebrate the one-hundred-and-fiftieth anniversary of the Russian Orthodox presence in Belgium in 2012 with triumphant reports in the Russian press and on Russian television.

We can justly be proud of what has been achieved. But we should be careful – very careful. In my sincere opinion, if in the next five to ten years we do not radically reconsider our position and fail to take any measures to rectify it, then by 2040, the number of parishes will again have shrunk to two or three, and the number of members to 30% of the current total.

The simple fact of the matter is that this rapid growth is not the outcome of the successful preaching and living of the Christian gospel among the local Russian or French or Dutch-speaking population. It is almost one and only cause is a massive inflow of Russian-speaking immigrants. Today's Russian-Belgian Orthodoxy consists almost completely, not of the descendants of the first (post-revolutionary) wave, not of the second (post-war) or third (dissident) waves, but of representatives of the so-called fourth wave, i.e. those arriving after the break-up of the Soviet Union.

Knowing the history of the first Russian emigration in Belgium, in particular, the percentage of the third (of fourth) generation descendants of the original post-1917 immigration that have remained in the Orthodox Church, I am under no illusions. The 'loss' between the emigration wave of 1917–1922, and the third and fourth generation is of the order of 85–90%. But for a small number of families for whom the preservation of the Russian tradition has been part of their aristocratic identity, the figure could well have been 95%.

The main causes of this 'burnout' are, I think, two. The first is that, in the present day, in every Christian denomination, there is a considerable loss from one generation to another. Where a church is functioning reasonably properly, preaching and witnessing the gospel to the outside world, this loss is made up by new converts from outside. In the Russian-Belgian Orthodoxy the same inter-generational loss occurs, but with no natural source of replenishment, other than new Russian-speaking immigrants. Yes, there was a certain replenishment in the past: in the 1970s and 1980s Orthodoxy enjoyed some success among French-speaking Belgian intellectuals, frustrated and anxious at the liturgical changes after Vatican II. For this group Archbishop Basil (Krivoshein) created four or five French-speaking parishes in or around Brussels. Only one still survives as a full parish. All the others have dwindled to nothing. Two are being kept open a bit artificially, as they have priest salaries attached, but as Russian-speaking parishes. Today the seriously active French-speaking parishes in Brussels are in the jurisdiction of the Patriarchate of Constantinople. The same jurisdiction also has three Dutch-speaking parishes. We have none, though in one church, Dutch serves as a secondary language in the otherwise Slavonic liturgy. Otherwise, the outflow has been continuous since 1945. Without the massive influx of immigrants, first of Orthodox Poles in the second half of the 1980s, and then, in the early 1990s, Russian-speaking 'refugees', most of them from the Central Asian republics of the former Soviet Union, there would probably no longer be a Russian Orthodox Church in Belgium. In the best case there might have remained one church to serve embassy employees, Russian students and businessmen, but no more than that – a situation similar to that in Belgium of the Lutheran churches of Sweden, Denmark and Germany.

The second reason for this 'burnout' is that the Russian Orthodox Church in this country plays a double function: apart from its strictly religious function it also acts as a 'club' and information centre for people who have not found (or not yet found) their way into the local culture. A key defining feature of the Russian-speaking immigration into Belgium between 1990–2000 (distinctive from the earlier Greek and later Romanian migrations) was the general social downshifting experienced by these emigrants, the majority of them from the Asian republics (Kazakhstan, Azerbaijan, Kyrgyzstan, etc.) of the former USSR. Many retained their refugee status for years, living off a combination of relatively generous social benefits plus undeclared work as low-paid cleaners, handymen and babysitters. The Russian church was the one place where they could set aside this social inferiority status. And there is nothing wrong with this. But as soon as these people, and especially their children, reach a decent level of linguistic proficiency, obtain Belgian nationality and find jobs, there is no longer any need of the Russian Orthodox Church to support self-esteem – indeed what is to keep the next generation in the church, with an ethnic culture they no longer own and a liturgical language which they badly understand?[2]

In other words, how do we make the transition from 'refugee church', to a church of socially integrated people? The turning point lies, it seems to me, where the need of this second function (information, social orientation and support of self-esteem) no longer exists. This is a pretty much inevitable process, which is already starting, but could in the next 10–20 years reduce the number of members and jeopardise the very existence of a certain number of parishes.[3]

Let me mention one final factor, less visible at first glance, which is, I believe, a litmus test of a healthy (or unhealthy) situation in the diocese. That is the ability of the Christians to produce full-time priests and monks to serve themselves out of their own ranks. The Russian diaspora in Belgium since the 1917 has not produced a single priest or monk in this category.[4]

Frankly, I do not think that the 'burnout process' of the present emigration, which is repeating that of the first emigration, can be stopped. But we can perhaps significantly slow down the process:

- We can openly make it clear to those members of the Russian Orthodox Church in Belgium, who are unable to analyse the situation for themselves, that we are approaching a transition point between 'refugee church' and church integrated into its surrounding society. That is, we now have to exist primarily for people whose main reason for their remaining in the church is their faith in Christ, and their desire to participate in the sacraments and move towards spiritual maturity, with no need for the church as their primary social structure.

- We need to insist on the fact that in the list of our priorities, 'to be a Christian' takes first place, 'to be Orthodox' second place and 'to be Russian or Russian-speaking', takes only third place. It is time to understand that our Lord does not care a bit what language we pray in, and that Russians are no more God's chosen people than, say, the Belgians or the Chinese.

- We need to strive for that level of spiritual life in which it is natural for a young man to consider dedicating his life full-time to the church. In other words, a situation in which holiness is the only justification for our retaining in Western Europe our particular denominational identity.

- We, that is the Russian church, ought to insist that any Russian Orthodox resident in Belgium, should, by the fifth year of his or her stay in this country, be fluent in at least one of the national languages. Failure to do so – and in particular when combined with conscious 'squatting' on social assistance – should be regarded as a sin, with all its consequences.

- We need to insist on the fact that every educated member of our church, cleric or layman, should be able to 'testify to the hope that is in us' in at least one of the local languages.

- One circumstance that cannot be changed, but must be considered squarely is that among the new generation of Russian-speaking parishioners, those arriving already churched and with Christian acquaintances and networks at home have been the exception rather than the rule. This distinguishes us from the Greek or Romanian diasporas: almost all the 'Belgian Greeks' and 'Belgian Romanians' arrived here already churched. They also remain in touch with their homeland, have relatives there, spend holidays, visit them and churches and monasteries they know. For most of the current members of the Russian Orthodox Church in Belgium, to travel to Russia, where they have no roots, is just as hard as visiting any other country. The outcome is that for them and for their children, Russian Orthodoxy is in fact Russian-Belgian Orthodoxy, lived in a very small group – a bit like a village isolated in the taiga. And as with any isolated village, a sort of incest sets in sooner or later, leading to degeneration and death. In this situation it is possible that instead of trying – from a distance and from scratch – to build relations with Orthodoxy in Russia (the country in which our members at one stage of their lives chose not to live in and still do not want to live,[5] and whose language their children, let alone grandchildren, will inevitably lose), it would be more profitable to engage a relationship with an Orthodoxy that is accessible to Western Europeans. I am thinking here in particular of Mount Athos, or surrogates such as the monastery of Maldon in England. Actually, the small group of more visionary and intelligent clergy and laity are already stepping in this direction. Yes, we are going to have to break now with Russian folklore and, in the next generation, with the Russian language. But to preserve Orthodoxy, is it not better to make this sacrifice, rather than lose the next generation to Orthodoxy by insisting on the Russian language?

So far we have talked about our own, so to speak, internal problems. But it would be incorrect to leave aside the question of what indeed is our role in the confession and preaching of Christianity beyond our linguistic and cultural boundaries. Is the raison d'*être* of the Russian Orthodox Church in Belgium limited to spiritual 'maintenance' of the Russian-speaking population? If we believe that we are called to a missionary, preaching activity in the West (and can indeed any church live a full life without a confessing openness to the society in which it exists?), then we are faced with a number of fundamental issues.

First of all we have to define – if not dogmatically, at least on a practical level – our position in relation to the Christian environment that surrounds us. The 'party line' remains that Orthodoxy is the only correct form of Christianity. But I ask: is this the testimony the Lord sent us into this country to give? Is institutional (Russian) Orthodoxy sole bearer of Christian truth? Or do we need to consider ourselves as part of the (wider) picture of Christianity in Belgium and in Europe – a picture in which other churches for historical reasons have a leadership role? Let's not dictate to the Lord the boundaries of His church but leave Him to show them to us.

These are issues we cannot ignore or circumvent. 'Come and see,' the Lord said to His first disciples. But come and see what? Our parishes are, for non-Russian speakers, closed internal worlds; impenetrable and inaccessible from the outside. In the whole of Brussels there is not a single church of the Russian Orthodox Church (and throughout the country – only one), to which I can invite a Belgian seeking the fullness of Christian truth, who will not suffer an immediate and profound disappointment. Put simply, for 'come and see' to work, three factors are important: one, the level of spiritual life; two, language; and three, social and cultural level. Let us consider each of these separately.

Spiritual level

The vast majority of converts to Orthodoxy among native Western Europeans have arrived in the church because of a religious leader who managed to make a deep impression on them. The two obvious examples, both now deceased, are Metropolitan Anthony of Sourozh (London) and St John (Maximovitch) (San Francisco). To their number we can possibly add our own Archbishop Basil (Krivoshein), who led the Russian Orthodox Church in Belgium from 1960 to 1985 and was instrumental in the founding of several local language parishes.[6]

Not to put too fine a point on it: the spiritual level needed to sustain life of the 'ethnic' parish, to fulfil its need for identity, requires little more than the most accurate simulation of standard religious practice in the home country. But the spiritual level needed to attract Western non-Orthodox, is totally different. Archbishop Basil (Krivoshein) left this world in 1985 and since then the Russian Orthodox Church in Belgium has experienced an acute shortage of people of genuinely high quality spiritual life. Yes, we have two or three priests whose spiritual and intellectual level makes them worthy companions of intelligent Catholic Europeans. But in terms of average spiritual temperature, you will find a much sadder situation. I am acutely aware of this ambiguity in my own path within Orthodoxy. The attraction was the patristic ascetic theology that I read of in books. Becoming a member of the Russian Orthodox Church in Belgium, however, I have met only a very small number people living lives that come anywhere near the excellent theory. Worse than that, despite the frequent berating of European morality out of Moscow, the moral level I have found in the Russian Orthodox Church in Belgium does not exceed that of European society as a whole, and is probably lower than that of the local Roman Catholic Church. I have seen more than I would have liked, among Russian-Belgian Orthodox, of organization of illegal entry into the country, intentional deception of public services to gain refugee status and attendant social benefits, marriage in order to gain citizenship, reluctance, even after obtaining the necessary rights, to take regular work and pay regular taxes. I stress once again that this way of life is contrary, not only to the high ideals of patristic asceticism and morality, but equally to the ethos of the average European, including the bourgeois Catholics, whose lack of spirituality and amorality is denounced from the pulpit by local Orthodox preachers. I note parenthetically that such morality turns off not only local Belgians, but even those few Russians who legally came to Belgium to work or study. The natural desire to avoid social downshifting and what is a demoralising environment for many prevents them becoming permanent parishioners of the Russian Orthodox Church in this country.

Language

I will do no more than state that we are very far from a situation
where all diocesan priests are fluent in the language of their
country of residence. The fact that the local persons who
converted to Orthodoxy in the 1970s and 1980s and were
then priested, did not speak in Russian, only exacerbates the
abnormal situation and the cultural division between French-
speaking and Russian-speaking Orthodoxy within the Russian
Orthodox Church.

Social and cultural level

It is well known that the people interested in Belgium in the
Orthodox Church are generally educated people belonging to
the middle or upper bourgeoisie, with the ability and inclination
to theological debate. Exceptions are rare. Most Russian
Orthodox in Belgium are less educated, do not speak the local
language, are incapable of serious discussions, and are socially
one or two classes below. As for the knowledge of the members
of the Russian Orthodox Church of the local religious culture,
it is usually close to zero. Russian Orthodox in Belgium are
nearly totally unfamiliar not only with the theology, liturgical
practice, and history of the Roman Catholic Church in their
country of adoption (which can be understood), but with the
architecture and design of the Catholic Church: with church
art; with the iconography of saints. Even the local saints of the
first millennium, that is of the 'undivided' church, are hardly
known to the Russian Orthodox.

Let me add one more remark: the Russian Church in times of
persecution aroused sympathy among Europeans, and for many
the idea of belonging to the church of the martyrs exercised
a certain attraction. Later with the renewal of the church in
Russia in the late 1980s and 1990s there was an invigorating
sense of belonging to a resurgent church. But those days are past.
Even leaving aside the recent series of scandals, skilfully played
up by the media – the overall style of the modern Orthodox
Church (at least that of the members of its senior clergy) is
not coincident with that sought for by European Christianity.
Extreme luxury,[7] autocracy,[8] the desire for symphony with a

government portrayed in the Western press as anti-democratic and corrupt – all this creates additional obstacles to any Orthodox 'mission' in the West. In this country, where bishops travel on the subway, trust in a pastor is in inverse proportion to the size of his limousine.

But it seems to me incorrect to see the missionary work only as a conversion of non-Orthodox to Orthodoxy. There is another form of missionary work in which it is possible for a member of the Russian Orthodox Church to lead an active and creative life with positive perspectives. This is the area of the non-institutional deployment of Orthodoxy, that is, its penetration into the consciousness and, more importantly, into the religious experience of people nominally remaining in the Roman Catholic Church; helping rehabilitate and strengthen the spiritual life of our Western brothers by correcting certain theological, moral, ascetic abnormalities.[9] This includes Orthodox being able to speak out – both in private conversation, and even in public – on things on which Catholics are thinking, but are afraid to speak, so as not to be accused of insulting liberal democratic idols. Long and constantly enriched experience of such communication with non-Orthodox is essential to my own understanding of my own task.

I personally believe that the future of Orthodoxy in Europe lies primarily in this approach. Not in increasing the number of parishes and parishioners (a growth which is not going to happen), nor in the growth of the number of state-paid Orthodox clergy (in the coming decades it will be a miracle if we can at least maintain the status quo). Nor should we count on any significant influx of local people. The only thing which is able to give, in my mind, really good fruits in any 'Orthodox mission', is to multiply the number of serious Catholics (especially among priests and religious) who are ready and open to receive from Orthodoxy what is the best in it, and which can supplement what is lacking or has gone weak in their own tradition.

Will we make it? There is no guarantee. But one thing is clear – if we try to ignore the obvious difficulties and dangers of our present situation, we have no reason to hope for divine grace. We will have only ourselves to blame if the next generation of

Russian-Belgian Orthodoxy fades and dissipates. Yes, the Lord blesses and helps in difficult and even hopeless situations, but on the condition that those involved in the situation do not hide their heads in the sand or, worse, sing their own praises while doing so.

CHRISTIANITY:
JOY, FREEDOM AND ABSENCE OF GUILT VS SUFFERING PENITENCE, HUMILITY AND PATIENCE

I wrote this article just after Easter 2019 to explain to one of our priests my unhappiness with the constant emphasis on suffering-repentance-humility-patience which forms the basis of much Orthodox preaching. I gave the article to a Roman Catholic friend and a Greek Orthodox friend – my reactions to their criticisms are worked into the final text given here. Unfortunately I never received a reply from the priest I originally penned it for.

If there is a single Bible verse which sums up my Christian hope, it is the sentence in St John's Gospel: 'I have come that men might have life, and have it in all its fullness' (John 10:10, NEB). For me Christianity is all about coming as far as possible, and as soon as possible, into the fullness of human being as God intended it, both in relationship to our fellow human beings and to Him, 'abiding' in Christ (John 15:4) with the Holy Spirit informing our lives. A marker of beginning to attain that state is joy, a joy whose source you don't quite recognise, but it is there, and increasingly so.

My Roman Catholic friend suggests that I ought to use love, rather than joy as a critical marker. To which I reply: If we take the nine gifts of the Spirit – love, joy, peace, patience, kindness, goodness, gentleness, faithfulness, self-control – it seems to me that there are two which are more 'feely' – joy and peace – while the rest are a bit more 'observational': we find ourselves being kinder, more gentle, more loving. I have always been very careful with 'love': yes, it is a marker, but in its true, Christian form, it is not terrible 'feely'. Perhaps I should have said 'joy and peace as crucial markers'. Certainly peace ought to be a salient feature of the life of grace: 'Peace I leave with you; my peace I give unto you.' (John 14:27, KJV) Joy gets less attention from Christ, though His 'Enter thou into the joy of thy Lord' (Matt. 25:21, KJV) could be an indirect reference.

Joy does not happen just like that. True joy, like true love, is a gift of God, a fruit of the Spirit living in us. In more Protestant – though perfectly biblical – language, it is the work of grace. While God is free to come and go as He pleases and in whom He pleases, the general Christian experience down the ages is that fullness of life in Christ is the fruit of a long process of purification, of making place for Christ to come and live in us deeply, down into the depth of our being. It is a double process of reconciliation first and then salvation: 'being reconciled through the death of His Son [...] , we shall be saved by his life' (Romans 5:10 NEB). This process of salvation peels away our inner resistances, letting ourselves be transformed from selfish monads into members of Christ in the community of the people of God, in the fullness of the humanity God has made us for.[1]

This is in response to a call, an invitation ('You did not choose me, but I chose you' John 15:16, NIV), which turns into a sense of presence, often felt as a sense of being 'in the right place' when we read the Scriptures, pray the prayers of the church or take part in the liturgy. I note incidentally that this call often includes an 'I want you, despite...'. The despite can be that you are not living to traditional social patterns, or have been in trouble with the law. This 'despite' element makes it imperative for any Christian guide to have a keen sense of what is important to correct quickly in a conversion situation and what can wait (like 'regularising' a living-together situation with a church marriage).

This purification is a painful process (see 'suffering' below), which demands increasingly a letting go of our own will, of our own efforts to build identities that please us, in the trust and hope that, by laying these aside, and letting ourselves be remade (the 'new creation' of 2 Corinthians 5:17), we in fact progress towards a life in Christ that is genuinely rich and full.

This process of throwing away our old identity and letting Christ give us a new one in Him (the 'new name' of Revelation 2:17), while vital, must be trod carefully. If there is a gap between relinquishing the old identity and taking on the new one, 'seven other more wicked spirits' (Matthew 12:45, NEB) can enter in the void.

It is also important not to find our identity in our sinfulness. For this reason I am against the adding of the words 'upon me a sinner' at the end of the Jesus Prayer. It is not the original version of the prayer, and for me it is not our essential identity in Christ as people saved by Him.

My Greek Orthodox critic insisted here that while we should not force the words 'upon me a sinner' onto people, neither should we exclude their being available for use. There are times when we have an overwhelming sense of sinfulness as part of the purification and growing process.

It is, I believe, important for us to sense, to have a foretaste of what the fullness of this life is to be. And while complete fullness may not be possible this side of the grave, we are right to claim as much of it as is possible here and now. Not a selfish looking for comfort, but remaining open to a call to something greater, purer, richer. Yes, there will be negative experiences along the way, and periods of emptiness. But it seems to me that we need to sense the ultimate τελος (end, goal) if we are to bear the negativity and emptiness. Perhaps as we go on, we sense it in different ways, more discreetly, in a more 'infused' way.

An important step here is the key shift in Christian life when we stop obeying God out of fear, but begin to do so out of an inner necessity in response to His love (in ascetic language moving from *praxis* to *theoria*). At this stage in particular we realise that we are brothers and sisters of Christ and members of God's household and have a certain freedom: as in my natural father's house, so in God's house I do not live in constant fear of His wrath; yes I respect Him, as I respect and honour my human father, but I am also very conscious of being son of God, brother of Christ and heir of the kingdom, and inhabit His house with the same confidence and sense of freedom.

This process of moving into Christ is one that will work only if we are prepared to invest our entire physical and psycho-spiritual energy. In many cases this can involve facing blockages to this energy caused by false attitudes towards our sexual and other drives, some of them unfortunately ecclesiogenic.[2] How we are to invest this full physical and psycho-spiritual energy is something I admit to being still unclear on. I confess to asking whether Yoga, Kundalini and similar disciplines, as well as energy-related medicines, do not have something essential to teach us here.

Sometimes the Orthodox Church gives the impression that it exists solely for the purpose of doing liturgy, and indeed that the liturgy is the pivotal point for all Christian life. I hesitate: for me liturgy has to maintain a permanent relationship and balance with a private prayer life. Christians have, in critical situations, been able to survive for long periods without liturgy, but not without prayer. Where liturgy is freely available, then its purpose is not just as personal spiritual medicine, but as a way of bringing the entire life of the world, both in church and outside, into the presence of God.

For me the acid test of a Christian church and a Christian community is this: is it ready and able to give all its members the space to develop their abilities to the full and to move as close to God as is possible this side of the grave?

I ran into trouble here with my Roman Catholic critic who states 'For me the locus of the test should be theocentric, emphatically not anthropocentric. In other words I want the church to be "whatever God wants it to be", whether that is convenient for me or for other people, whether it is helpful for me, or for other people, or not. And, in accordance with the programme of "Abandonment to Divine Providence" (have you read that?) whatever it actually is, is what God wants it to be. For me this is a precious principle: the primacy of that which exists over that which does not. Clearly the experience of the Incarnation was supremely unhelpful for a very large number of people – they rejected Jesus Christ. Nevertheless it was God's will that it should be exactly as it was. So for me the impact on people's self-realization cannot really be the test – I must find another.'

To this I reply: 'I may have done myself a disservice, by using the language of self-realization manuals. Let me take it another way round: if God provides His people with x units of energy and y talents, I think we can reasonably assume that it is with the expectation that they are to be used to His glory. I think we can also reasonably assume that "What God wants it to be" is in fact for the good – indeed for the best – of His creation. Otherwise we can get trapped into preaching a message which boils down to: God made you, you have to obey Him and do what He wants (quickly understood as: in the way, I preacher, tell you), regardless of how you feel about it. A bit like being drafted into the army by force – now knuckle down and obey. I got whiffs of this at times at a Protestant charismatic church which I belonged to for a couple of years, where I once whispered under my breath "helots in a despot's army". This is not the relationship, I believe, God wants with His people. He wants it with adult, responsible people, who are able to sense the real benefits of discipleship, having "come unto perfect man, unto the measure of the stature of the fullness of Christ" (Ephesians 4:13, KJV). God has taken a huge, but vital risk, in making us free beings and – perhaps we can even say – Himself vulnerable to His own creation.

I feel uneasy with your Abandonment to Divine Providence concept. I would want to reword it as "whatever is, is what God allows it to be" and that "God is in the present situation right now: it is the only reality He wants to work in".'

It is in this perspective that, I believe, we have to be very careful with certain elements which are widely found in Russian Orthodox discourse and practice. Let me deal with four of them: suffering (страдание), penitence (покаяние), humility (смирение) and patience (or longsuffering) (терпение). They are interrelated. The order in which I treat them is pretty haphazard. In each case, it seems to me, discernment is required when speaking of them. Careless handling of them can block, or indeed, render impossible fullness of life in Christ, both individually and corporately.

Suffering

Suffering is an inevitable part of our human lot. Suffering is essentially the physical and/or psychological pain caused by the gap between where we are and where we should be. It is a vital marker – people who have lost the ability to feel pain, such us lepers and users of certain painkillers, lose an essential vital protection.

Some maintain that illness or other difficult situations are God's way of calling us back to Himself when we have forsaken Him. I do not deny this, but I see no warrant in Scripture or the fathers to assume an automatic relationship. The fact that you are sick does not automatically mean you have strayed from God. Yes, no doubt God can use sickness to bring us to our senses, to make us less reliant on our own selves. I would suggest that a marker of where God is indeed at work here is where one senses a way forward, in which God will be glorified. To someone spiritually sensitive, there is a sort of inner logic in what is happening. The temporary hardship or blockage leads into new paths (someone unable to be a priest finds he can minister to God in other ways, a career failure makes someone rethink their priorities: is worldly success so important?). But at times there seems like no logic, we hurt and we shout to, and at, God.

Speaking with my Greek friend, we centred on the idea of 'breakdown' – that often in Christian lives, individual and corporate, it is necessary that God smash overly restrictive structures we have created for ourselves. We need to 'reboot' into a broader world. The caterpillar has to become a butterfly.

My own experience here is that we can 'shout at' God. We can tell Him straight that we are hurting, that we do not understand a situation. We can tell it 'as it comes', without using prissy language. I would also add at this stage that, if we want to 'read' sickness from a spiritual standpoint, we must also include the psychosomatic element in our diagnoses. A lot of sickness – including cancer – is caused by long-term exposure to negative situations. And that in certain cases a 'practical' solution may be preferable to a 'spiritual one' – the answer may not be more prayer or patience (терпение) but to chuck an unfulfilling job or ditch a misbehaving partner.

A lot of suffering today is psycho-spiritual, caused by people's inability to live balanced lives, in many cases being unable to live out their natural drives, emotional and other, in a full and healthy fashion. Fear of censure, requirements to conform to ideologies and mindsets one does not really believe in, and lack of space (money and time) to exercise one's creativity to the full, prevent people from expressing their God-given selves and talents.[3] The church must, it seems to me, be a place where this is possible. I am not convinced it is.

A word on the 'mystery' of suffering. Yes, freely accepted it can have a redemptive character. St Paul speaks of 'filling up in my flesh what is still lacking in regard to Christ's afflictions, for the sake of his body, which is the church' (Colossians 1:24, NIV). Saints of all ages have felt the call to participate in Christ's sufferings for the salvation of the church and of humankind, some – at least in the Roman Catholic Church – also as reparation for situations where God has been seriously dishonoured.

More fundamentally, at some stage in the Christian life, we have to allow ourselves to be caught up in the essential mystery of cross and resurrection. As the epistle reading at every baptism and at the holy Saturday liturgy, immediately before the first announcement of the resurrection, tell us 'We were therefore buried with him through baptism into death in order that, just as Christ was raised from the dead through the glory of the Father, we too may live a new life' (Romans 6:4, NIV). Initially we apply this in relation to the individual sins that are wiped away in our baptism (and in the 're-baptism' of confession). But increasingly we become aware of something much deeper: that the only way that suffering and sin can be halted – if I am not to pass on the hurts I received in my childhood onto my own children, if anger at injustice is not to lead to new injustices – is through my bringing these into the cross and resurrection process. And ultimately, in a way we adumbrate more than we can explain it theologically, we realise that the cross and resurrection is not just a one-off historical event but an ongoing practice, we know that our bringing our own pain and hurts into this process allows us and others to be 'remade', 'recreated'.

And indeed if our bearing of suffering is not to be simply 'holy masochism' imposed on us by a cruel God, we have to enter into this logic, following Christ who 'for the sake of the joy that was set before him endured the cross' (Hebrews 12:2, NEB). It is in this dynamic that I hesitate to see suffering as a value in itself: it is of use only in taking us to a situation beyond itself, where 'there will be no more death or mourning or crying or pain' (Revelation 21:4, NIV).

Penitence

There are two fundamental concepts in religious practice: 'repentance' and 'penitence'. Generally the image evoked by the Russian term покаяние is the latter, even if it also translates the former. However, the only concept that exists in the New Testament is 'repentance', that is *metanoia*, a fundamental change-around of attitude and mindset. In principle, this is a one-off affair, which even if involving tears temporarily, ends up with a sense of freedom and joy. It is not a constant attitude of feeling bad in front of God and *misérabilité*. Mary Magdalen did not spend the rest of her life feeling miserable. While she may not have danced the polka every evening, I suspect a sense of enormous gratefulness of being accepted and having space to exercise her considerable capacity to love deeply. In practice *metanoia* is an iterative process, as we peel away the onion, layer by layer, becoming increasingly aware, in God's time, of our own inner sinfulness and shortcoming.

We need, however, to be particularly careful as we peel away more of the onion. The popular concept of penitence is closely linked with guilt for conscious sins of commission and omission, but the deeper we go, the more the blockages we encounter are not of our own being, reflecting the traumata and hurt imposed on us by an often cruel world. If we are to heal and move beyond these in Christ, we have to move beyond the guilt-repentance link-up and simply accept that we are hurt by reason of others, that it is the cross that Christ gives us to bear, and which we accept, reluctantly, but ultimately with a sort of joy as we recognise it as a path of salvation.

An ongoing sense of guilt is not part of the Christian experience. Yes, we sinned in the past, but it is the sense of guilt towards God that Christ has set us free from. A gentle pain, a spiritual scar, will always remain from our past sins, but no more. Christian preaching must be very careful not to play with feelings of guilt, and in particular not to use them to block a sense of freedom in Christ.

Here I clashed with my Roman Catholic critic, who writes: 'Here I fundamentally disagree. I think an ongoing sense of guilt is part of the Christian experience, something that should grow rather than disappear. I know this is a minority view but I am very attached to it.'

My reply: 'I'm not comfortable here. I want to insist on new creation, the fundamental, radical newness that life in Christ offers. If you like, we are being totally recycled: "let your minds be remade and your whole nature thus transformed" (Romans 12:2, NEB). The call is to "walk in newness of life" (Romans 6:4). We need to be constantly looking forward: "No one who puts his hand to the plough and looks back is fit for service in the kingdom of God" (Luke 9:62, NIV). Clinging guilt over past sins prevents this. We teach that sins confessed are put away and are behind us. In confession a priest will sometimes tear up the piece of paper on which a person has written their sins. Guilt should last up to the time of confession, but no longer. Yes, we remain acutely aware of our fragility and our weak points. But it seems to me St Peter's injunction to "Be sober, be vigilant" (1 Peter 5:8, KJV), the prayer "Lead us not into temptation", and God's grace, are enough.

This does not mean that, perhaps later on the path, we do not get glimpses into the horror and bleakness of sin, of what we have left behind, but our call is to be new creations (2 Corinthians 5:17). To let the light of Christ shine into the very depth of our beings: "in him there is no darkness" (1 John 1:5, NIV).

I sense a nasty relationship between "guilt" and "fear". Fear is not a feature of the walk with God: "perfect love drives out fear" (1 John 4:18, NIV), "to enable us to serve him without fear in holiness and righteousness before him all our days" (Luke 1:74–75, NIV).'

Peeling away the depths can be a painful and difficult experience, in particular as we start to open the deeper cellars of our subconscious to Christ's light, cellars from which the evil one has to be thrown out. It is important that we not be ashamed in front of Christ for what is in there. In a very real sense, we need to come back to the Edenic state of being 'naked and not ashamed'.

Humility

Humility (смирение) is a fundamental Christian attitude, following Christ who 'humbled himself becoming obedient unto death, even death upon the cross' (Philippians 2:8, KJV). I insist, though, that it is an attitude incumbent on every single Christian, from patriarch to beggar. It must never, never be preached as a tool for maintaining a pecking order, with 'be humble' being crypto-speak for 'shut up and do as I tell you' or 'my job is to preach, yours is to listen and accept unquestioningly'. Dorothy of Gaza in his 'Instructions' makes a clear distinction between 'humility' and 'servility' (Instructions X. 10, § 106). Nor should смирение be used as an excuse for failing to use one's psychic strength and talents to the full to God's glory. It is no excuse for cleaning the floor when you could be helping teach catechism, or putting up with second-rate spiritual guidance or refusing to question a preacher's sloppy theology.

Patience

'Love' indeed 'beareth all things … endureth all things' (1 Corinthians 13:7, KJV). However, the same caveat applies as for humility, that a call for patience should not be used to stifle the naming of incompetence or injustice and, where possible, taking action against it. It must not be used as a tool for maintaining a questionable status quo.

I note considerable criticism from our Protestant brothers, particularly in America, of Orthodoxy's unreadiness to question the status quo. Many complain that Orthodoxy spends all its time riling at what it sees as sexual immorality, but keeps deathly silent at social injustice. It asks whether Russian Orthodoxy has not compromised itself here by its financial dependence on a not particularly pure-handed oligarchy. Could the Russian Orthodox Church, it asks, have produced a Dietrich Bonhoeffer, an Oscar Romero or a Martin Luther King?

AFTERWORD

How will the story go on from here?
I frankly don't know. Not a little will depend on how this book is received.

In any event I am happy to dialogue with serious readers. The primary routes are via Live Journal (ursusanglicanus) or Facebook (Michael Lomax), where the texts in this book were first published. In both I apply a policy of filtering, in order to separate private ('friends only') and public comment, and also block neophytes and a certain breed of fundamentalists, whom my broader approach will trouble. So to get the full me you will need to have me accept you as a friend.

I read most European languages and Russian, and answer comfortably in English, French and German. But please, please, if you are not really fluent in English, use your own language. I will almost certainly get it into better English than you will.

NOTES

2010

1 Literally 'little father'. A common, fairly informal, way of addressing a priest in the Russian Orthodox Church

2011

[1] A starets, plural startsi, feminine staritsa is a spirit-filled elder. Traditionally, startsi have been revered by Russians for their holiness and visited for spiritual advice

2012

[1] See also my essay 'Comparative Theology: The Need for a Paradigm Shift' later in this book

[2] From: Celtic Christianity, Translated and Introduced by Oliver Davies, The Paulist Press, 1999, p. 283

2013

[1] Samuel Crossman (1623-1683) – Hymns Ancient and Modern no. 102

[2] Dorothée de Gaza, Oeuvres spirituelles, Sources Chrétiennes, 1963

[3] Verbum Förlag, Stockholm, 1996

[4] In fact, paradoxically, I suspect, judging from writers like Serguei Fudel, that the most 'free' and 'mature' period of Russian church life was in the 1920s and 1930s, with the weakening of the external structures. Conversely, the consolidation of the Russian Orthodox Church's structures since about 2000 seems to have done little to increase its spiritual maturity.

2014

[1] The short-form version of Psalm 104, based on the LXX. Service Book of the Holy Orthodox-Catholic Apostolic Church, compiled and translated by Isabel Hapgood, 1922, p. 1

2015

[1] Les Mouches, 1943

2017

[1] The standard Slavonic (old church Russian) word for 'repentance' as in 'Repent, for the Kingdom of God is at hand', but with a strong overtone of remorse and breast-beating, and rather far from the original Greek metanoia, which is more 'fundamental change of mindset'.

[2] Zondervan, 2010

2018

[1] For example: Fr Alexander Rozanov: 'Diaries of a Village Priest', published in 1882, covering the period 1840–1880 (Russian version available on https://azbyka.ru/fiction/zapiski-selskogo-svyashhennika/), or the autobiography of Nikita Hilyarov-Platonov (1824–1887), a trained theologian who spent much of his life in church/government missions examining education and religious life in the countryside (Russian version available on http://az.lib.ru/g/giljarowplatonow_n_p/text_1886_iz_perezhitogo1.shtml.)

[2] Axios' (Greek for 'worthy') is the cry with which a congregation greets a newly-ordained deacon or priest when being vested in his liturgical garments by the bishop. 'Anaxios' means 'unworthy'.

2019

[1] An Akathist is a type of hymn usually recited by Orthodox Christians, dedicated to a saint, holy event, or one of the persons of the Holy Trinity.

Comparative Theology

[1] On the traditional dividing points I note: filioque (whatever the 'wrongness' in principle of adding a couple of words to the creed, there is a general understanding of why the words were added, and generally this difference is no longer seen as a major stumbling block); Immaculate Conception (while the 'biology' of how Mary is 'immaculate' differs, her purity, her role in salvation and her intercessory power are generally accepted in both the Orthodox and Roman Catholic churches); the bodily resurrection of the Mother of God (while the mechanics vary – in Roman Catholic theology she does not die, in Orthodox theology she does – the net result is the same: she has ascended as a first fruit of humanity and with a special position next to Christ in heaven. Both Orthodox and Roman Catholic theology and iconography attribute the places 'at my right or my left' [Matthew 20:23] to Mary and John the Baptist); and papal infallibility (see main text above).

[2] Dogmatic theology has its uses here. For example, the definitions of the Second Ecumenical Council on the divinity of Christ and the Fourth Ecumenical Council on Christ having two natures, are vital for the concept of divinisation, an essential element of Orthodox spirituality. It is the decisions of the Seventh Ecumenical Council that confirm the validity of icons as a valuable tool, among others, for attaining this.

[3] Here I have to criticise what seems to me a blinkered approach by my own church, which reads Protestantism in terms of traditional European Lutheranism, with little reference to the free, non-Episcopalian Protestantism which is sweeping South America, Korea and China, and which, with its more traditional moral emphases, could prove a useful ally.

[4] The standard Orthodox term for a relaxation of church rules, on a 'lesser of two evils basis', such as relaxation of fasting rules to allow a physically weak person to take communion, or permltting divorce and remarriage in certain cases.

Orthodoxy in Belgium

[1] There were in fact another three or four mini-parishes. Part of their raison d'être was political: it served the local Moscow Patriarchate archbishop to show to the Soviet authorities that he had more parishes than the other 'non-Moscow' Russian jurisdictions.

[2] Church Slavonic is, to a Russian, of a level of difficulty not dissimilar to Chaucer to an Englishman.

[3] The classic pattern, as one priest explained to me, is a girl in her early twenties, daughter of refugees, with good schooling in French, who marries outside the church. There will probably be a church wedding, she will bring the children to be baptised, perhaps come to the big festivals, bring eggs and cakes to be blessed at Easter, but slowly but surely will fall away. Part of the problem, in my mind, has been a 'diabolization' of other Christian confessions, which means that young people either partner with an Orthodox or a total unbeliever, but almost never with believers from other confessions.

[4] Several local priests have been ordained in recent years. All are part-time, all but one were aged 40 or over at ordination. Three have university degrees, three are builders. None has gone through seminary.

[5] There was, about five years ago, a well-funded Russian government plan to repatriate refugees, which came to nothing.

[6] I'm playing to the gallery here a bit. The man remains to me something a mystery. An excellent commentator on the Fathers, the best ever exponent of St Gregory Palamas, but whose memory here has faded to near zero.

[7] Especially automobiles. The Patriarch has tried to intervene, but his own riding a large Mercedes, at the orders, he says, of the Russian authorities concerned for his safety, hardly helps.

[8] For me this is the single largest 'killer' of the Russian Orthodox witness outside Russia – and doing a lot of damage inside too.

[9] This and the next sentence are, I realise, a little one-sided, and 'playing to the gallery'. I have not added that there is a fair bit that Orthodoxy needs to learn from the West. It is not, unfortunately, ready yet for this message.

Christianity, Joy, Freedom and Absence of Guilt vs Suffering Penitence, Humility and Patience

[1] Some brands of Protestantism fail to honour this two-step process, seeing the initial conversion experience as sufficient, and with insufficient attention to the slow salvation process. While many people are indeed knocked by a strong conversion experience into a profound change of life, this tends to express itself essentially at the moral level (don't smoke anymore, don't drink anymore, don't misbehave with women anymore), often not without a certain ensuing self-righteousness. Wiser Protestants recognise this limitation and a need for deeper conversion. A well-known Methodist – and deep conversion is part of the Methodist founding experience – found the golden mean in Protestant language by saying: John or Joan was converted once, and then over and over again.

[2] Ἐκκλησία here, of course, in terms of church-as-institution.

[3] A concern of mine here is the number of Orthodox priests and spiritual men who get cancer. Should we link it to the effect of constantly 'taking on' of other people's sins through confession and of an acute awareness in deep prayer of the sickness of the world, or more prosaically to the stress caused by the general unhealthiness of a priest's life – constant money problems, difficult relationships with an often despotic hierarchy, physically unhealthy conditions of church services, etc.? I suspect in the first case they tend to recover (St Sophrony of Essex and my own former dukhovnik); in the latter case they do not.